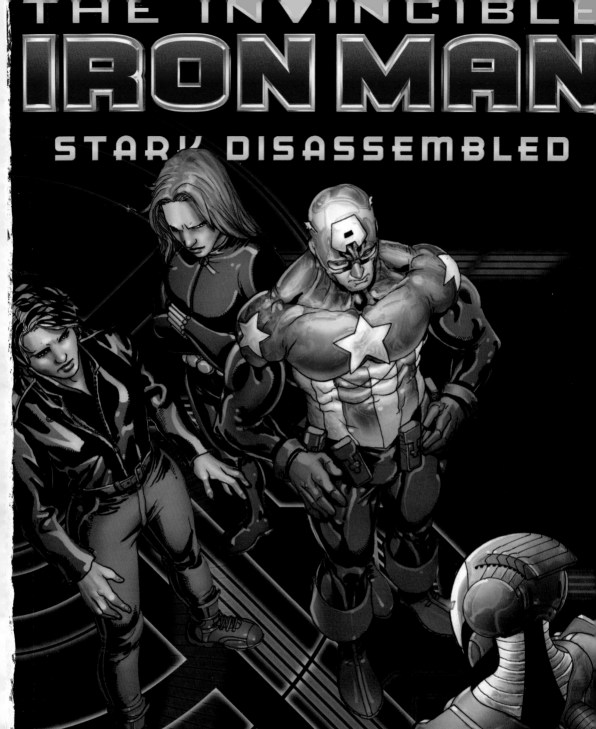

THE INVINCIBLE
IRON MAN
STARK DISASSEMBLED

INVINCIBLE IRON MAN VOL. 4: STARK DISASSEMBLED. Contains material originally published in magazine form as INVINCIBLE IRON MAN #20-24. First printing 2010. Hardcover ISBN# 978-0-7851-4554-
Softcover ISBN# 978-0-7851-3686-6. Published by MARVEL WORLDWIDE, INC., a subsidiary of MARVEL ENTERTAINMENT, LLC. OFFICE OF PUBLICATION: 417 5th Avenue, New York, NY 10016. Copyright ©
2009 and 2010 Marvel Characters, Inc. All rights reserved. Hardcover: $19.99 per copy in the U.S. and $22.50 in Canada (GST #R127032852). Softcover: $15.99 per copy in the U.S. and $17.99 in Canada (GS
#R127032852). Canadian Agreement #40668537. All characters featured in this issue and the distinctive names and likenesses thereof, and all related indicia are trademarks of Marvel Characters, Inc. No similari
between any of the names, characters, persons, and/or institutions in this magazine with those of any living or dead person or institution is intended, and any such similarity which may exist is purely coincidenta
Printed in the U.S.A. ALAN FINE, EVP - Office of the President, Marvel Worldwide, Inc. and EVP & CMO Marvel Characters B.V.; DAN BUCKLEY, Chief Executive Officer and Publisher - Print, Animation & Digit
Media; JIM SOKOLOWSKI, Chief Operating Officer; DAVID GABRIEL, SVP of Publishing Sales & Circulation; DAVID BOGART, SVP of Business Affairs & Talent Management; MICHAEL PASCIULLO, VP Merchandisin
& Communications; JIM O'KEEFE, VP of Operations & Logistics; DAN CARR, Executive Director of Publishing Technology; JUSTIN F. GABRIE, Director of Publishing & Editorial Operations; SUSAN CRESPI, Editoria
Operations Manager; ALEX MORALES, Publishing Operations Manager; STAN LEE, Chairman Emeritus. For information regarding advertising in Marvel Comics or on Marvel.com, please contact Ron Stern, VP
Business Development, at rstern@marvel.com. For Marvel subscription inquiries, please call 800-217-9158. **Manufactured between 5/21/10 and 6/30/10 (hardcover), and 5/31/10 and 12/23/10 (softcover**

THE INVINCIBLE IRON MAN
STARK DISASSEMBLED

WRITER: **MATT FRACTION**
ARTIST: **SALVADOR LARROCA**
COLORS: **FRANK D'ARMATA**
LETTERS: **VC'S JOE CARAMAGNA**
COVER ART: **SALVADOR LARROCA** & **RIAN HUGHES**
ASSISTANT EDITOR: **ALEJANDRO ARBONA**
EDITOR: **RALPH MACCHIO**

COLLECTION EDITOR: **JENNIFER GRÜNWALD**
ASSISTANT EDITOR: **ALEX STARBUCK**
ASSOCIATE EDITOR: **JOHN DENNING**
EDITOR, SPECIAL PROJECTS: **MARK D. BEAZLEY**
SENIOR EDITOR, SPECIAL PROJECTS: **JEFF YOUNGQUIST**
SENIOR VICE PRESIDENT OF SALES: **DAVID GABRIEL**
BOOK DESIGNER: **RODOLFO MURAGUCHI**

EDITOR IN CHIEF: **JOE QUESADA**
PUBLISHER: **DAN BUCKLEY**
EXECUTIVE PRODUCER: **ALAN FINE**

PREVIOUSLY:

The man that was Tony Stark is dead.

Norman Osborn, the leader of the corrupt government agency known as H.A.M.M.E.R., made a grab for all the power and information Stark once had. As the former director of the intelligence and peacekeeping agency S.H.I.E.L.D., Tony couldn't let the database of superhuman secret identities, and the secrets of his proprietary Iron Man repulsor technology, fall into Osborn's hands...or the consequences would be disastrous. He protected the information the only way possible. He deleted every trace of it — including his own mind.

Now Tony's brain doesn't even know how to make his body breathe — he put himself in a persistent vegetative state. But not before entrusting his right-hand woman, Pepper Potts, with a suit of armor and repulsor generator of her own. And Maria Hill, Tony's former second in command at S.H.I.E.L.D., retrieved a very sensitive hard drive — contents unknown — from a Stark facility with the help of intelligence op the Black Widow.

Working together, Pepper, Maria and the Widow have gathered with Captain America and Dr. Don Blake — a.k.a. Thor, the mighty Norse god of thunder — to take the next step...

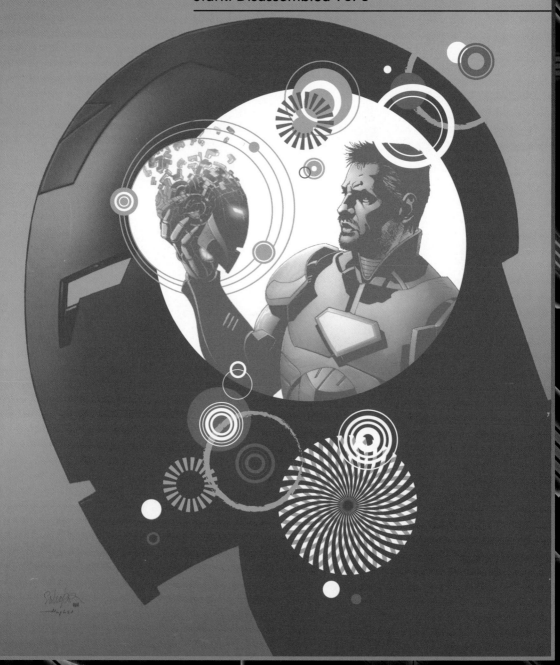

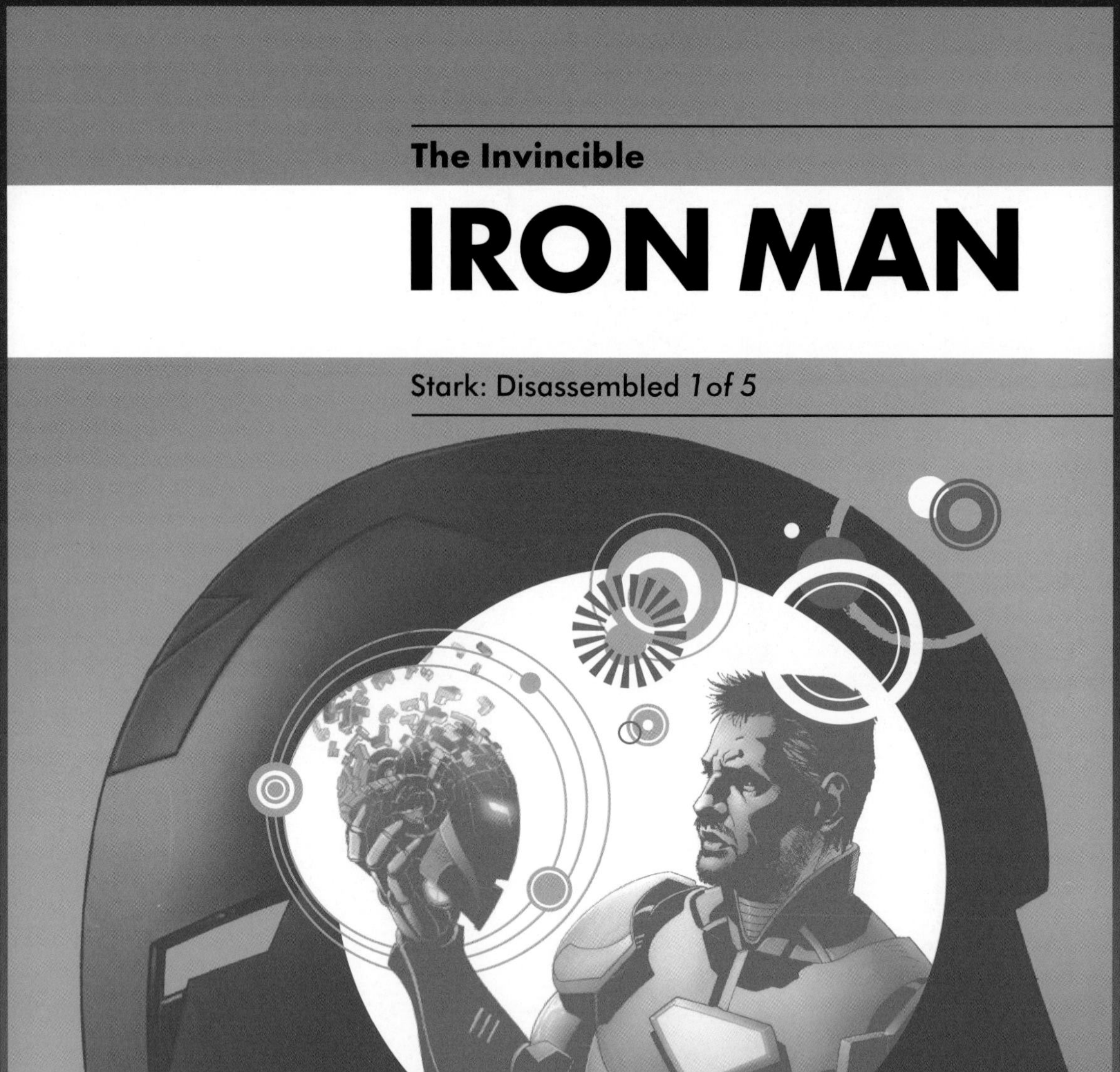
The Invincible
IRON MAN
Stark: Disassembled 1 of 5

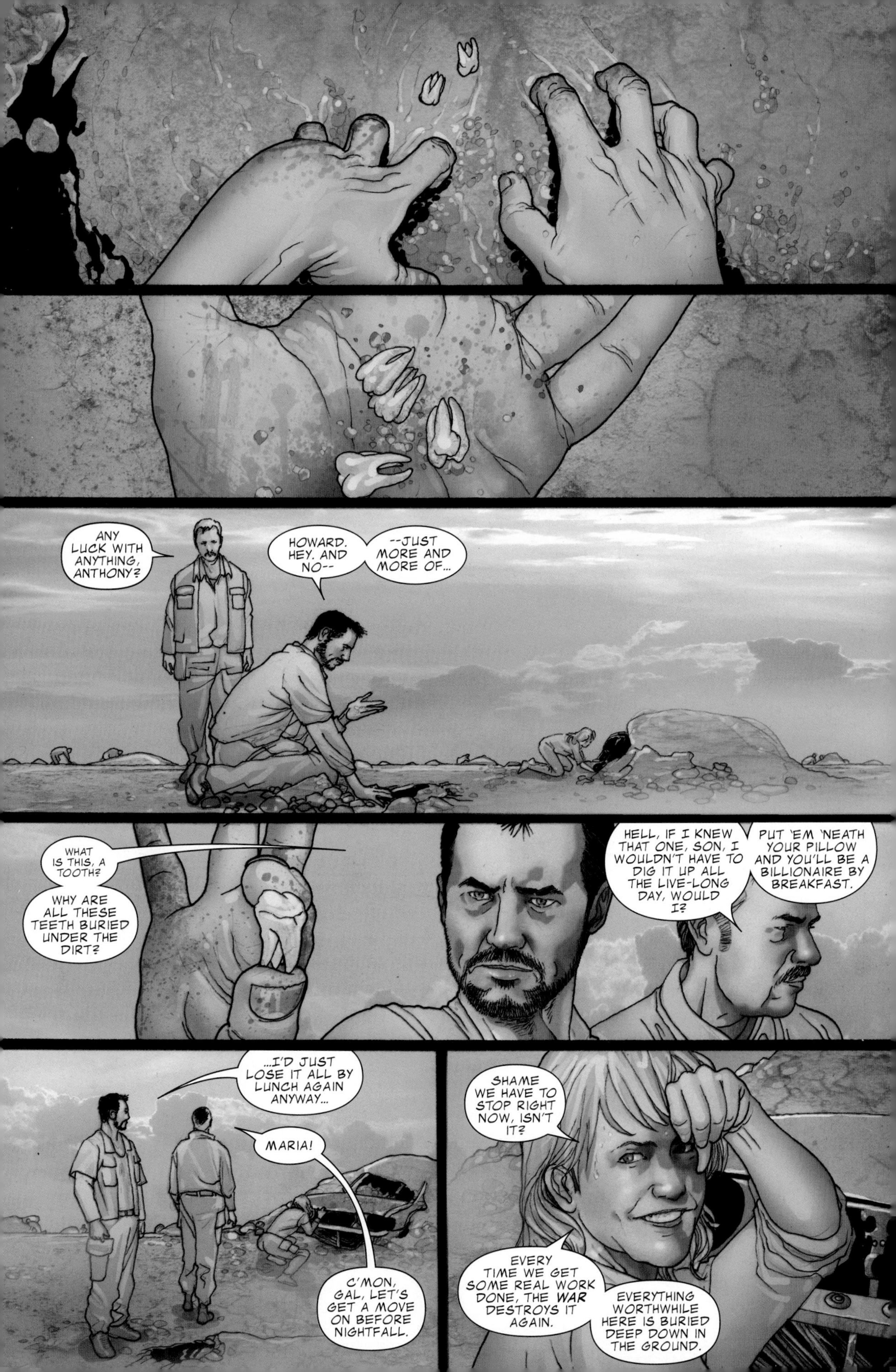
ANY LUCK WITH ANYTHING, ANTHONY?
HOWARD. HEY. AND NO--
--JUST MORE AND MORE OF...
WHAT IS THIS, A TOOTH?
WHY ARE ALL THESE TEETH BURIED UNDER THE DIRT?
HELL, IF I KNEW THAT ONE, SON, I WOULDN'T HAVE TO DIG IT UP ALL THE LIVE-LONG DAY, WOULD I?
PUT 'EM 'NEATH YOUR PILLOW AND YOU'LL BE A BILLIONAIRE BY BREAKFAST.
...I'D JUST LOSE IT ALL BY LUNCH AGAIN ANYWAY...
MARIA!
C'MON, GAL, LET'S GET A MOVE ON BEFORE NIGHTFALL.
SHAME WE HAVE TO STOP RIGHT NOW, ISN'T IT?
EVERY TIME WE GET SOME REAL WORK DONE, THE WAR DESTROYS IT AGAIN.
EVERYTHING WORTHWHILE HERE IS BURIED DEEP DOWN IN THE GROUND.

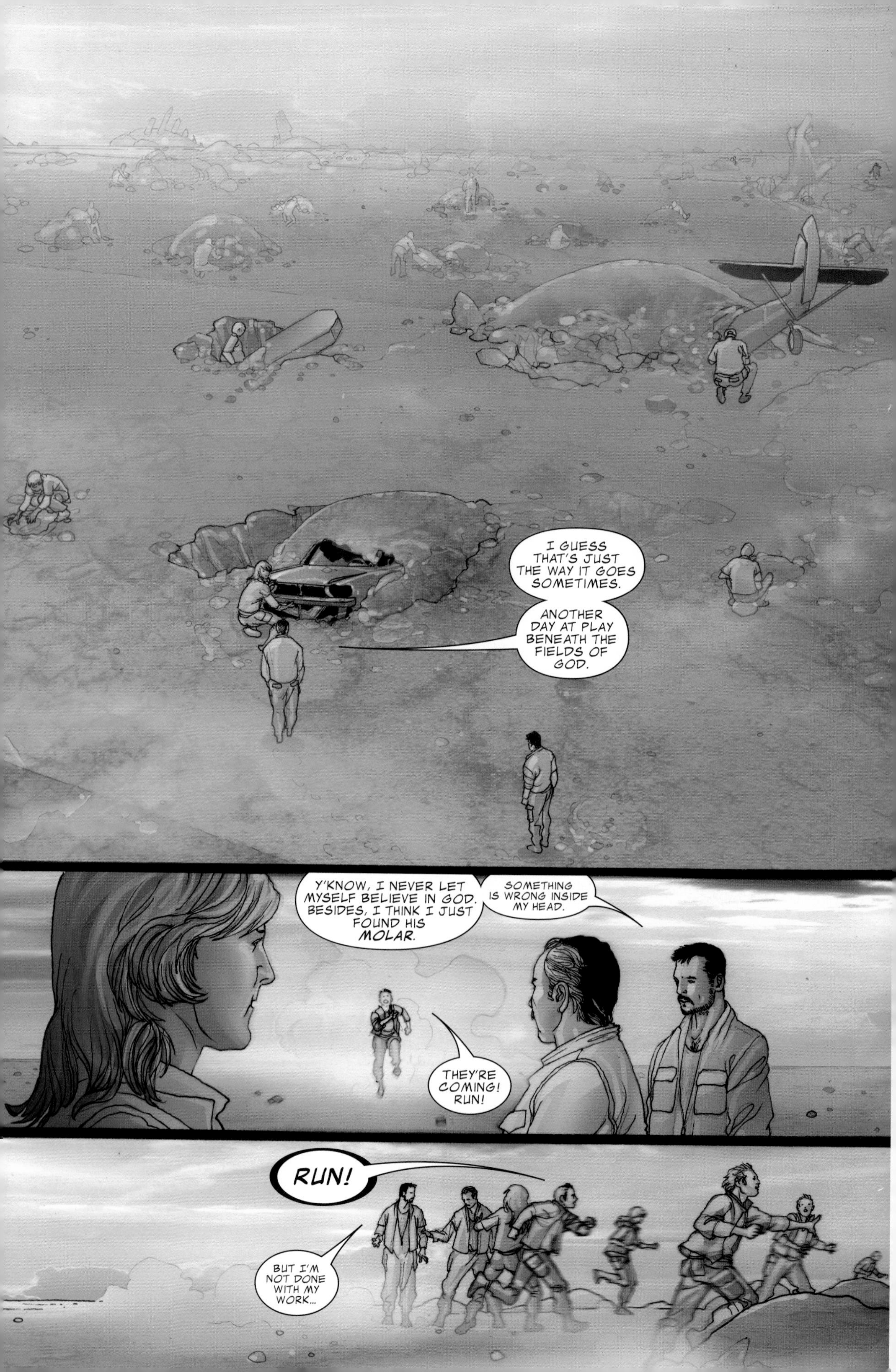
I GUESS THAT'S JUST THE WAY IT GOES SOMETIMES.
ANOTHER DAY AT PLAY BENEATH THE FIELDS OF GOD.
Y'KNOW, I NEVER LET MYSELF BELIEVE IN GOD. BESIDES, I THINK I JUST FOUND HIS *MOLAR*.
SOMETHING IS WRONG INSIDE MY HEAD.
THEY'RE COMING! RUN!
RUN!
BUT I'M NOT DONE WITH MY WORK...

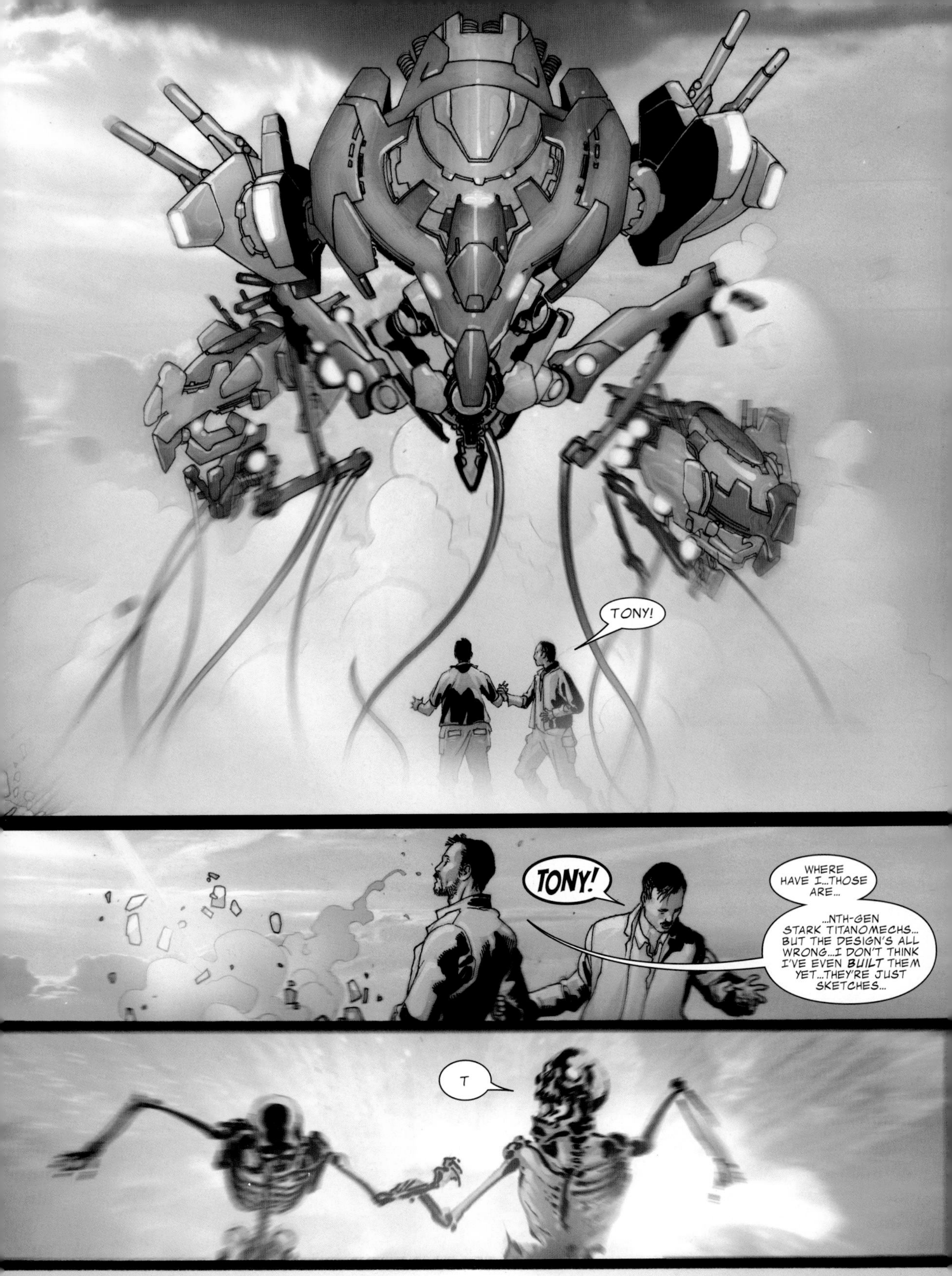
TONY!
TONY!
WHERE HAVE I...THOSE ARE...
...NTH-GEN STARK TITANOMECHS... BUT THE DESIGN'S ALL WRONG...I DON'T THINK I'VE EVEN *BUILT* THEM YET...THEY'RE JUST SKETCHES...
T

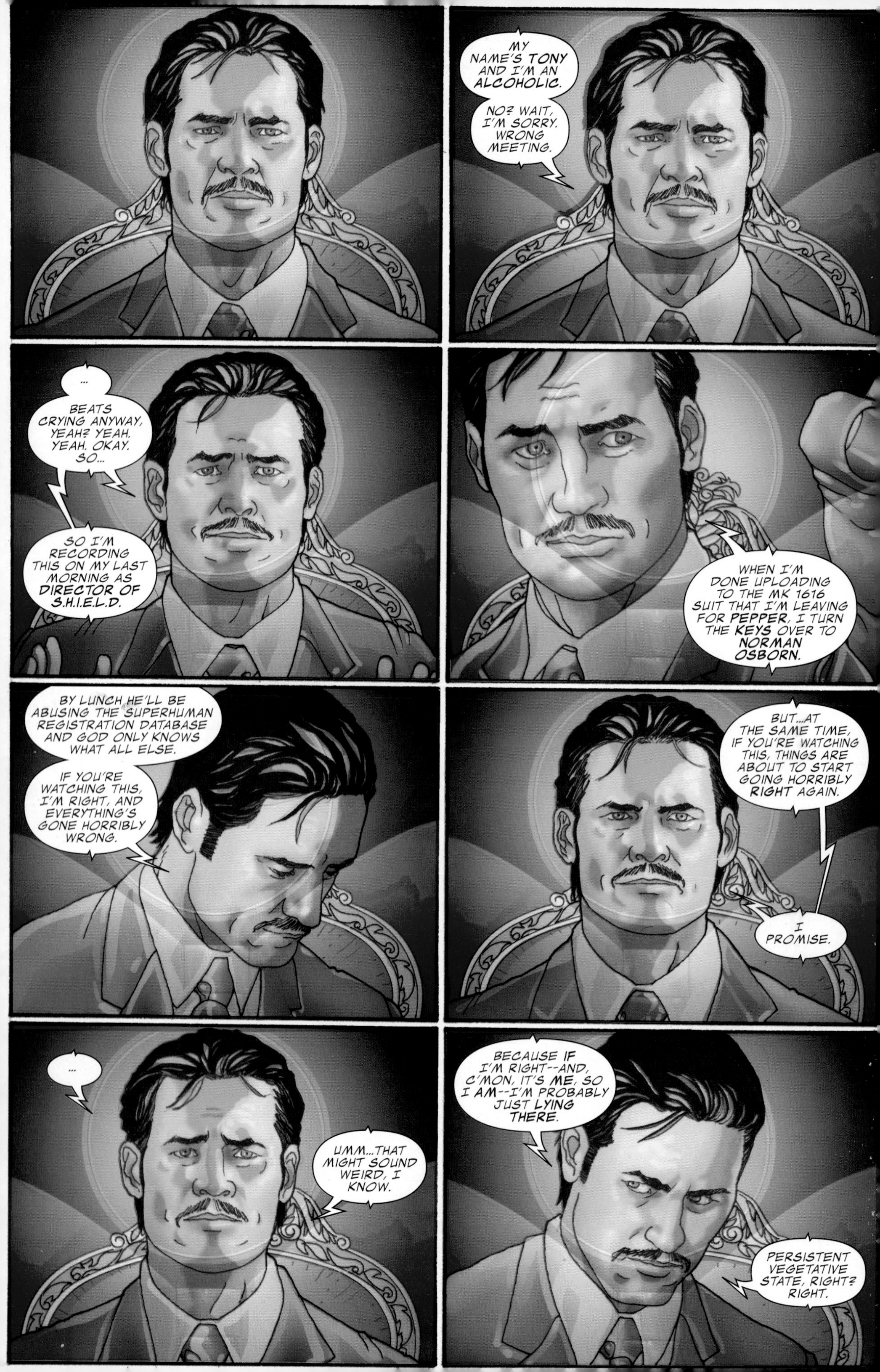
MY NAME'S TONY AND I'M AN ALCOHOLIC.
NO? WAIT, I'M SORRY. WRONG MEETING.
...
BEATS CRYING ANYWAY, YEAH? YEAH. YEAH. OKAY. SO...
SO I'M RECORDING THIS ON MY LAST MORNING AS DIRECTOR OF S.H.I.E.L.D.
WHEN I'M DONE UPLOADING TO THE MK 1616 SUIT THAT I'M LEAVING FOR PEPPER, I TURN THE KEYS OVER TO NORMAN OSBORN.
BY LUNCH HE'LL BE ABUSING THE SUPERHUMAN REGISTRATION DATABASE AND GOD ONLY KNOWS WHAT ALL ELSE.
IF YOU'RE WATCHING THIS, I'M RIGHT, AND EVERYTHING'S GONE HORRIBLY WRONG.
BUT...AT THE SAME TIME, IF YOU'RE WATCHING THIS, THINGS ARE ABOUT TO START GOING HORRIBLY RIGHT AGAIN.
I PROMISE.
...
UMM...THAT MIGHT SOUND WEIRD, I KNOW.
BECAUSE IF I'M RIGHT--AND, C'MON, IT'S ME, SO I AM--I'M PROBABLY JUST LYING THERE.
PERSISTENT VEGETATIVE STATE, RIGHT? RIGHT.

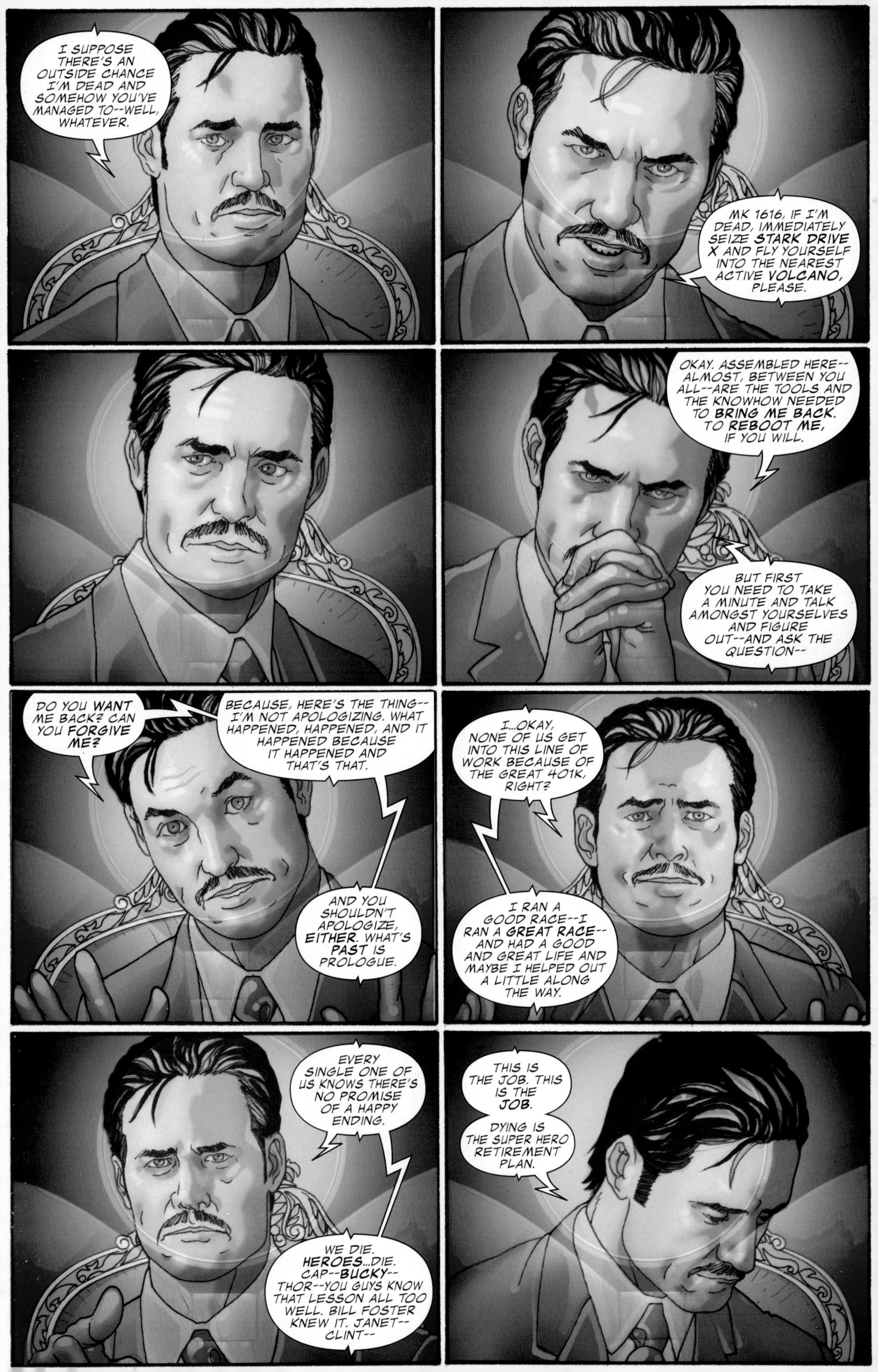
I SUPPOSE THERE'S AN OUTSIDE CHANCE I'M DEAD AND SOMEHOW YOU'VE MANAGED TO--WELL, WHATEVER.
MK 1616, IF I'M DEAD, IMMEDIATELY SEIZE STARK DRIVE X AND FLY YOURSELF INTO THE NEAREST ACTIVE VOLCANO, PLEASE.
OKAY. ASSEMBLED HERE--ALMOST, BETWEEN YOU ALL--ARE THE TOOLS AND THE KNOWHOW NEEDED TO BRING ME BACK. TO REBOOT ME, IF YOU WILL.
BUT FIRST YOU NEED TO TAKE A MINUTE AND TALK AMONGST YOURSELVES AND FIGURE OUT--AND ASK THE QUESTION--
DO YOU WANT ME BACK? CAN YOU FORGIVE ME?
BECAUSE, HERE'S THE THING--I'M NOT APOLOGIZING. WHAT HAPPENED, HAPPENED, AND IT HAPPENED BECAUSE IT HAPPENED AND THAT'S THAT.
AND YOU SHOULDN'T APOLOGIZE, EITHER. WHAT'S PAST IS PROLOGUE.
I...OKAY, NONE OF US GET INTO THIS LINE OF WORK BECAUSE OF THE GREAT 401K, RIGHT?
I RAN A GOOD RACE--I RAN A GREAT RACE--AND HAD A GOOD AND GREAT LIFE AND MAYBE I HELPED OUT A LITTLE ALONG THE WAY.
EVERY SINGLE ONE OF US KNOWS THERE'S NO PROMISE OF A HAPPY ENDING.
WE DIE. HEROES...DIE. CAP--BUCKY--THOR--YOU GUYS KNOW THAT LESSON ALL TOO WELL. BILL FOSTER KNEW IT. JANET--CLINT--
THIS IS THE JOB. THIS IS THE JOB.
DYING IS THE SUPER HERO RETIREMENT PLAN.

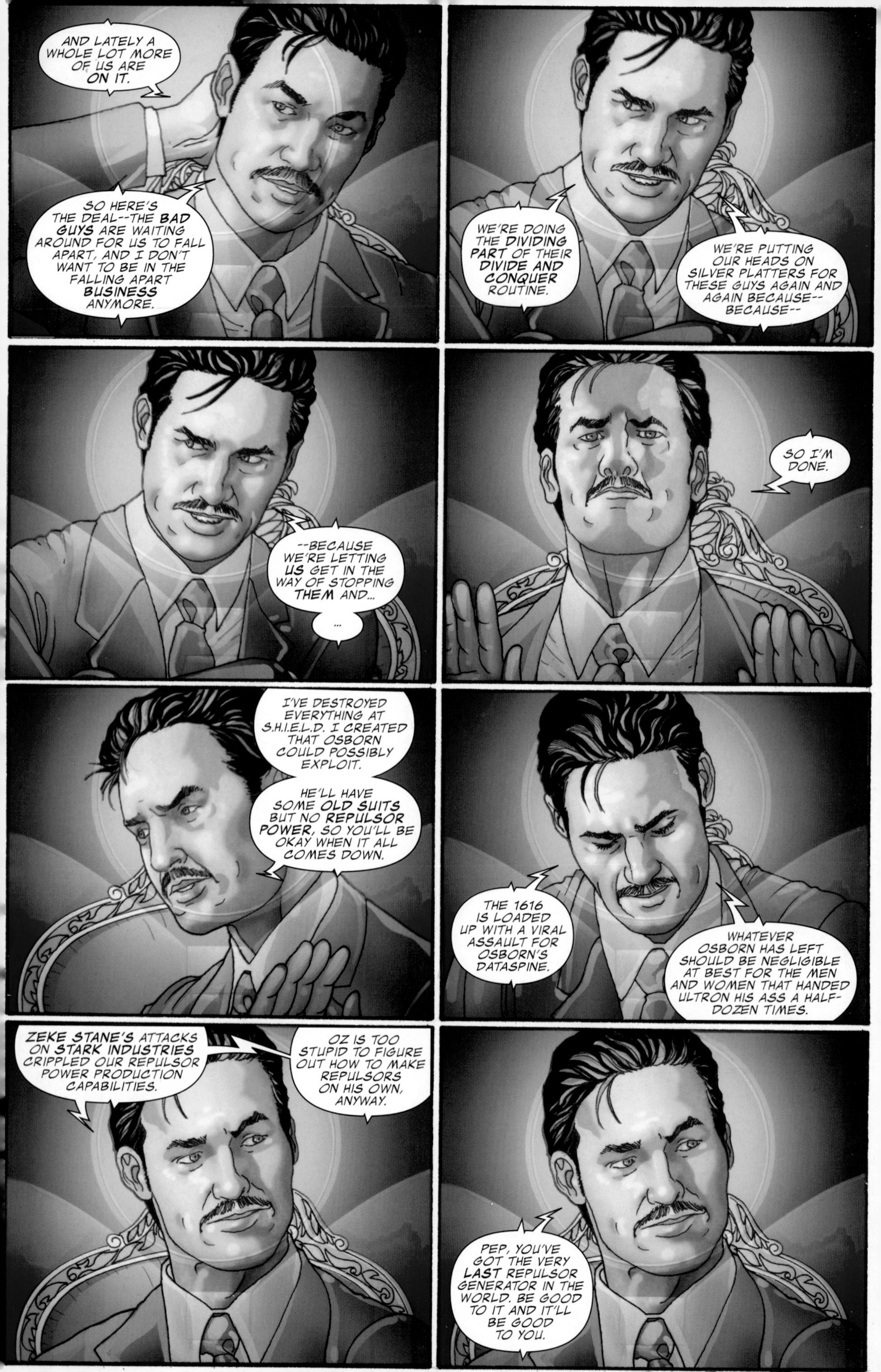
AND LATELY A WHOLE LOT MORE OF US ARE ON IT.
SO HERE'S THE DEAL--THE BAD GUYS ARE WAITING AROUND FOR US TO FALL APART, AND I DON'T WANT TO BE IN THE FALLING APART BUSINESS ANYMORE.
WE'RE DOING THE DIVIDING PART OF THEIR DIVIDE AND CONQUER ROUTINE.
WE'RE PUTTING OUR HEADS ON SILVER PLATTERS FOR THESE GUYS AGAIN AND AGAIN BECAUSE-- BECAUSE--
--BECAUSE WE'RE LETTING US GET IN THE WAY OF STOPPING THEM AND...
...
SO I'M DONE.
I'VE DESTROYED EVERYTHING AT S.H.I.E.L.D. I CREATED THAT OSBORN COULD POSSIBLY EXPLOIT.
HE'LL HAVE SOME OLD SUITS BUT NO REPULSOR POWER, SO YOU'LL BE OKAY WHEN IT ALL COMES DOWN.
THE 1616 IS LOADED UP WITH A VIRAL ASSAULT FOR OSBORN'S DATASPINE.
WHATEVER OSBORN HAS LEFT SHOULD BE NEGLIGIBLE AT BEST FOR THE MEN AND WOMEN THAT HANDED ULTRON HIS ASS A HALF-DOZEN TIMES.
ZEKE STANE'S ATTACKS ON STARK INDUSTRIES CRIPPLED OUR REPULSOR POWER PRODUCTION CAPABILITIES.
OZ IS TOO STUPID TO FIGURE OUT HOW TO MAKE REPULSORS ON HIS OWN, ANYWAY.
PEP, YOU'VE GOT THE VERY LAST REPULSOR GENERATOR IN THE WORLD. BE GOOD TO IT AND IT'LL BE GOOD TO YOU.

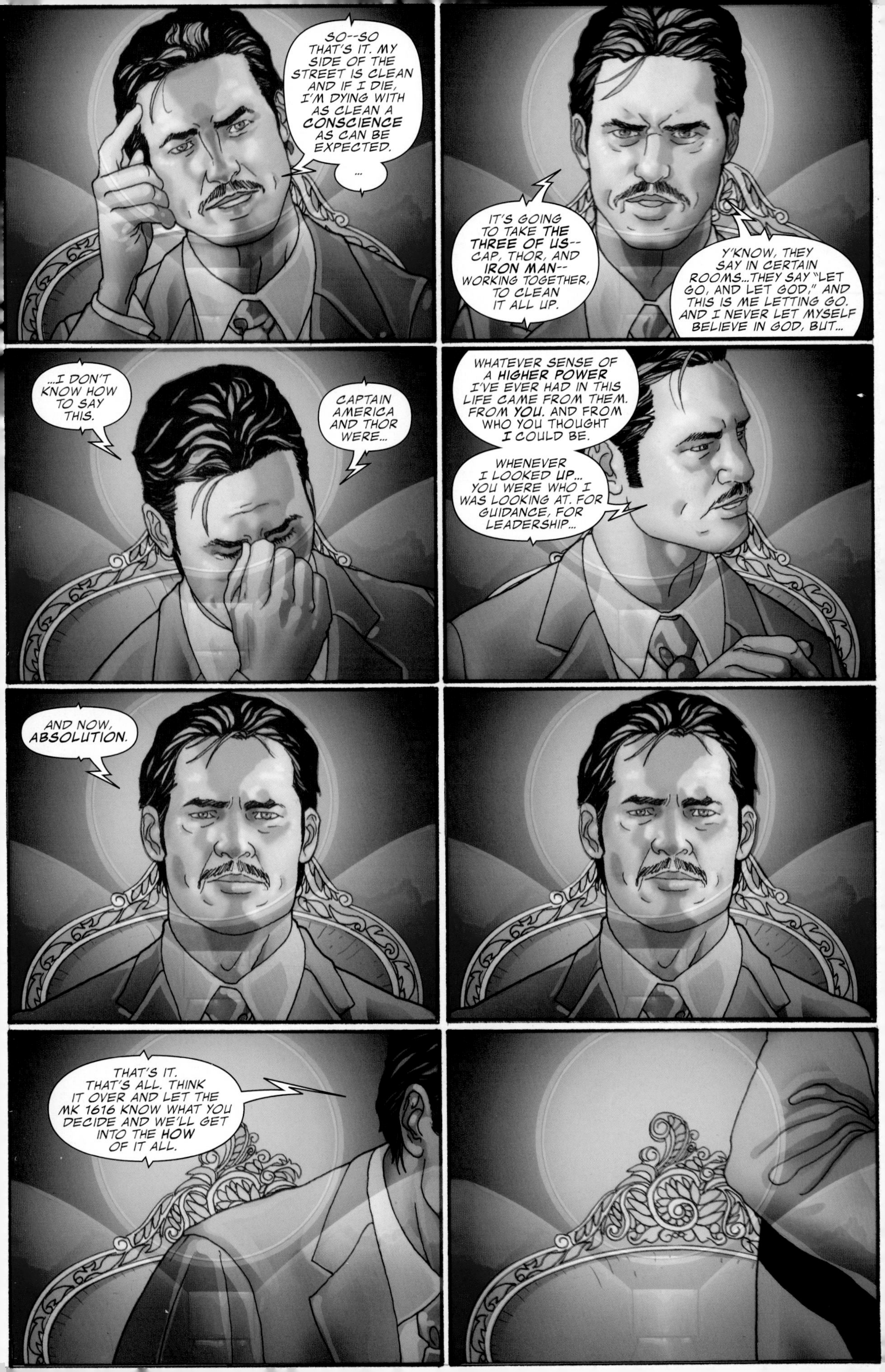
SO--SO THAT'S IT. MY SIDE OF THE STREET IS CLEAN AND IF I DIE, I'M DYING WITH AS CLEAN A CONSCIENCE AS CAN BE EXPECTED.
...
IT'S GOING TO TAKE THE THREE OF US--CAP, THOR, AND IRON MAN--WORKING TOGETHER, TO CLEAN IT ALL UP.
Y'KNOW, THEY SAY IN CERTAIN ROOMS...THEY SAY "LET GO, AND LET GOD," AND THIS IS ME LETTING GO. AND I NEVER LET MYSELF BELIEVE IN GOD, BUT...
...I DON'T KNOW HOW TO SAY THIS.
CAPTAIN AMERICA AND THOR WERE...
WHATEVER SENSE OF A HIGHER POWER I'VE EVER HAD IN THIS LIFE CAME FROM THEM. FROM YOU. AND FROM WHO YOU THOUGHT I COULD BE.
WHENEVER I LOOKED UP... YOU WERE WHO I WAS LOOKING AT. FOR GUIDANCE, FOR LEADERSHIP...
AND NOW, ABSOLUTION.
THAT'S IT. THAT'S ALL. THINK IT OVER AND LET THE MK 1616 KNOW WHAT YOU DECIDE AND WE'LL GET INTO THE HOW OF IT ALL.

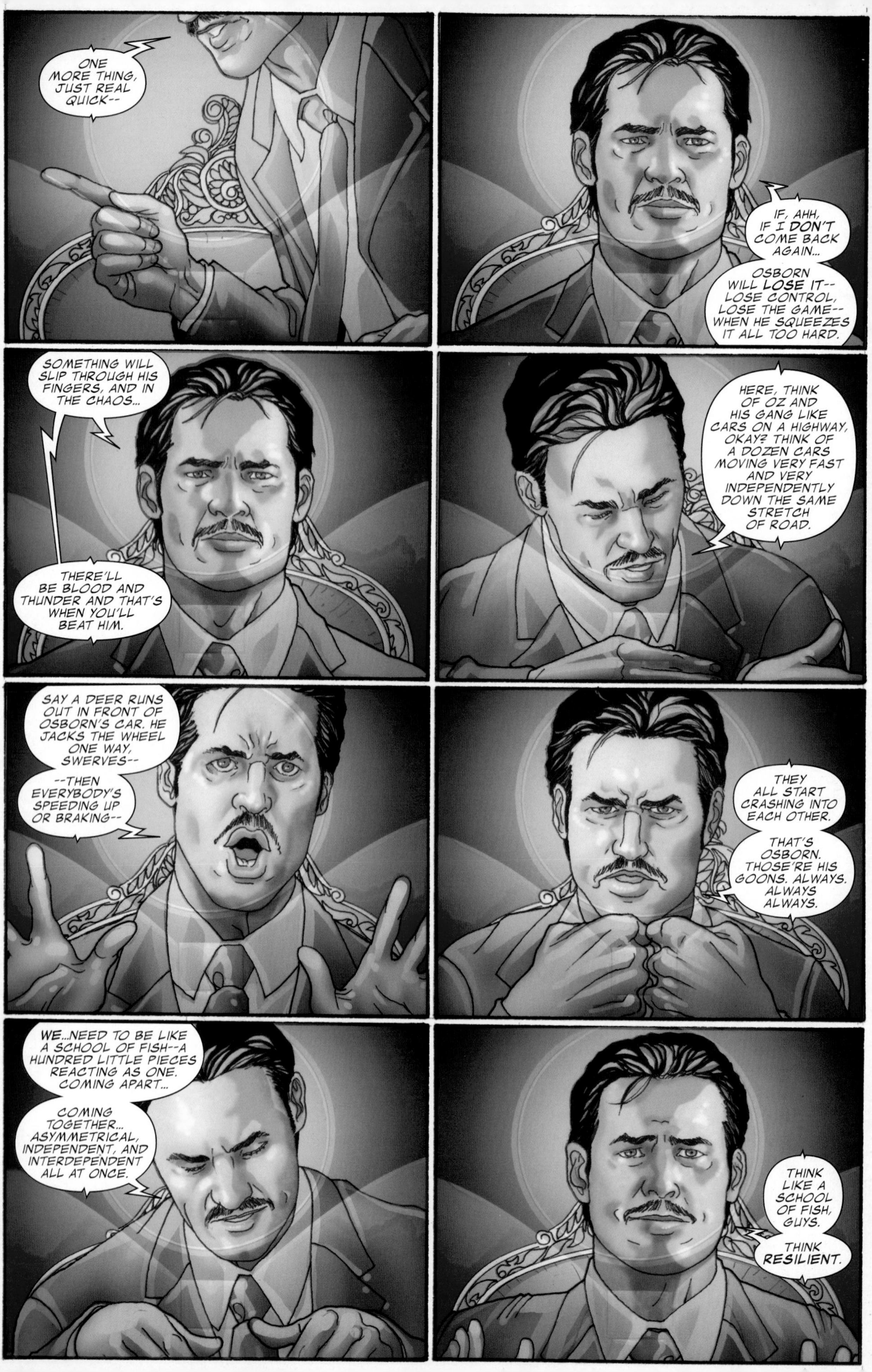
ONE MORE THING, JUST REAL QUICK--
IF, AHH, IF I DON'T COME BACK AGAIN...
OSBORN WILL LOSE IT--LOSE CONTROL, LOSE THE GAME--WHEN HE SQUEEZES IT ALL TOO HARD.
SOMETHING WILL SLIP THROUGH HIS FINGERS, AND IN THE CHAOS...
THERE'LL BE BLOOD AND THUNDER AND THAT'S WHEN YOU'LL BEAT HIM.
HERE, THINK OF OZ AND HIS GANG LIKE CARS ON A HIGHWAY, OKAY? THINK OF A DOZEN CARS MOVING VERY FAST AND VERY INDEPENDENTLY DOWN THE SAME STRETCH OF ROAD.
SAY A DEER RUNS OUT IN FRONT OF OSBORN'S CAR. HE JACKS THE WHEEL ONE WAY, SWERVES--
--THEN EVERYBODY'S SPEEDING UP OR BRAKING--
THEY ALL START CRASHING INTO EACH OTHER.
THAT'S OSBORN. THOSE'RE HIS GOONS. ALWAYS. ALWAYS ALWAYS.
WE...NEED TO BE LIKE A SCHOOL OF FISH--A HUNDRED LITTLE PIECES REACTING AS ONE. COMING APART...
COMING TOGETHER... ASYMMETRICAL, INDEPENDENT, AND INTERDEPENDENT ALL AT ONCE.
THINK LIKE A SCHOOL OF FISH, GUYS.
THINK RESILIENT.

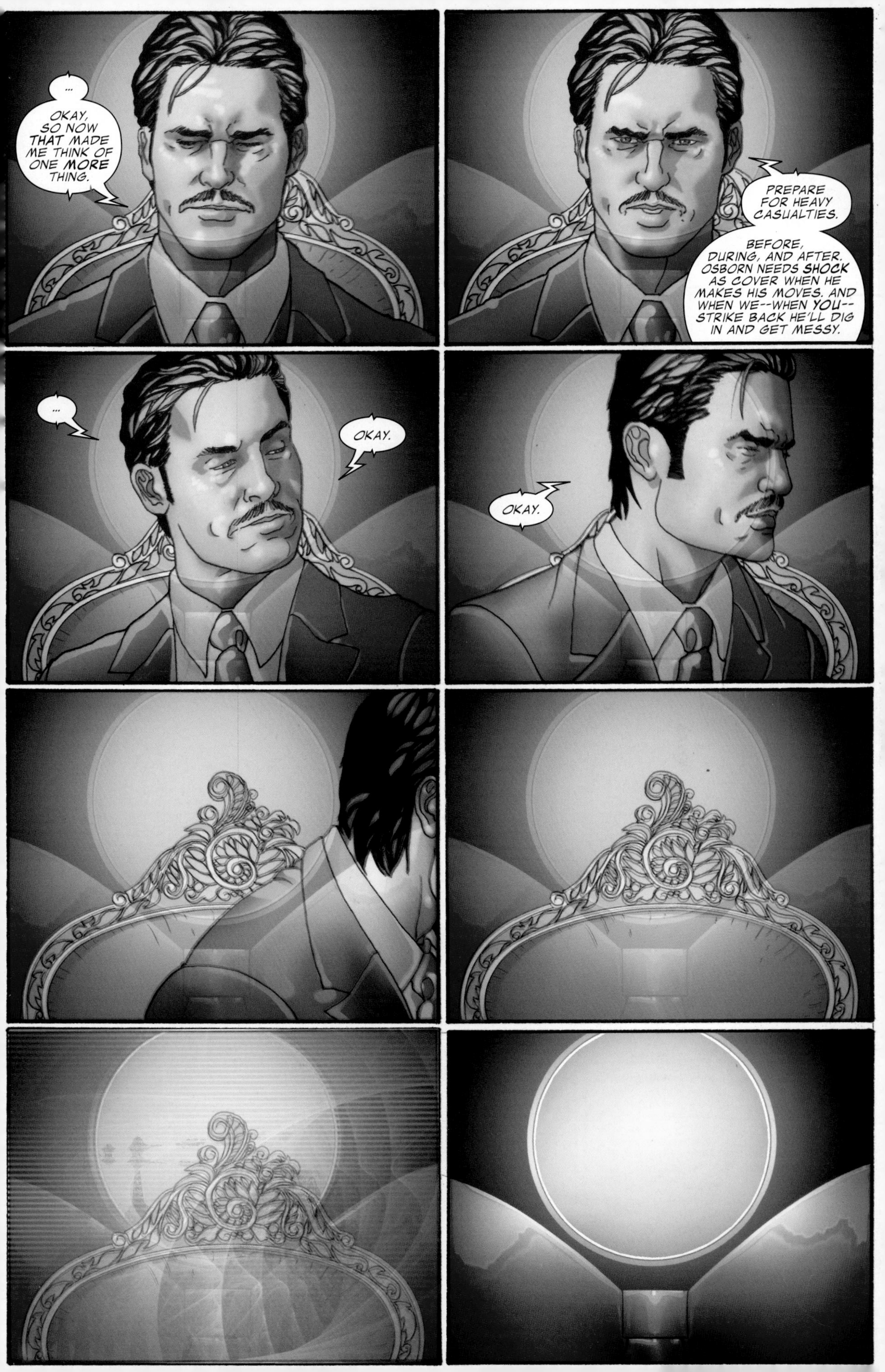
...
OKAY, SO NOW THAT MADE ME THINK OF ONE MORE THING.
PREPARE FOR HEAVY CASUALTIES.
BEFORE, DURING, AND AFTER. OSBORN NEEDS SHOCK AS COVER WHEN HE MAKES HIS MOVES. AND WHEN WE--WHEN YOU--STRIKE BACK HE'LL DIG IN AND GET MESSY.
...
OKAY.
OKAY.

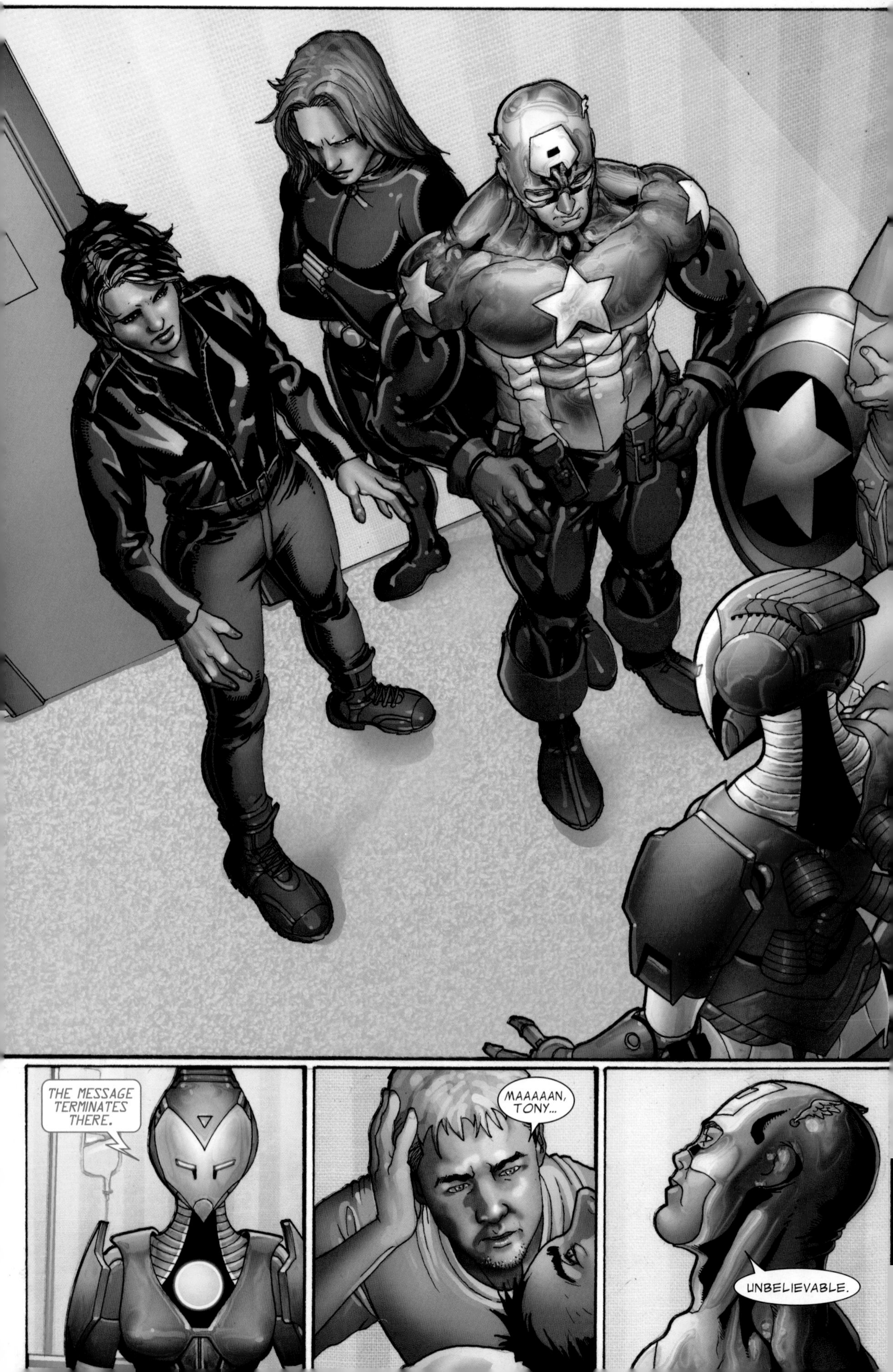
THE MESSAGE TERMINATES THERE.
MAAAAAN, TONY...
UNBELIEVABLE.

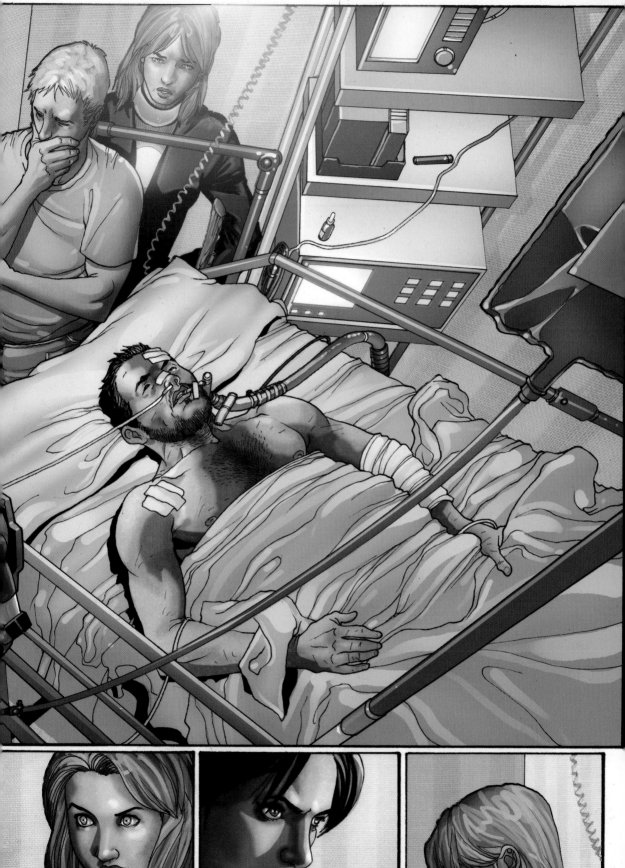

WAS HE THIS INSANE WHEN YOU WORKED FOR HIM, HILL?

MORE OR LESS, NAT. MORE OR LESS...

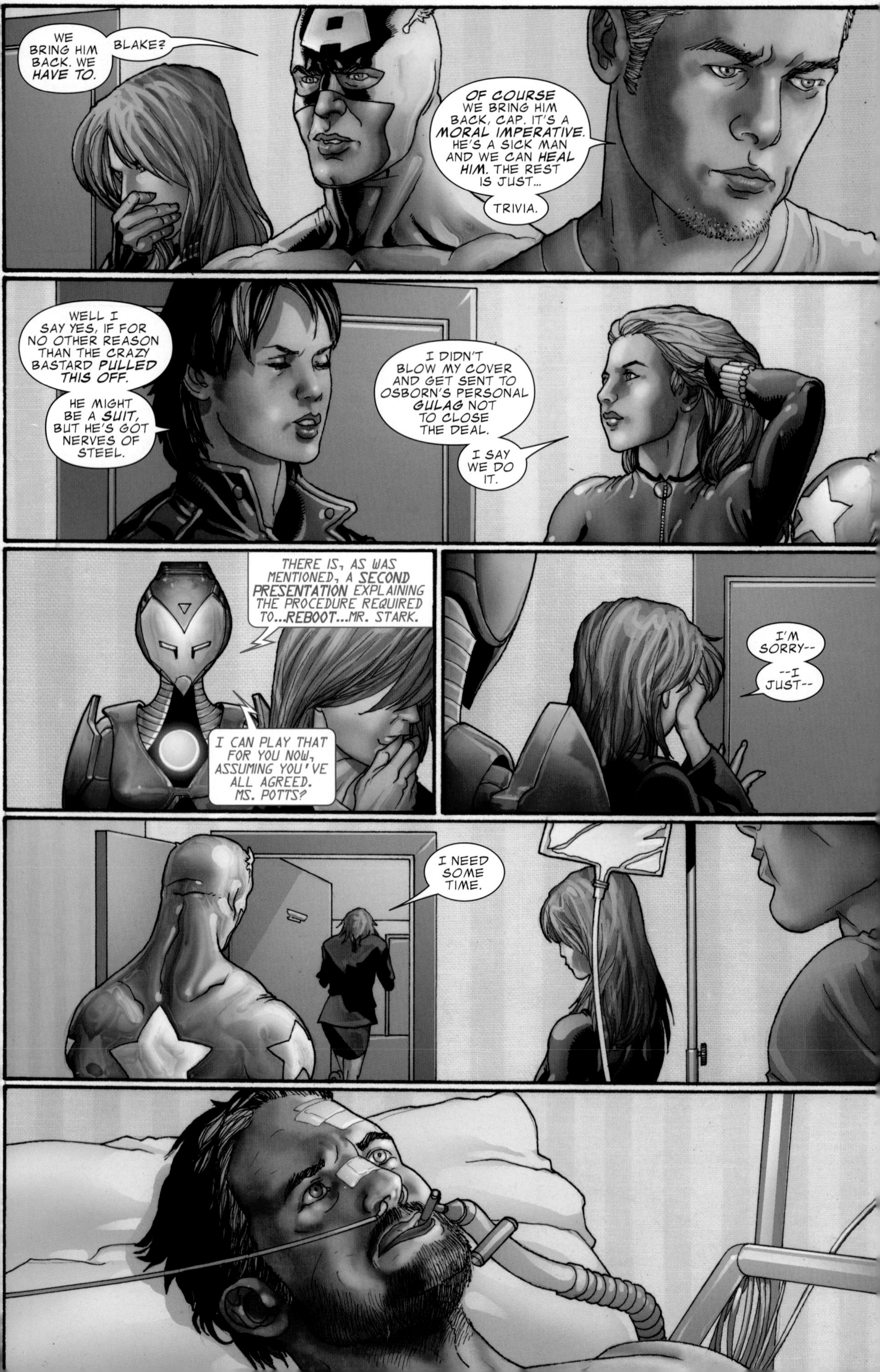
WE BRING HIM BACK. WE HAVE TO.
BLAKE?
OF COURSE WE BRING HIM BACK, CAP. IT'S A MORAL IMPERATIVE. HE'S A SICK MAN AND WE CAN HEAL HIM. THE REST IS JUST...
TRIVIA.
WELL I SAY YES, IF FOR NO OTHER REASON THAN THE CRAZY BASTARD PULLED THIS OFF.
HE MIGHT BE A SUIT, BUT HE'S GOT NERVES OF STEEL.
I DIDN'T BLOW MY COVER AND GET SENT TO OSBORN'S PERSONAL GULAG NOT TO CLOSE THE DEAL.
I SAY WE DO IT.
THERE IS, AS WAS MENTIONED, A SECOND PRESENTATION EXPLAINING THE PROCEDURE REQUIRED TO...REBOOT...MR. STARK.
I CAN PLAY THAT FOR YOU NOW, ASSUMING YOU'VE ALL AGREED. MS. POTTS?
I'M SORRY--
--I JUST--
I NEED SOME TIME.

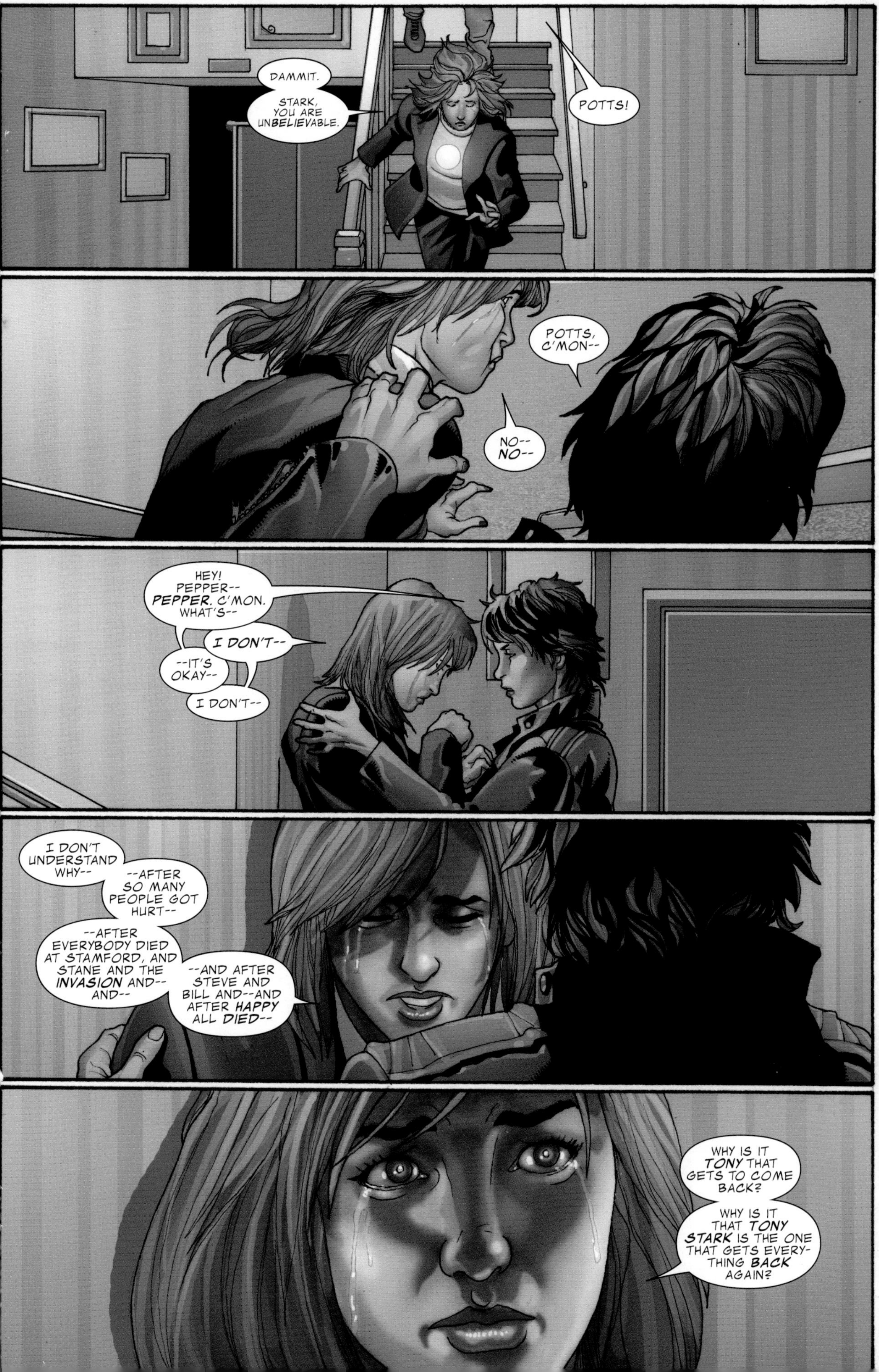
DAMMIT.
STARK, YOU ARE UNBELIEVABLE.
POTTS!
POTTS, C'MON--
NO-- NO--
HEY! PEPPER-- PEPPER. C'MON. WHAT'S--
I DON'T--
--IT'S OKAY--
I DON'T--
I DON'T UNDERSTAND WHY--
--AFTER SO MANY PEOPLE GOT HURT--
--AFTER EVERYBODY DIED AT STAMFORD, AND STANE AND THE INVASION AND-- AND--
--AND AFTER STEVE AND BILL AND--AND AFTER HAPPY ALL DIED--
WHY IS IT TONY THAT GETS TO COME BACK?
WHY IS IT THAT TONY STARK IS THE ONE THAT GETS EVERY-THING BACK AGAIN?

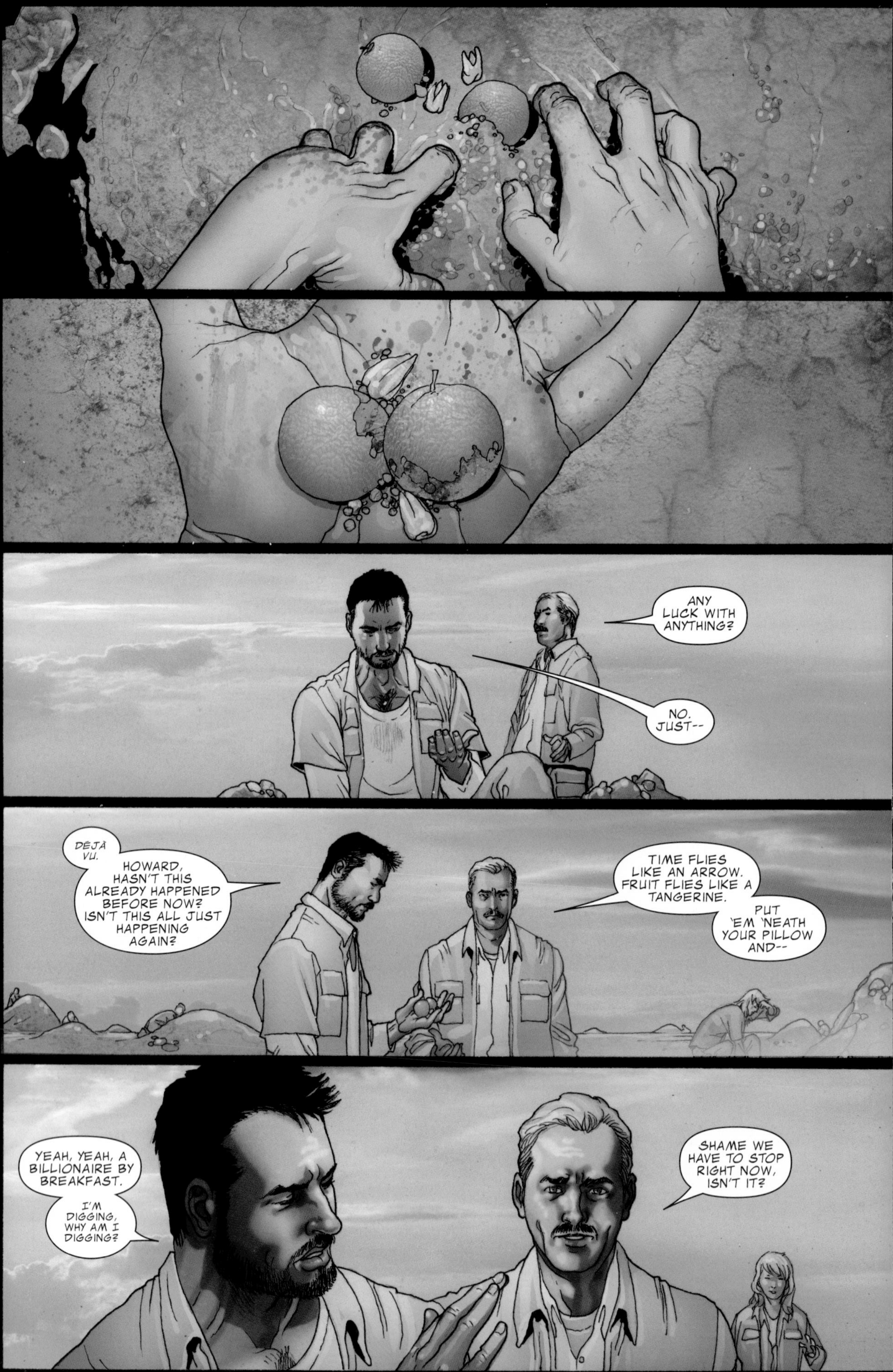
ANY LUCK WITH ANYTHING?
NO. JUST--
DÉJÀ VU.
HOWARD, HASN'T THIS ALREADY HAPPENED BEFORE NOW? ISN'T THIS ALL JUST HAPPENING AGAIN?
TIME FLIES LIKE AN ARROW. FRUIT FLIES LIKE A TANGERINE.
PUT 'EM 'NEATH YOUR PILLOW AND--
YEAH, YEAH, A BILLIONAIRE BY BREAKFAST.
I'M DIGGING, WHY AM I DIGGING?
SHAME WE HAVE TO STOP RIGHT NOW, ISN'T IT?

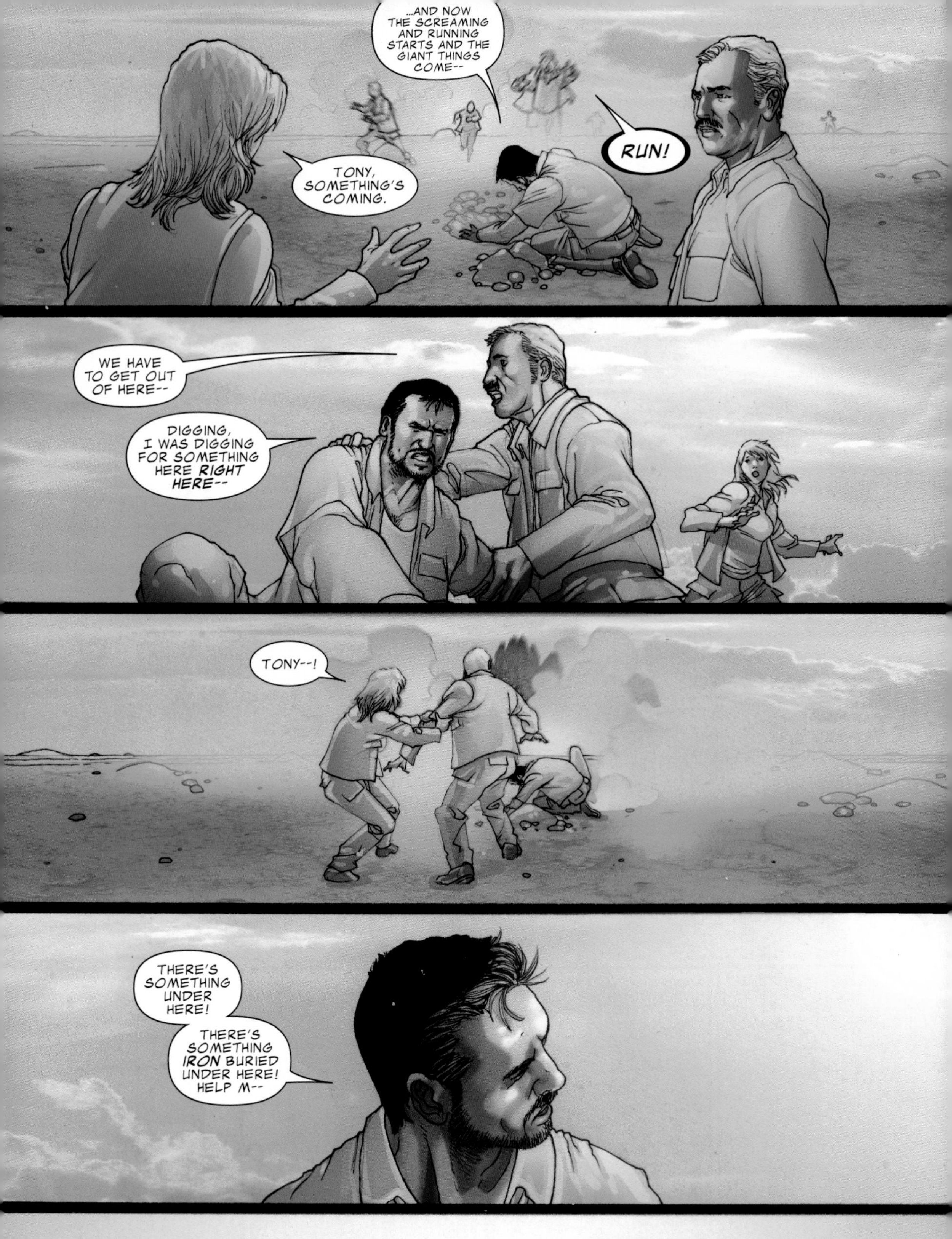
...AND NOW THE SCREAMING AND RUNNING STARTS AND THE GIANT THINGS COME--
TONY, SOMETHING'S COMING.
RUN!
WE HAVE TO GET OUT OF HERE--
DIGGING, I WAS DIGGING FOR SOMETHING HERE RIGHT HERE--
TONY--!
THERE'S SOMETHING UNDER HERE!
THERE'S SOMETHING IRON BURIED UNDER HERE! HELP M--

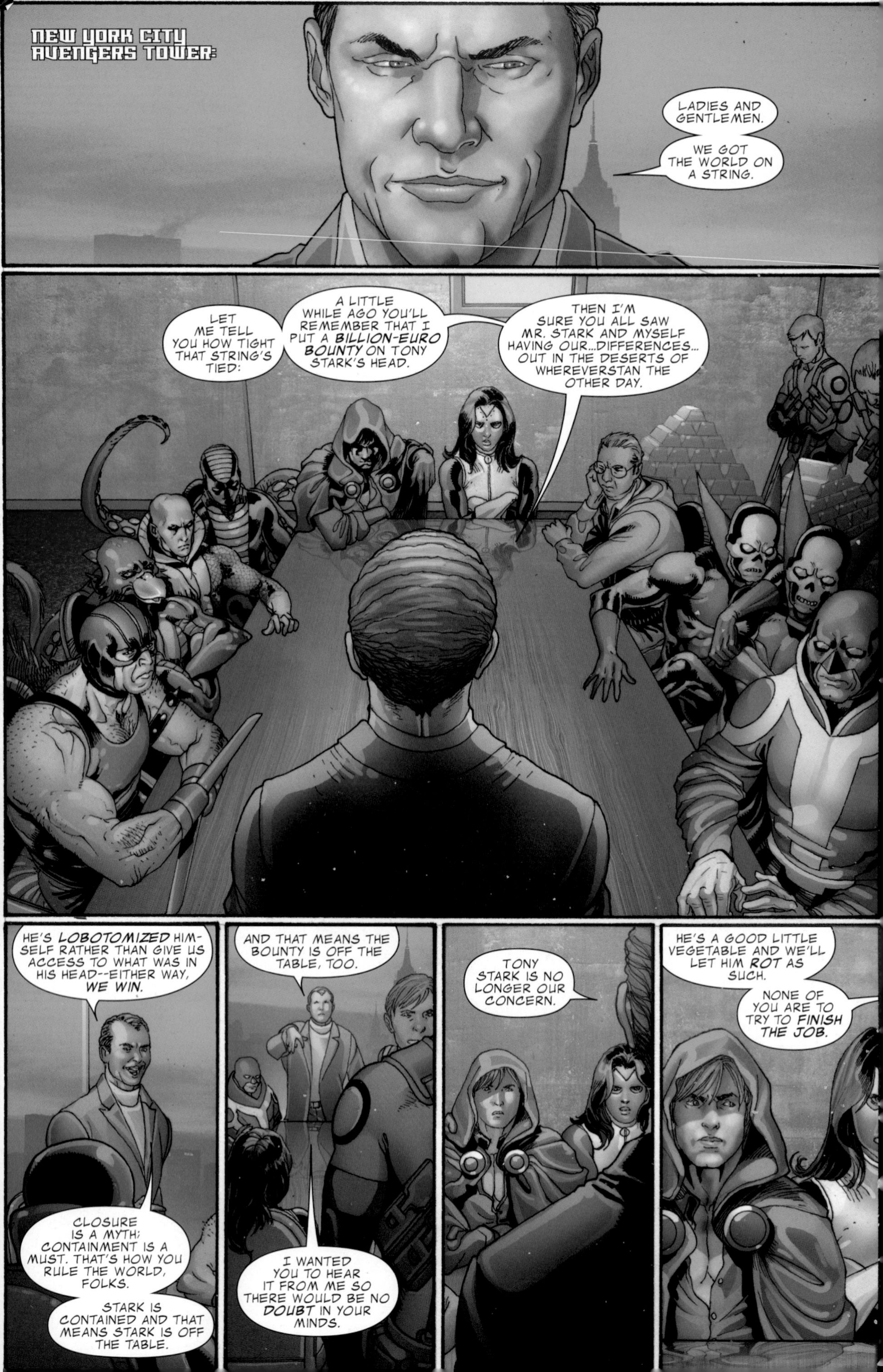
NEW YORK CITY
AVENGERS TOWER:
LADIES AND GENTLEMEN.
WE GOT THE WORLD ON A STRING.
LET ME TELL YOU HOW TIGHT THAT STRING'S TIED:
A LITTLE WHILE AGO YOU'LL REMEMBER THAT I PUT A BILLION-EURO BOUNTY ON TONY STARK'S HEAD.
THEN I'M SURE YOU ALL SAW MR. STARK AND MYSELF HAVING OUR...DIFFERENCES... OUT IN THE DESERTS OF WHEREVERSTAN THE OTHER DAY.
HE'S LOBOTOMIZED HIMSELF RATHER THAN GIVE US ACCESS TO WHAT WAS IN HIS HEAD--EITHER WAY, WE WIN.
CLOSURE IS A MYTH; CONTAINMENT IS A MUST. THAT'S HOW YOU RULE THE WORLD, FOLKS.
STARK IS CONTAINED AND THAT MEANS STARK IS OFF THE TABLE.
AND THAT MEANS THE BOUNTY IS OFF THE TABLE, TOO.
I WANTED IT YOU TO HEAR IT FROM ME SO THERE WOULD BE NO DOUBT IN YOUR MINDS.
TONY STARK IS NO LONGER OUR CONCERN.
HE'S A GOOD LITTLE VEGETABLE AND WE'LL LET HIM ROT AS SUCH.
NONE OF YOU ARE TO TRY TO FINISH THE JOB.

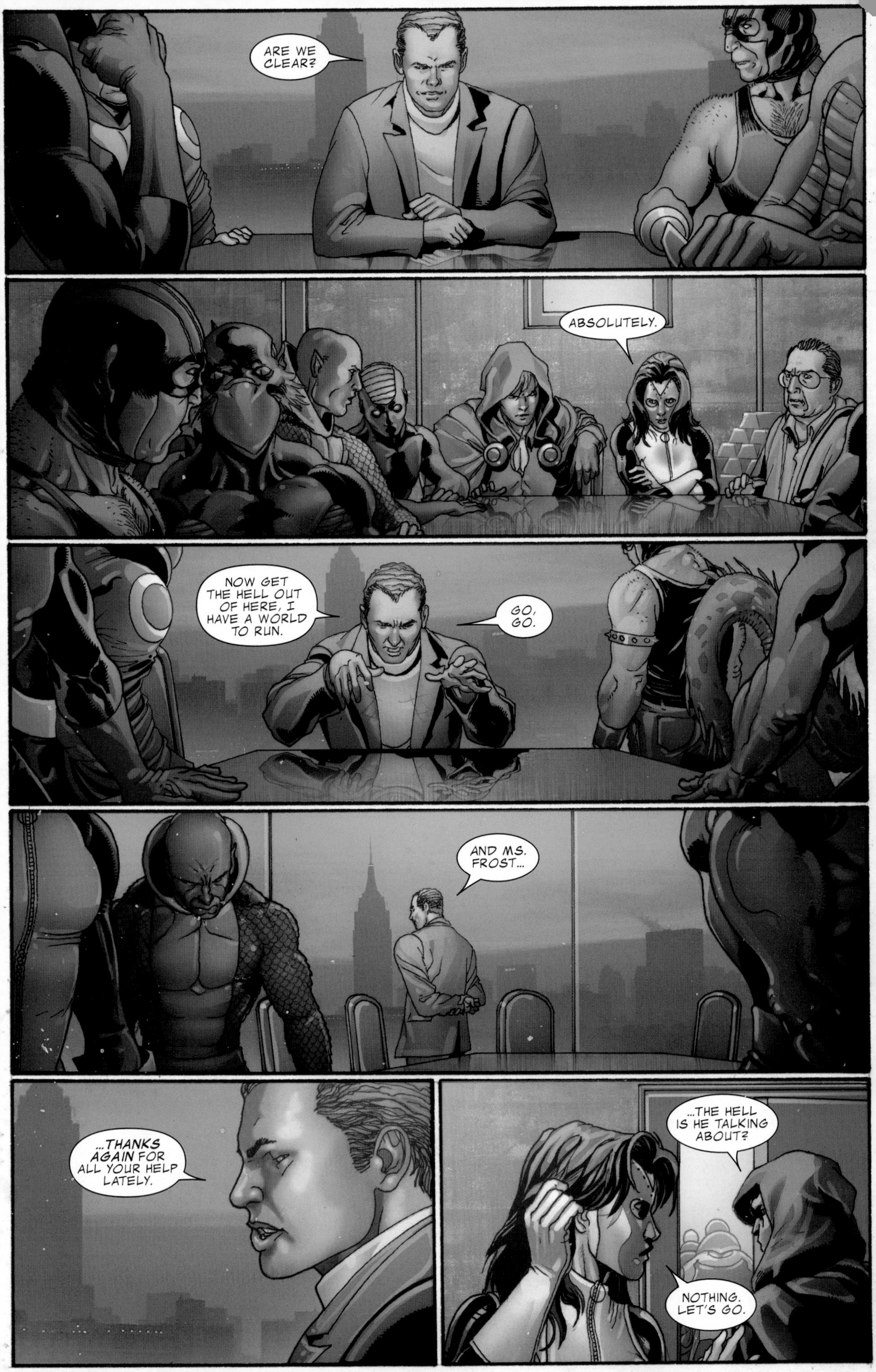
ARE WE CLEAR?
ABSOLUTELY.
NOW GET THE HELL OUT OF HERE, I HAVE A WORLD TO RUN.
GO, GO.
AND MS. FROST...
...*THANKS AGAIN* FOR ALL YOUR HELP LATELY.
...THE HELL IS HE TALKING ABOUT?
NOTHING. LET'S GO.

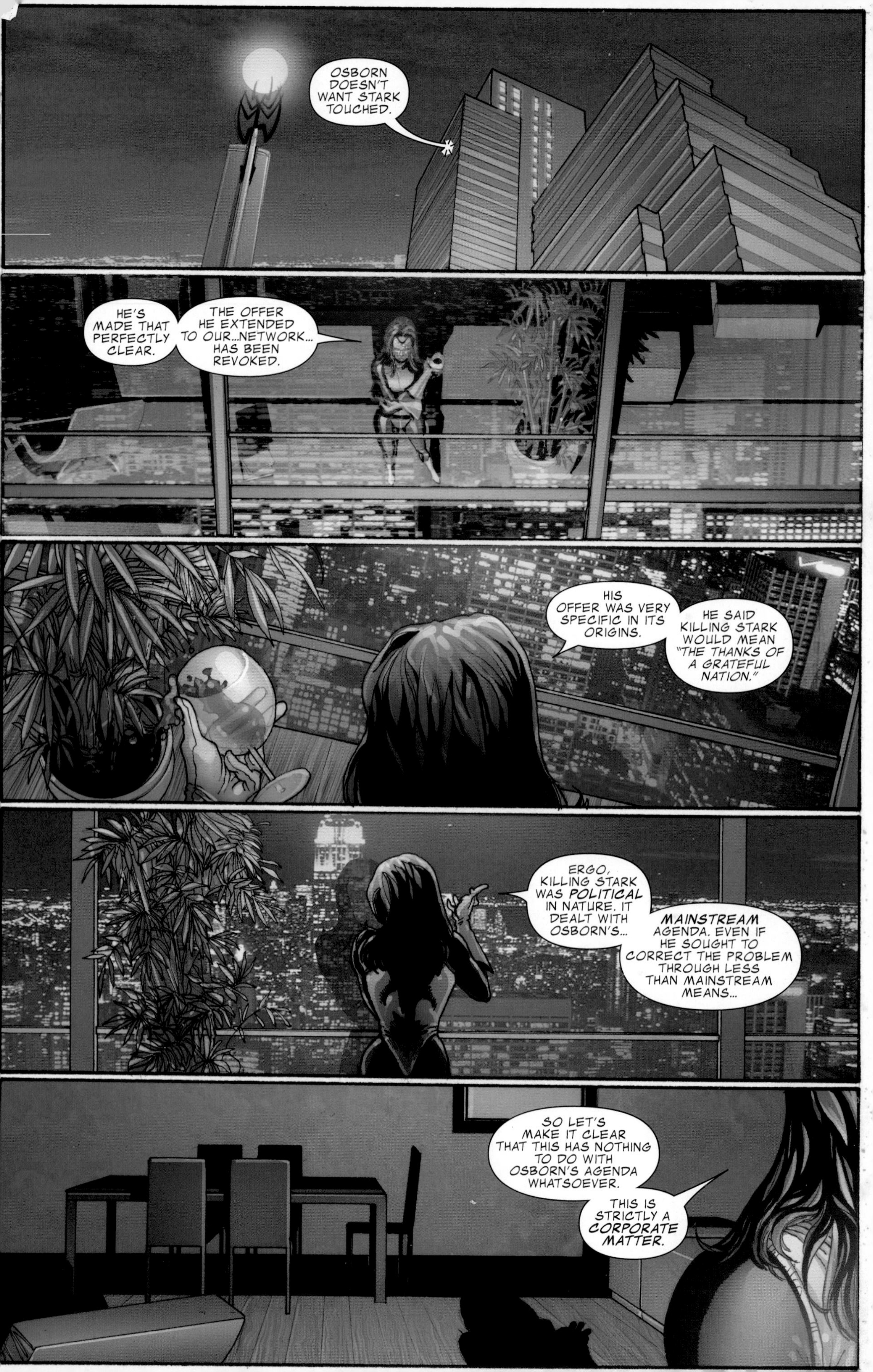
OSBORN DOESN'T WANT STARK TOUCHED.
HE'S MADE THAT PERFECTLY CLEAR.
THE OFFER HE EXTENDED TO OUR...NETWORK... HAS BEEN REVOKED.
HIS OFFER WAS VERY SPECIFIC IN ITS ORIGINS.
HE SAID KILLING STARK WOULD MEAN "THE THANKS OF A GRATEFUL NATION."
ERGO, KILLING STARK WAS POLITICAL IN NATURE. IT DEALT WITH OSBORN'S...
MAINSTREAM AGENDA. EVEN IF HE SOUGHT TO CORRECT THE PROBLEM THROUGH LESS THAN MAINSTREAM MEANS...
SO LET'S MAKE IT CLEAR THAT THIS HAS NOTHING TO DO WITH OSBORN'S AGENDA WHATSOEVER.
THIS IS STRICTLY A CORPORATE MATTER.

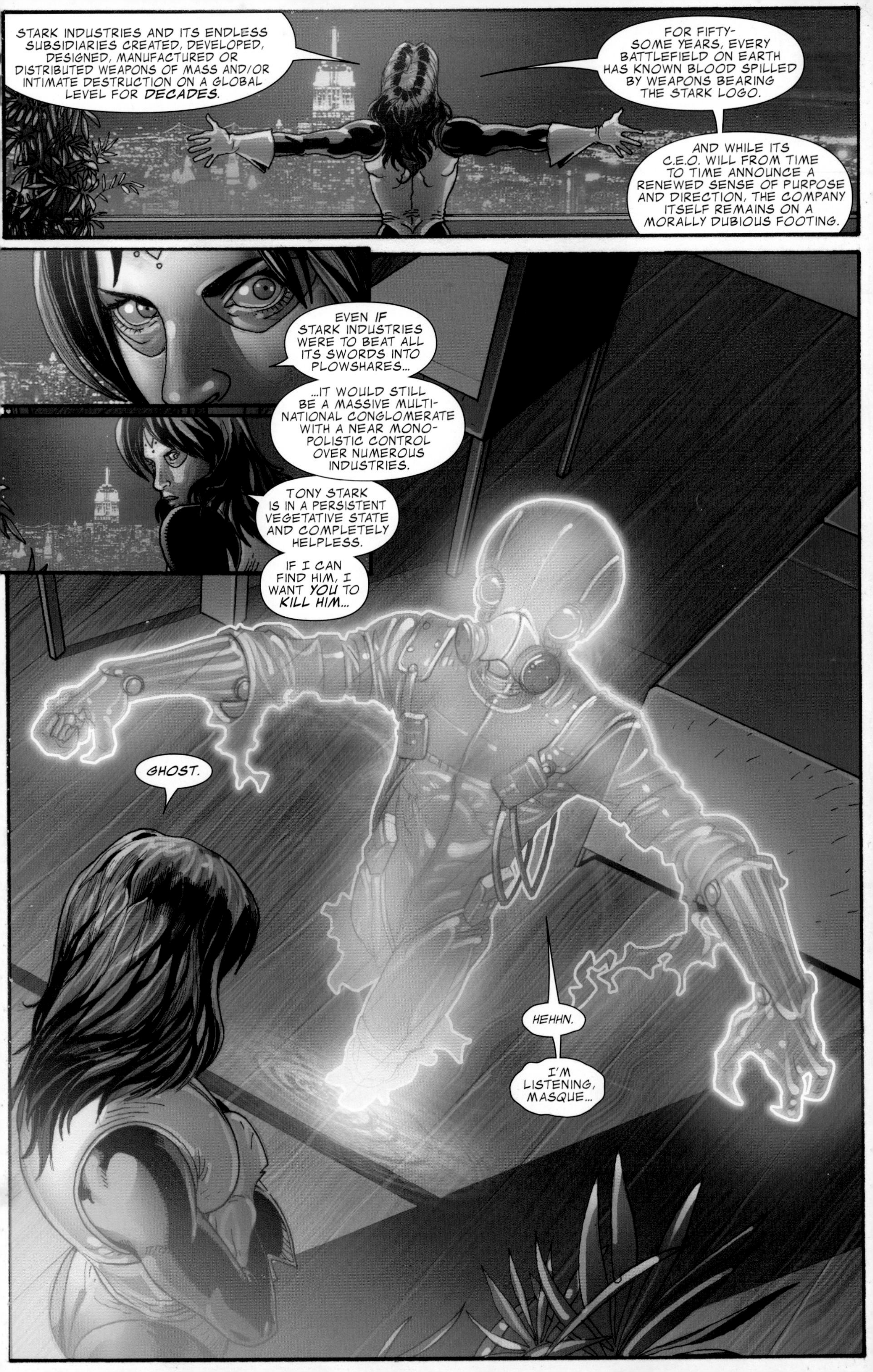
STARK INDUSTRIES AND ITS ENDLESS SUBSIDIARIES CREATED, DEVELOPED, DESIGNED, MANUFACTURED OR DISTRIBUTED WEAPONS OF MASS AND/OR INTIMATE DESTRUCTION ON A GLOBAL LEVEL FOR DECADES.
FOR FIFTY-SOME YEARS, EVERY BATTLEFIELD ON EARTH HAS KNOWN BLOOD SPILLED BY WEAPONS BEARING THE STARK LOGO.
AND WHILE ITS C.E.O. WILL FROM TIME TO TIME ANNOUNCE A RENEWED SENSE OF PURPOSE AND DIRECTION, THE COMPANY ITSELF REMAINS ON A MORALLY DUBIOUS FOOTING.
EVEN IF STARK INDUSTRIES WERE TO BEAT ALL ITS SWORDS INTO PLOWSHARES...
...IT WOULD STILL BE A MASSIVE MULTI-NATIONAL CONGLOMERATE WITH A NEAR MONO-POLISTIC CONTROL OVER NUMEROUS INDUSTRIES.
TONY STARK IS IN A PERSISTENT VEGETATIVE STATE AND COMPLETELY HELPLESS.
IF I CAN FIND HIM, I WANT YOU TO KILL HIM...
GHOST.
HEHHN.
I'M LISTENING, MASQUE...

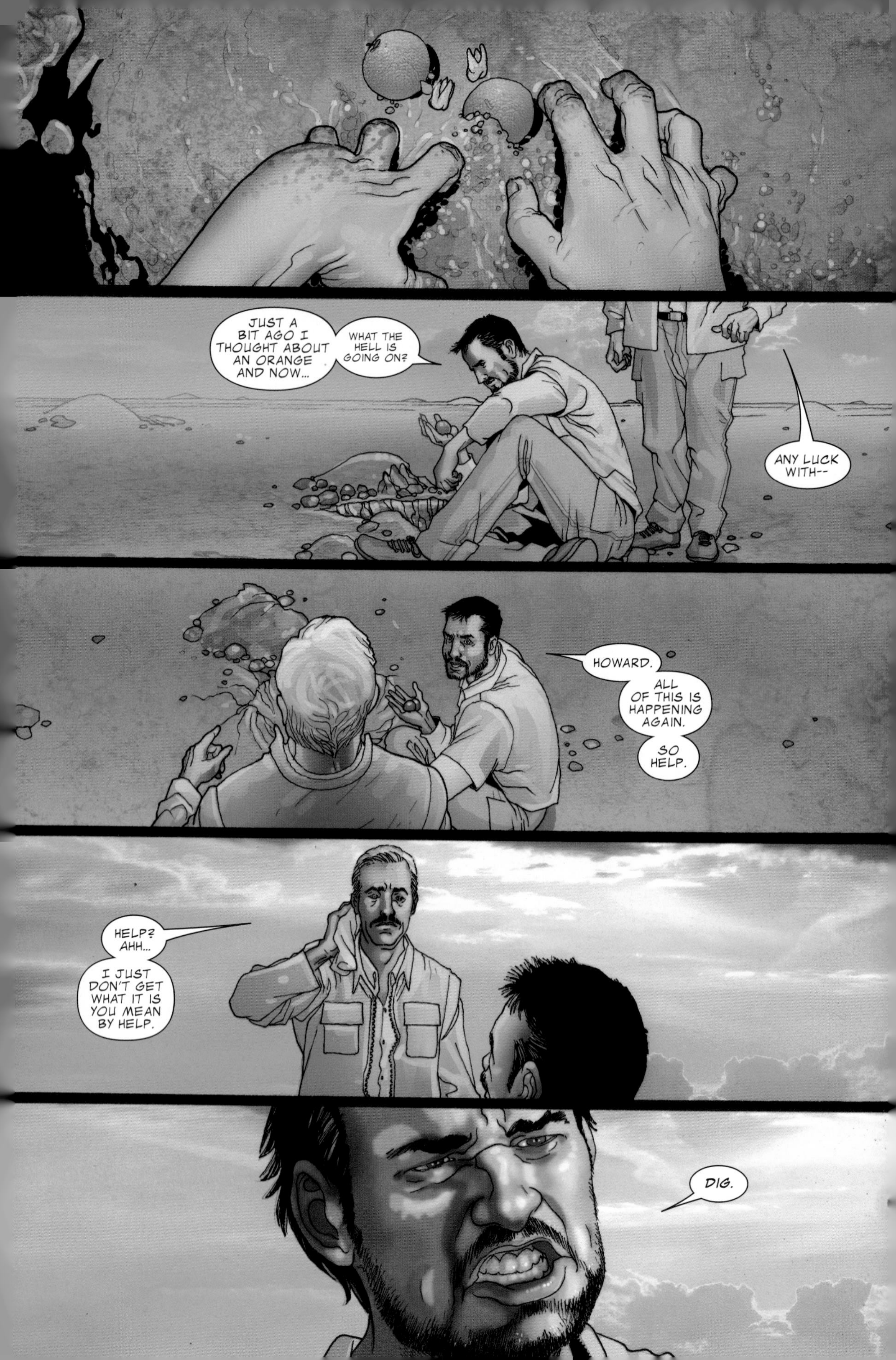
JUST A BIT AGO I THOUGHT ABOUT AN ORANGE AND NOW...
WHAT THE HELL IS GOING ON?
ANY LUCK WITH--
HOWARD.
ALL OF THIS IS HAPPENING AGAIN.
SO HELP.
HELP? AHH...
I JUST DON'T GET WHAT IT IS YOU MEAN BY HELP.
DIG.

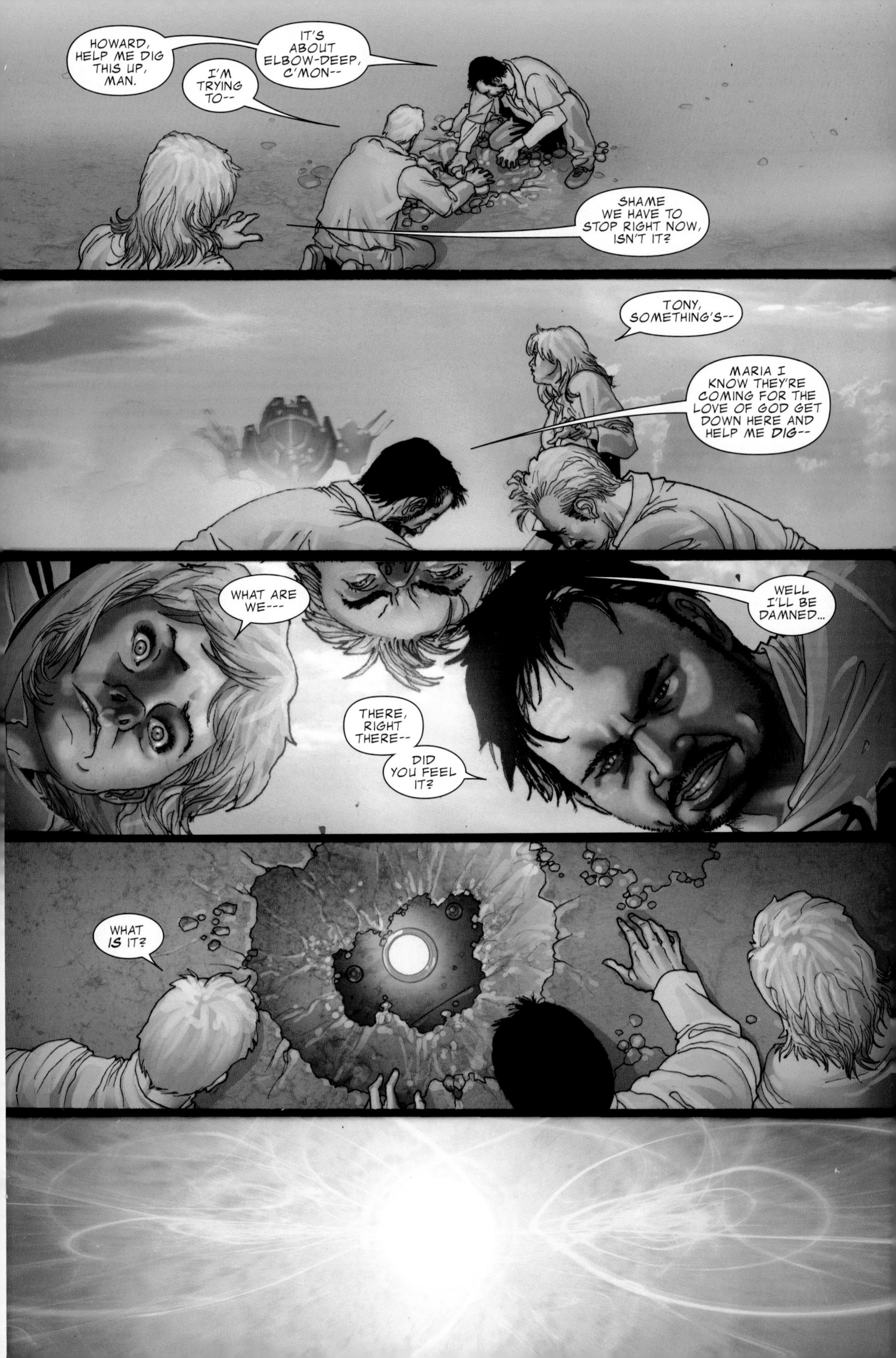
HOWARD, HELP ME DIG THIS UP, MAN.
IT'S ABOUT ELBOW-DEEP, C'MON--
I'M TRYING TO--
SHAME WE HAVE TO STOP RIGHT NOW, ISN'T IT?
TONY, SOMETHING'S--
MARIA I KNOW THEY'RE COMING FOR THE LOVE OF GOD GET DOWN HERE AND HELP ME DIG--
WHAT ARE WE---
WELL I'LL BE DAMNED...
THERE, RIGHT THERE--
DID YOU FEEL IT?
WHAT IS IT?

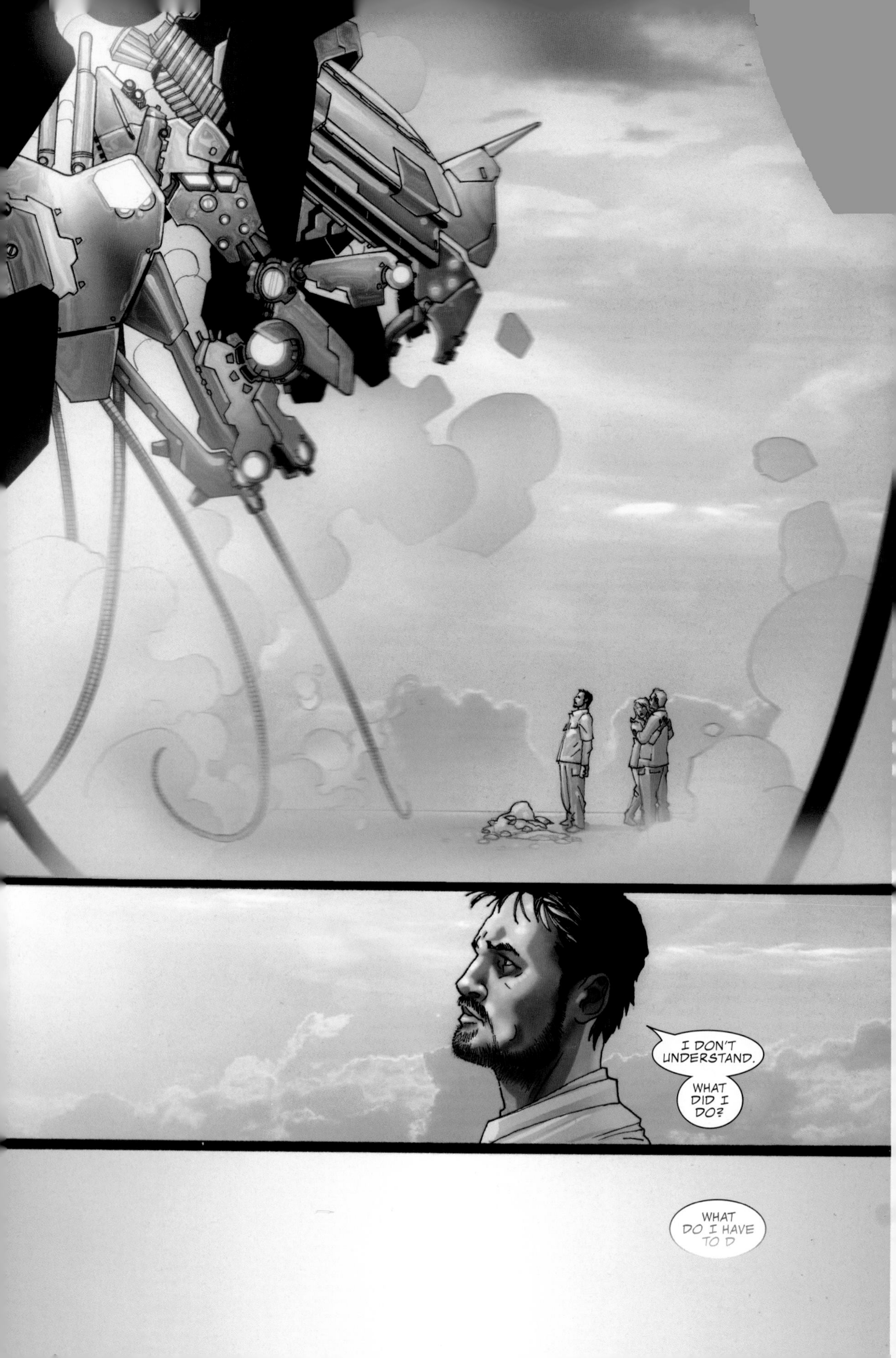
I DON'T UNDERSTAND.
WHAT DID I DO?
WHAT DO I HAVE TO D

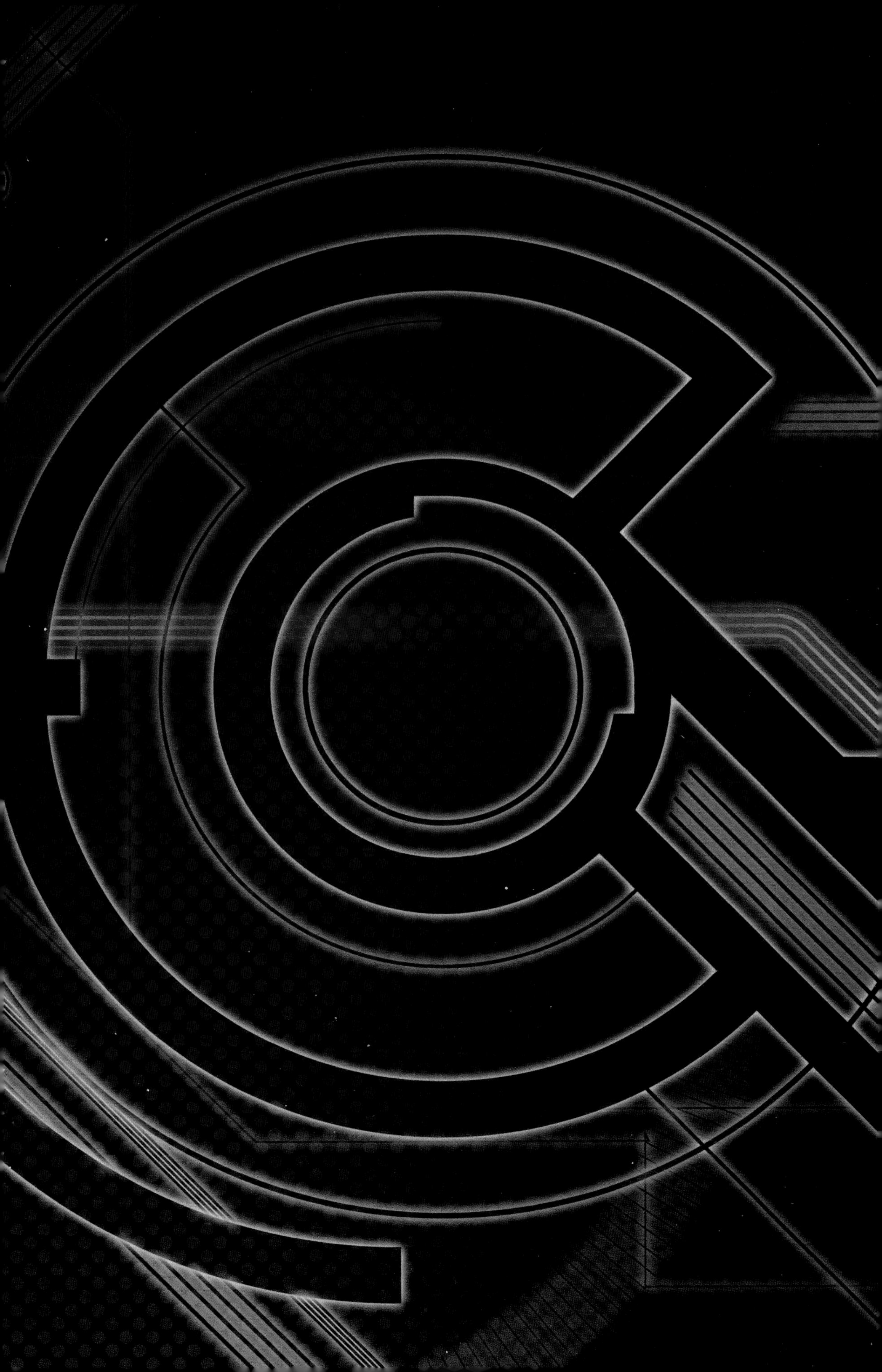

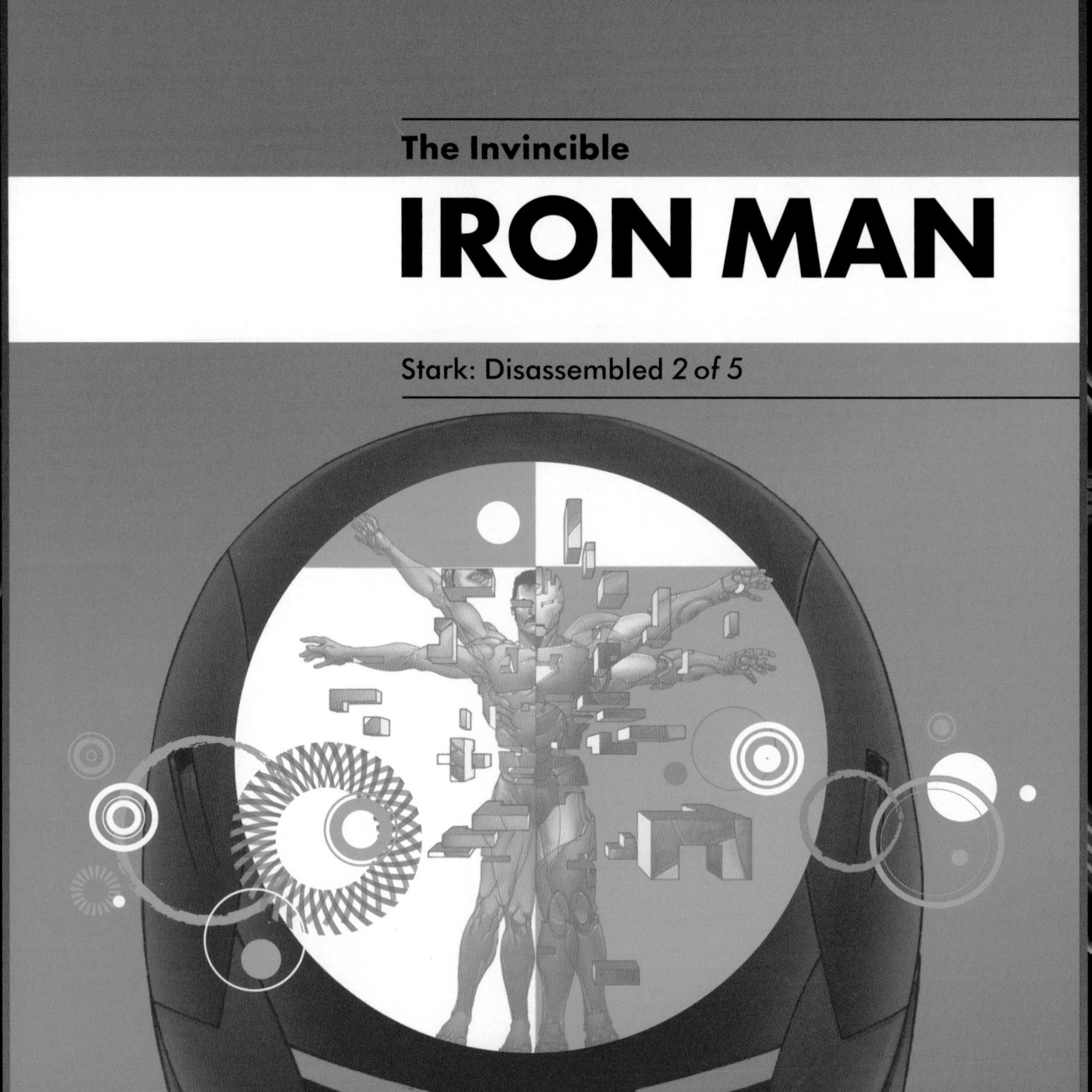
The Invincible
IRON MAN
Stark: Disassembled 2 of 5

21

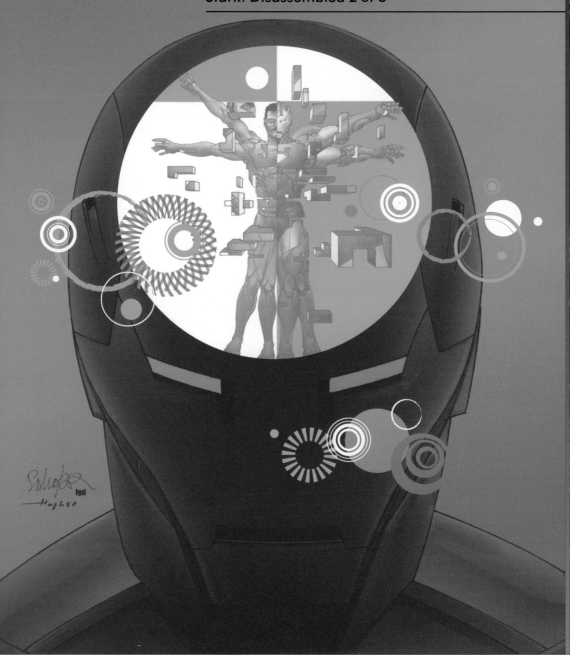

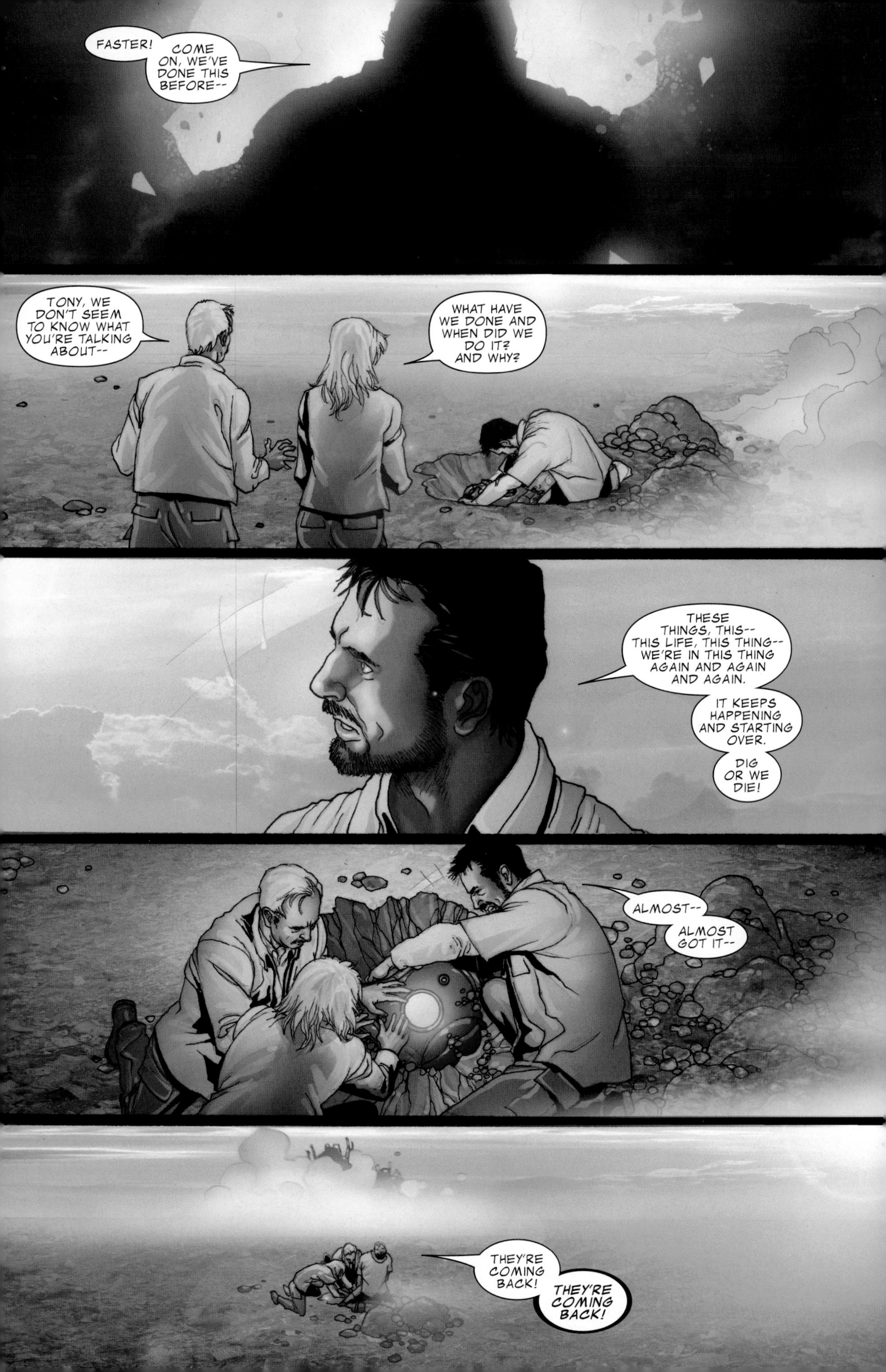
FASTER!
COME ON, WE'VE DONE THIS BEFORE--
TONY, WE DON'T SEEM TO KNOW WHAT YOU'RE TALKING ABOUT--
WHAT HAVE WE DONE AND WHEN DID WE DO IT? AND WHY?
THESE THINGS, THIS-- THIS LIFE, THIS THING-- WE'RE IN THIS THING AGAIN AND AGAIN AND AGAIN.
IT KEEPS HAPPENING AND STARTING OVER.
DIG OR WE DIE!
ALMOST--
ALMOST GOT IT--
THEY'RE COMING BACK!
THEY'RE COMING BACK!

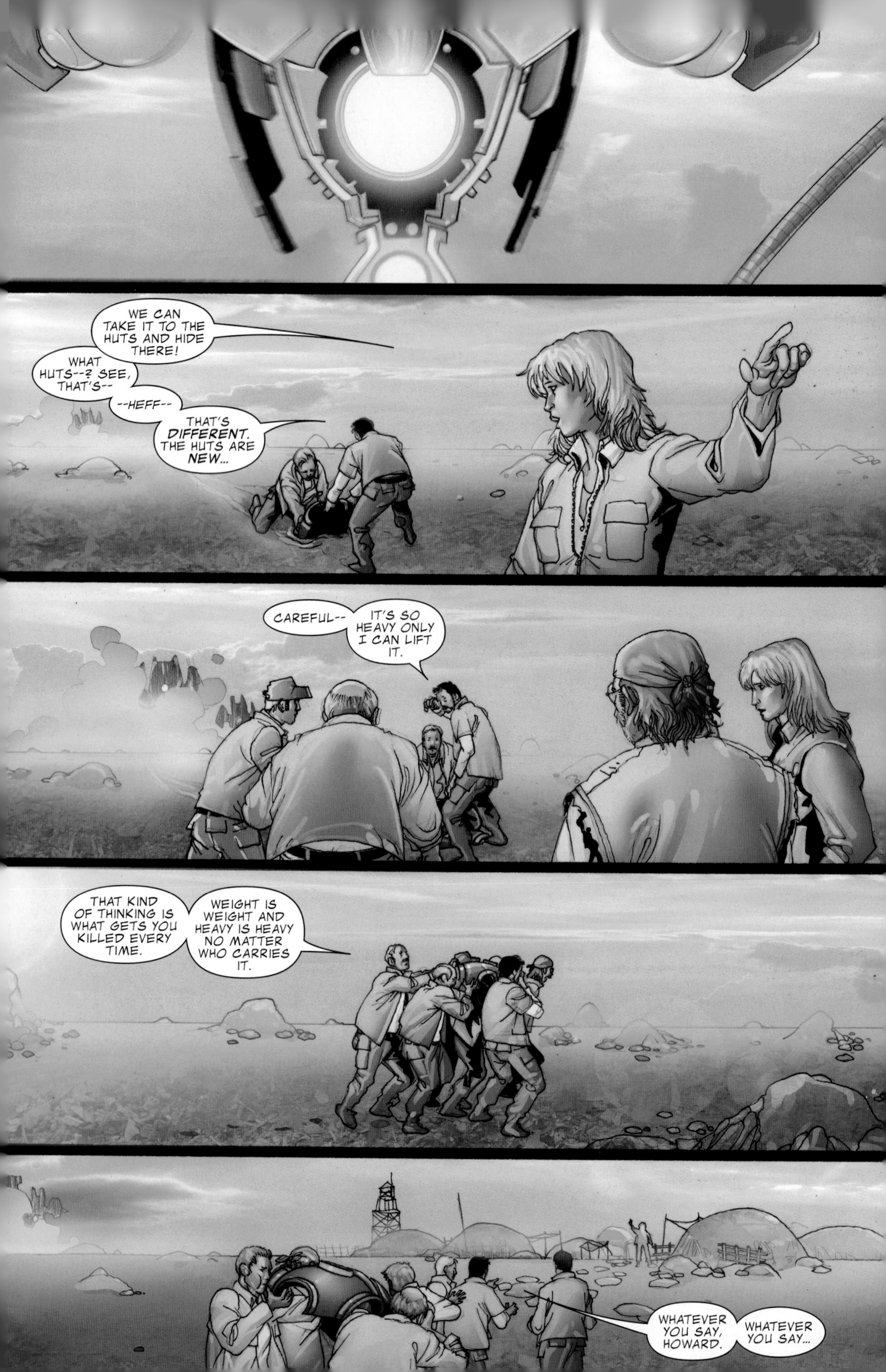

WE CAN TAKE IT TO THE HUTS AND HIDE THERE!
WHAT HUTS--? SEE, THAT'S--
--HEFF--
THAT'S *DIFFERENT*. THE HUTS ARE *NEW*...
CAREFUL--
IT'S SO HEAVY ONLY I CAN LIFT IT.
THAT KIND OF THINKING IS WHAT GETS YOU KILLED EVERY TIME.
WEIGHT IS WEIGHT AND HEAVY IS HEAVY NO MATTER WHO CARRIES IT.
WHATEVER YOU SAY, HOWARD.
WHATEVER YOU SAY...

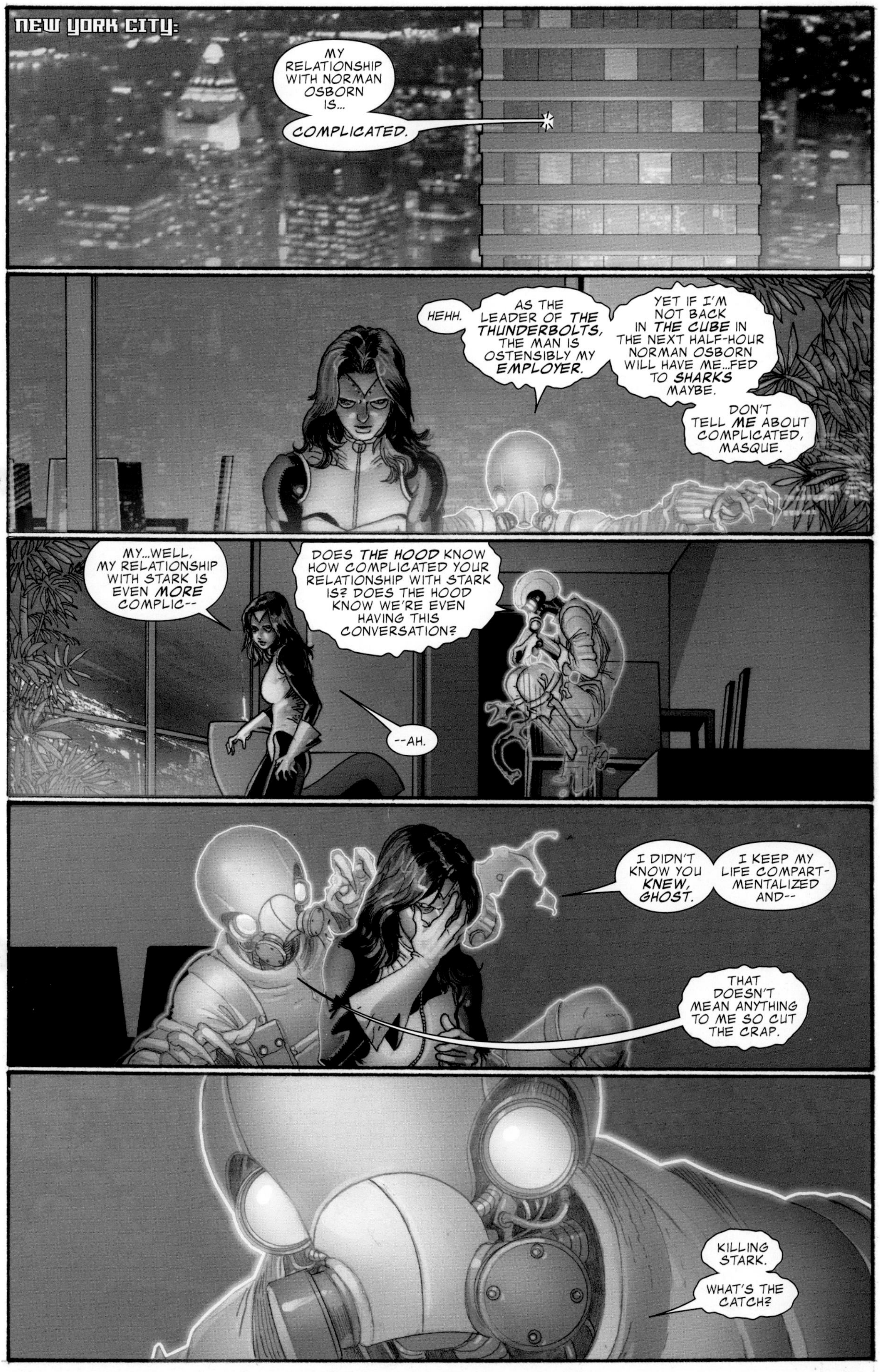
NEW YORK CITY:
MY RELATIONSHIP WITH NORMAN OSBORN IS...
COMPLICATED.
HEHH.
AS THE LEADER OF THE THUNDERBOLTS, THE MAN IS OSTENSIBLY MY EMPLOYER.
YET IF I'M NOT BACK IN THE CUBE IN THE NEXT HALF-HOUR NORMAN OSBORN WILL HAVE ME...FED TO SHARKS MAYBE.
DON'T TELL ME ABOUT COMPLICATED, MASQUE.
MY...WELL, MY RELATIONSHIP WITH STARK IS EVEN MORE COMPLIC--
DOES THE HOOD KNOW HOW COMPLICATED YOUR RELATIONSHIP WITH STARK IS? DOES THE HOOD KNOW WE'RE EVEN HAVING THIS CONVERSATION?
--AH.
I DIDN'T KNOW YOU KNEW, GHOST.
I KEEP MY LIFE COMPART-MENTALIZED AND--
THAT DOESN'T MEAN ANYTHING TO ME SO CUT THE CRAP.
KILLING STARK.
WHAT'S THE CATCH?

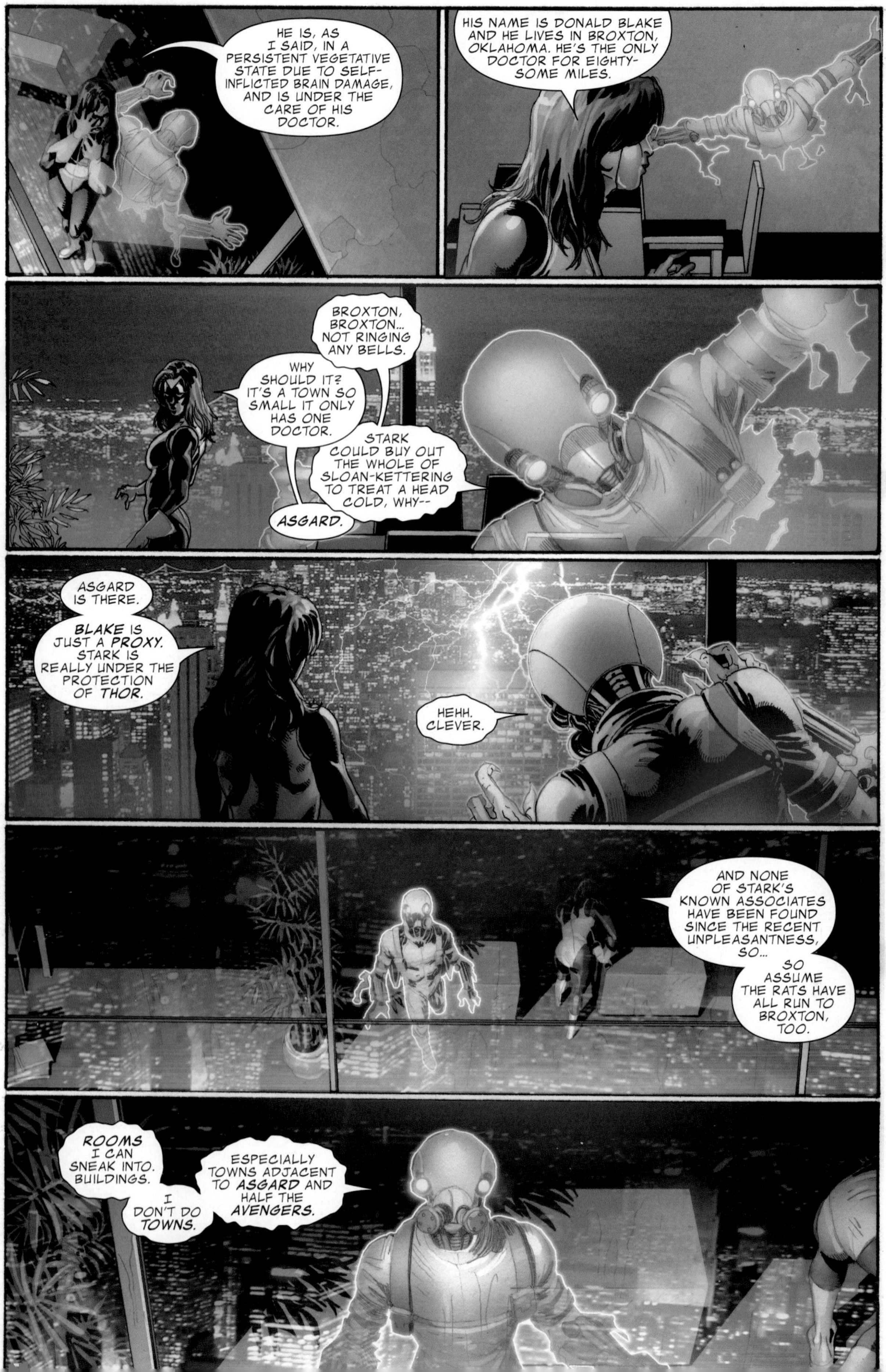
HE IS, AS I SAID, IN A PERSISTENT VEGETATIVE STATE DUE TO SELF-INFLICTED BRAIN DAMAGE, AND IS UNDER THE CARE OF HIS DOCTOR.
HIS NAME IS DONALD BLAKE AND HE LIVES IN BROXTON, OKLAHOMA. HE'S THE ONLY DOCTOR FOR EIGHTY-SOME MILES.
BROXTON, BROXTON... NOT RINGING ANY BELLS.
WHY SHOULD IT? IT'S A TOWN SO SMALL IT ONLY HAS ONE DOCTOR.
STARK COULD BUY OUT THE WHOLE OF SLOAN-KETTERING TO TREAT A HEAD COLD, WHY--
ASGARD.
ASGARD IS THERE.
BLAKE IS JUST A PROXY. STARK IS REALLY UNDER THE PROTECTION OF THOR.
HEHH. CLEVER.
AND NONE OF STARK'S KNOWN ASSOCIATES HAVE BEEN FOUND SINCE THE RECENT UNPLEASANTNESS, SO...
SO ASSUME THE RATS HAVE ALL RUN TO BROXTON, TOO.
ROOMS I CAN SNEAK INTO. BUILDINGS.
I DON'T DO TOWNS.
ESPECIALLY TOWNS ADJACENT TO ASGARD AND HALF THE AVENGERS.

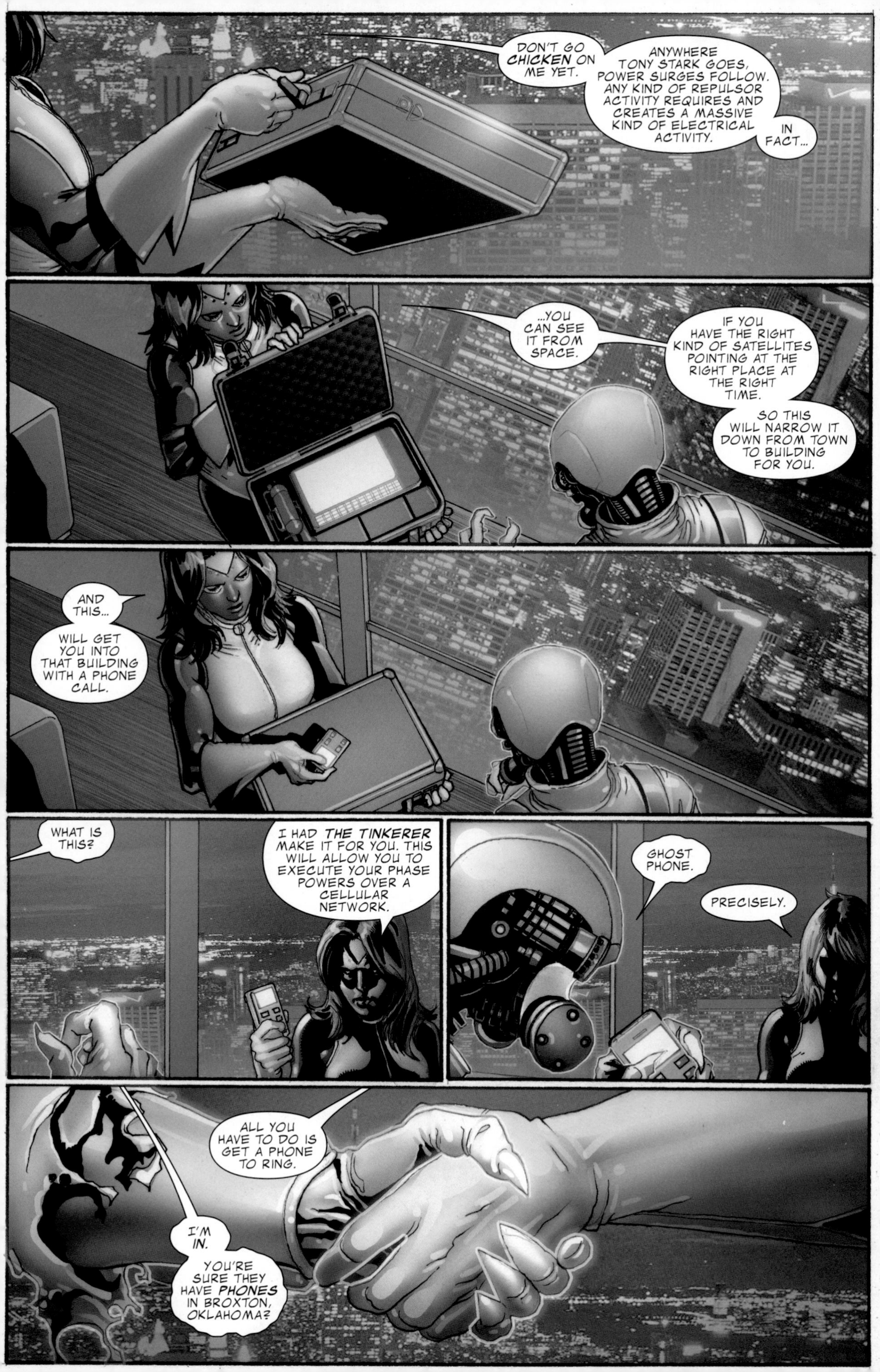
DON'T GO CHICKEN ON ME YET.
ANYWHERE TONY STARK GOES, POWER SURGES FOLLOW. ANY KIND OF REPULSOR ACTIVITY REQUIRES AND CREATES A MASSIVE KIND OF ELECTRICAL ACTIVITY.
IN FACT...
...YOU CAN SEE IT FROM SPACE.
IF YOU HAVE THE RIGHT KIND OF SATELLITES POINTING AT THE RIGHT PLACE AT THE RIGHT TIME.
SO THIS WILL NARROW IT DOWN FROM TOWN TO BUILDING FOR YOU.
AND THIS...
WILL GET YOU INTO THAT BUILDING WITH A PHONE CALL.
WHAT IS THIS?
I HAD THE TINKERER MAKE IT FOR YOU. THIS WILL ALLOW YOU TO EXECUTE YOUR PHASE POWERS OVER A CELLULAR NETWORK.
GHOST PHONE.
PRECISELY.
ALL YOU HAVE TO DO IS GET A PHONE TO RING.
I'M IN.
YOU'RE SURE THEY HAVE PHONES IN BROXTON, OKLAHOMA?

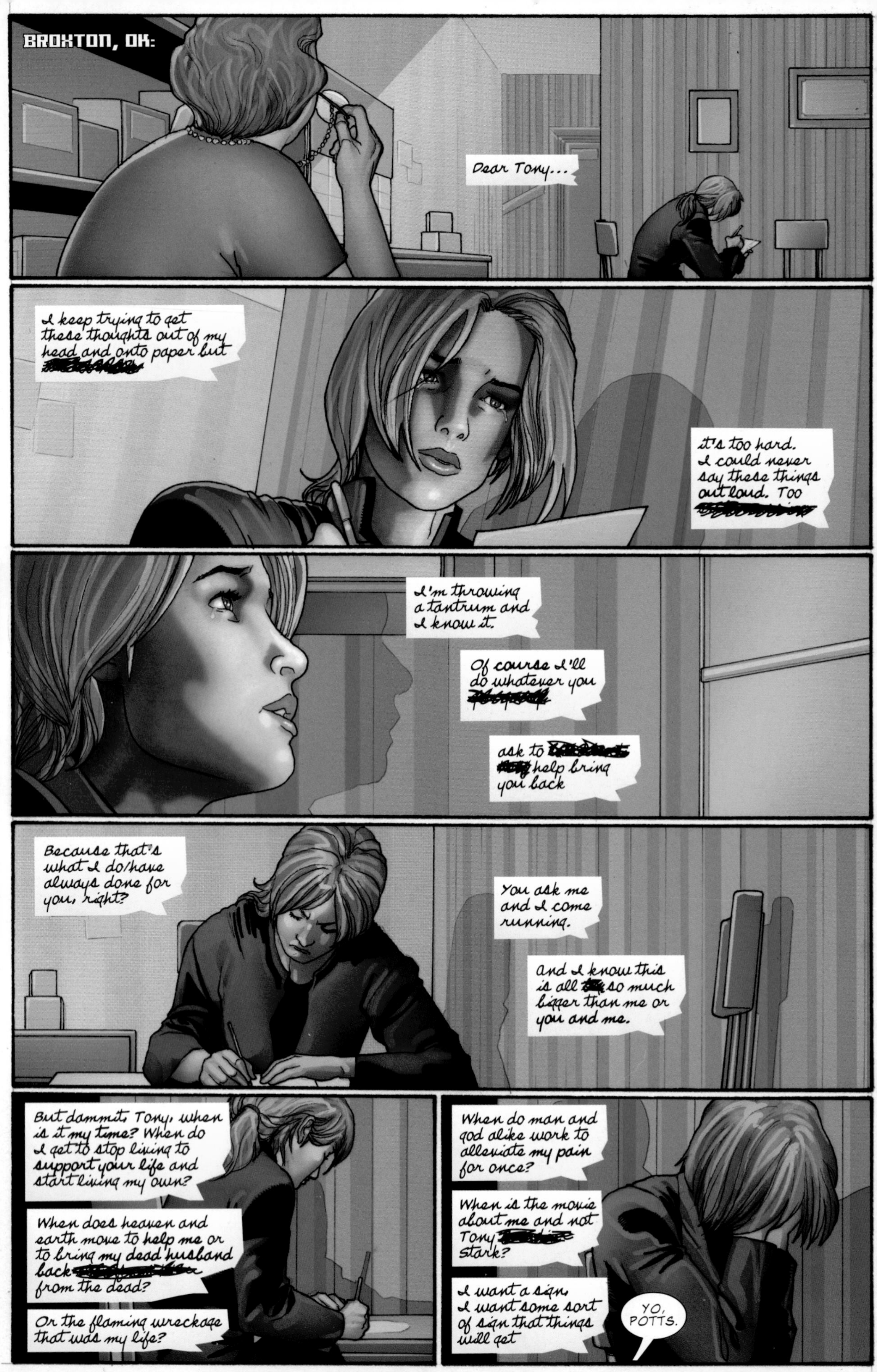
BROXTON, OK:
Dear Tony...
I keep trying to get these thoughts out of my head and onto paper but [redacted]
it's too hard. I could never say these things out loud. Too [redacted]
I'm throwing a tantrum and I know it.
Of course I'll do whatever you [redacted]
ask to [redacted] help bring you back
Because that's what I do/have always done for you, right?
You ask me and I come running.
And I know this is all [redacted] so much bigger than me or you and me.
But dammit, Tony, when is it my time? When do I get to stop living to support your life and start living my own?
When does heaven and earth move to help me or to bring my dead husband back [redacted] from the dead?
Or the flaming wreckage that was my life?
When do man and god alike work to alleviate my pain for once?
When is the movie about me and not Tony [redacted] Stark?
I want a sign. I want some sort of sign that things will get
YO, POTTS.

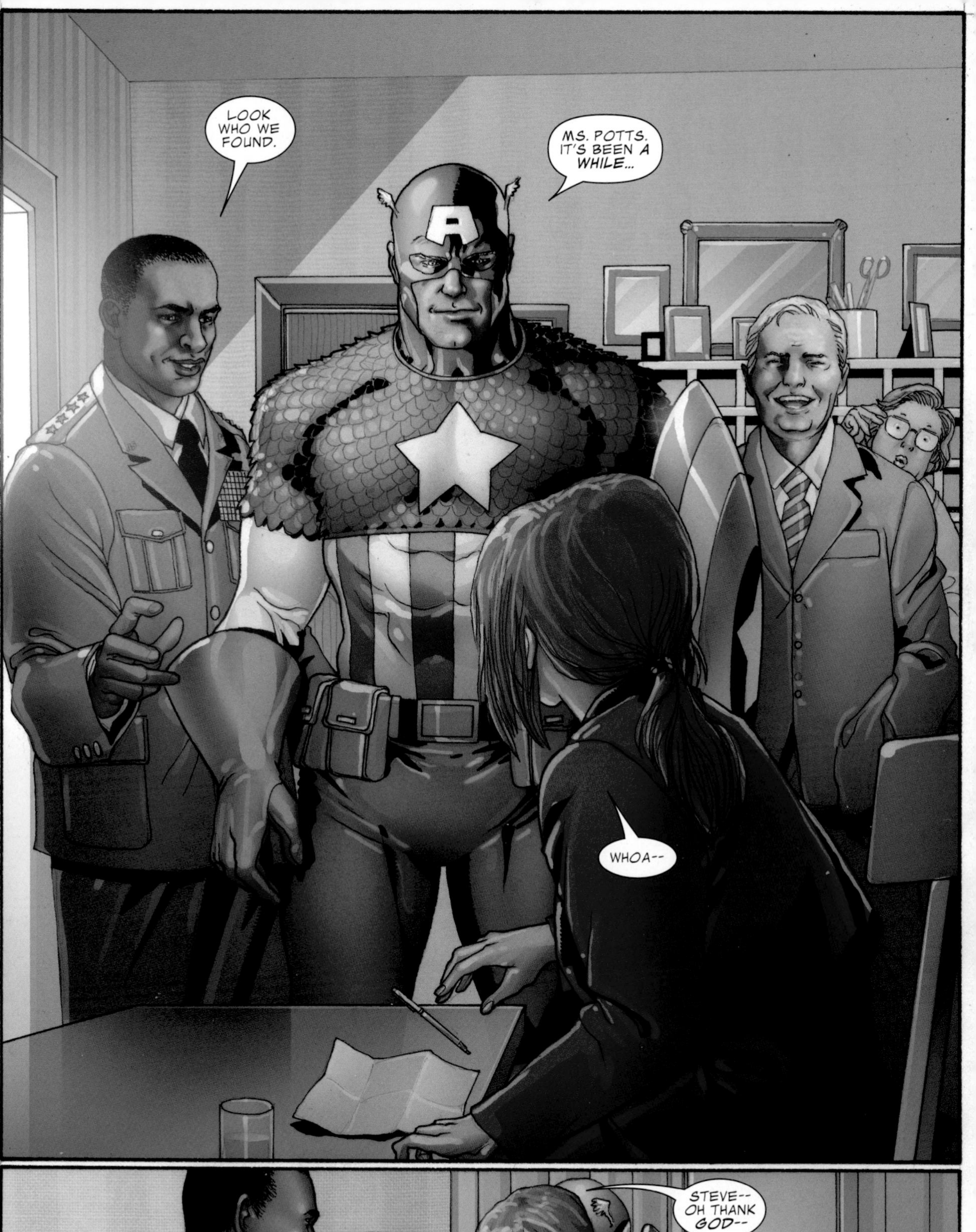
LOOK WHO WE FOUND.
MS. POTTS. IT'S BEEN A WHILE...
WHOA--

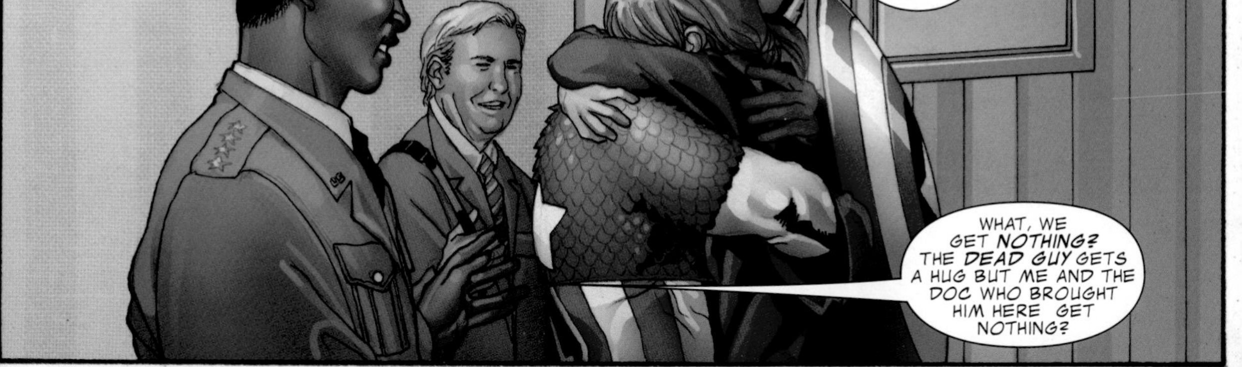
STEVE-- OH THANK GOD--
WHAT, WE GET NOTHING? THE DEAD GUY GETS A HUG BUT ME AND THE DOC WHO BROUGHT HIM HERE GET NOTHING?

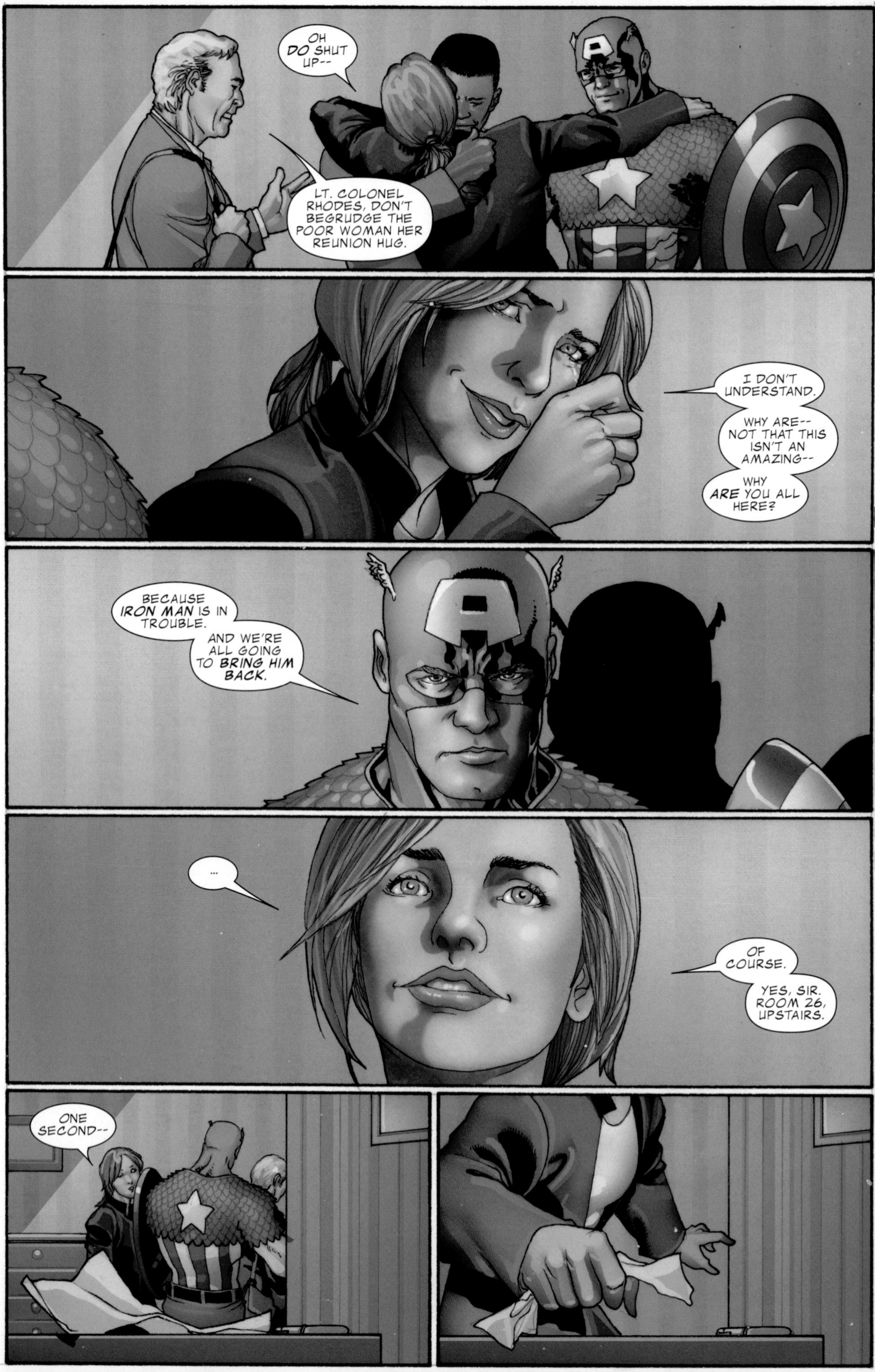
OH DO SHUT UP--
LT. COLONEL RHODES, DON'T BEGRUDGE THE POOR WOMAN HER REUNION HUG.
I DON'T UNDERSTAND.
WHY ARE-- NOT THAT THIS ISN'T AN AMAZING--
WHY ARE YOU ALL HERE?
BECAUSE IRON MAN IS IN TROUBLE.
AND WE'RE ALL GOING TO BRING HIM BACK.
...
OF COURSE.
YES, SIR. ROOM 26, UPSTAIRS.
ONE SECOND--

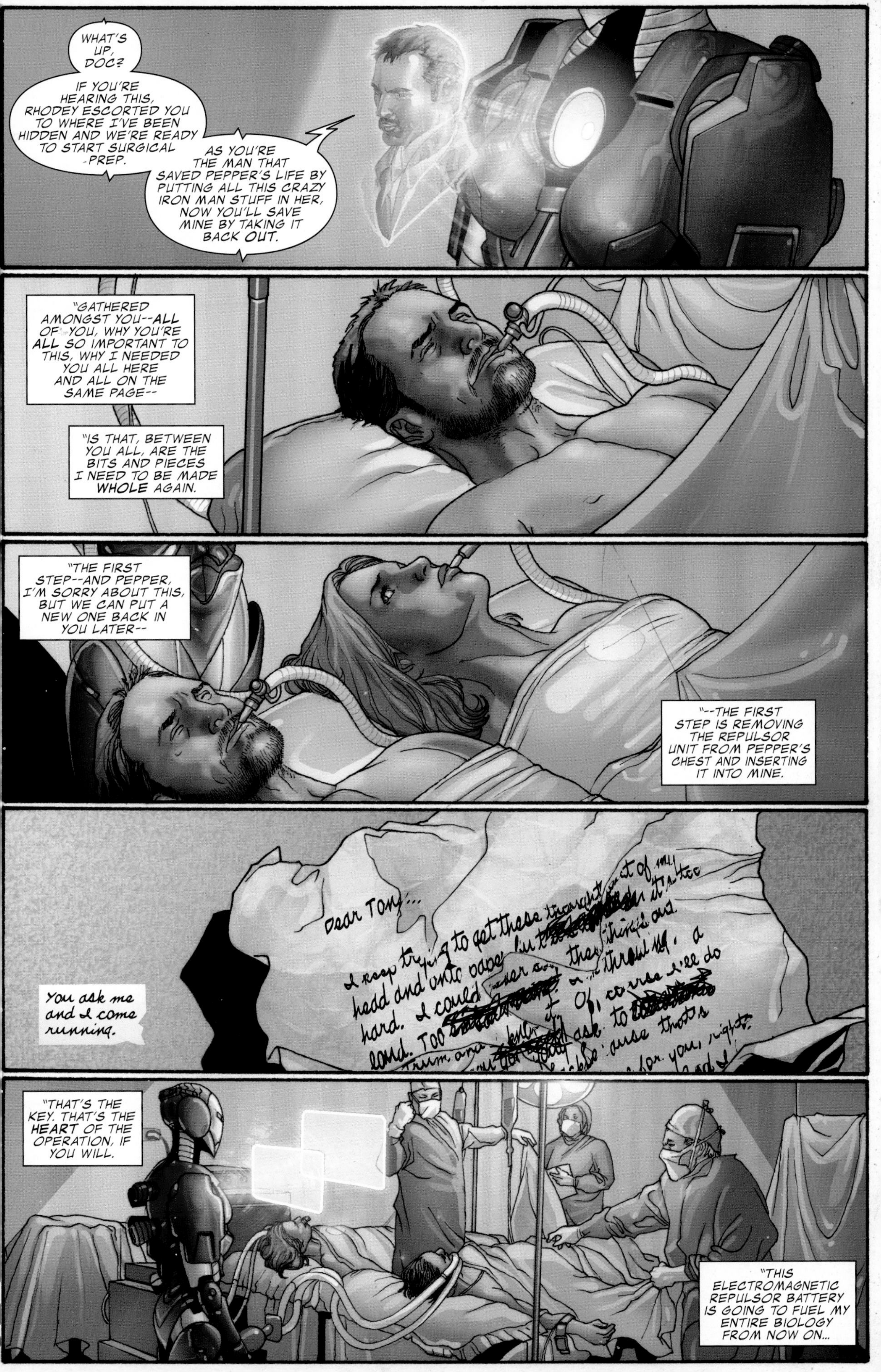
WHAT'S UP, DOC?
IF YOU'RE HEARING THIS, RHODEY ESCORTED YOU TO WHERE I'VE BEEN HIDDEN AND WE'RE READY TO START SURGICAL -PREP.
AS YOU'RE THE MAN THAT SAVED PEPPER'S LIFE BY PUTTING ALL THIS CRAZY IRON MAN STUFF IN HER, NOW YOU'LL SAVE MINE BY TAKING IT BACK OUT.
"GATHERED AMONGST YOU--ALL OF YOU, WHY YOU'RE ALL SO IMPORTANT TO THIS, WHY I NEEDED YOU ALL HERE AND ALL ON THE SAME PAGE--
"IS THAT, BETWEEN YOU ALL, ARE THE BITS AND PIECES I NEED TO BE MADE WHOLE AGAIN.
"THE FIRST STEP--AND PEPPER, I'M SORRY ABOUT THIS, BUT WE CAN PUT A NEW ONE BACK IN YOU LATER--
"--THE FIRST STEP IS REMOVING THE REPULSOR UNIT FROM PEPPER'S CHEST AND INSERTING IT INTO MINE.
Dear Tony...
You ask me and I come running.
"THAT'S THE KEY. THAT'S THE HEART OF THE OPERATION, IF YOU WILL.
"THIS ELECTROMAGNETIC REPULSOR BATTERY IS GOING TO FUEL MY ENTIRE BIOLOGY FROM NOW ON...

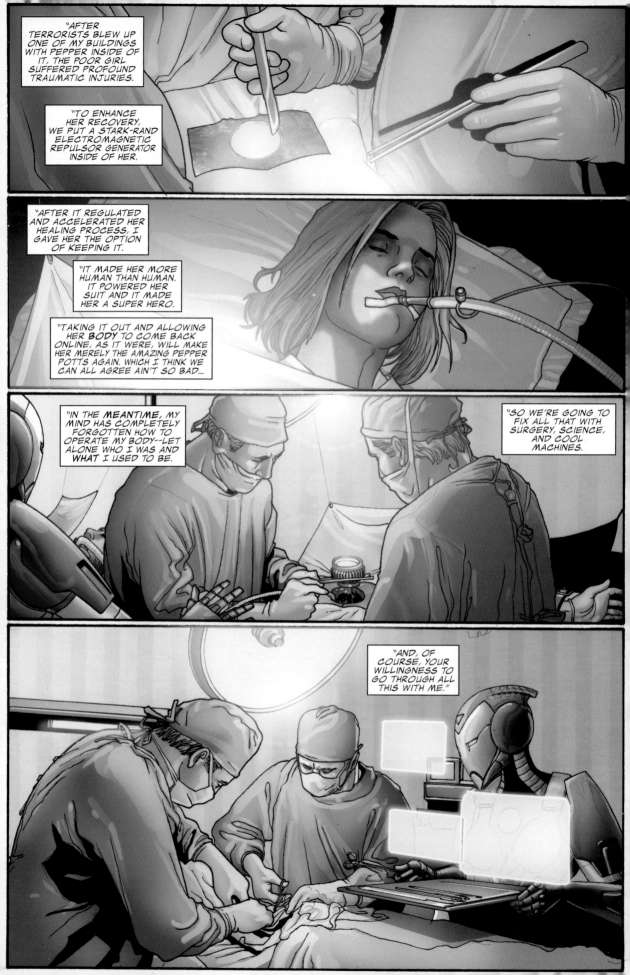

"AFTER TERRORISTS BLEW UP ONE OF MY BUILDINGS WITH PEPPER INSIDE OF IT, THE POOR GIRL SUFFERED PROFOUND TRAUMATIC INJURIES."

"TO ENHANCE HER RECOVERY, WE PUT A STARK-RAND ELECTROMAGNETIC REPULSOR GENERATOR INSIDE OF HER.

"AFTER IT REGULATED AND ACCELERATED HER HEALING PROCESS, I GAVE HER THE OPTION OF KEEPING IT.

"IT MADE HER MORE HUMAN THAN HUMAN. IT POWERED HER SUIT AND IT MADE HER A SUPER HERO.

"TAKING IT OUT AND ALLOWING HER *BODY* TO COME BACK ONLINE, AS IT WERE, WILL MAKE HER MERELY THE AMAZING PEPPER POTTS AGAIN. WHICH I THINK WE CAN ALL AGREE AIN'T SO BAD...

"IN THE *MEANTIME,* MY MIND HAS COMPLETELY FORGOTTEN HOW TO OPERATE MY BODY--LET ALONE WHO I WAS AND WHAT I USED TO BE.

"SO WE'RE GOING TO FIX ALL THAT WITH SURGERY, SCIENCE, AND COOL MACHINES.

"AND, OF COURSE, YOUR WILLINGNESS TO GO THROUGH ALL THIS WITH ME."

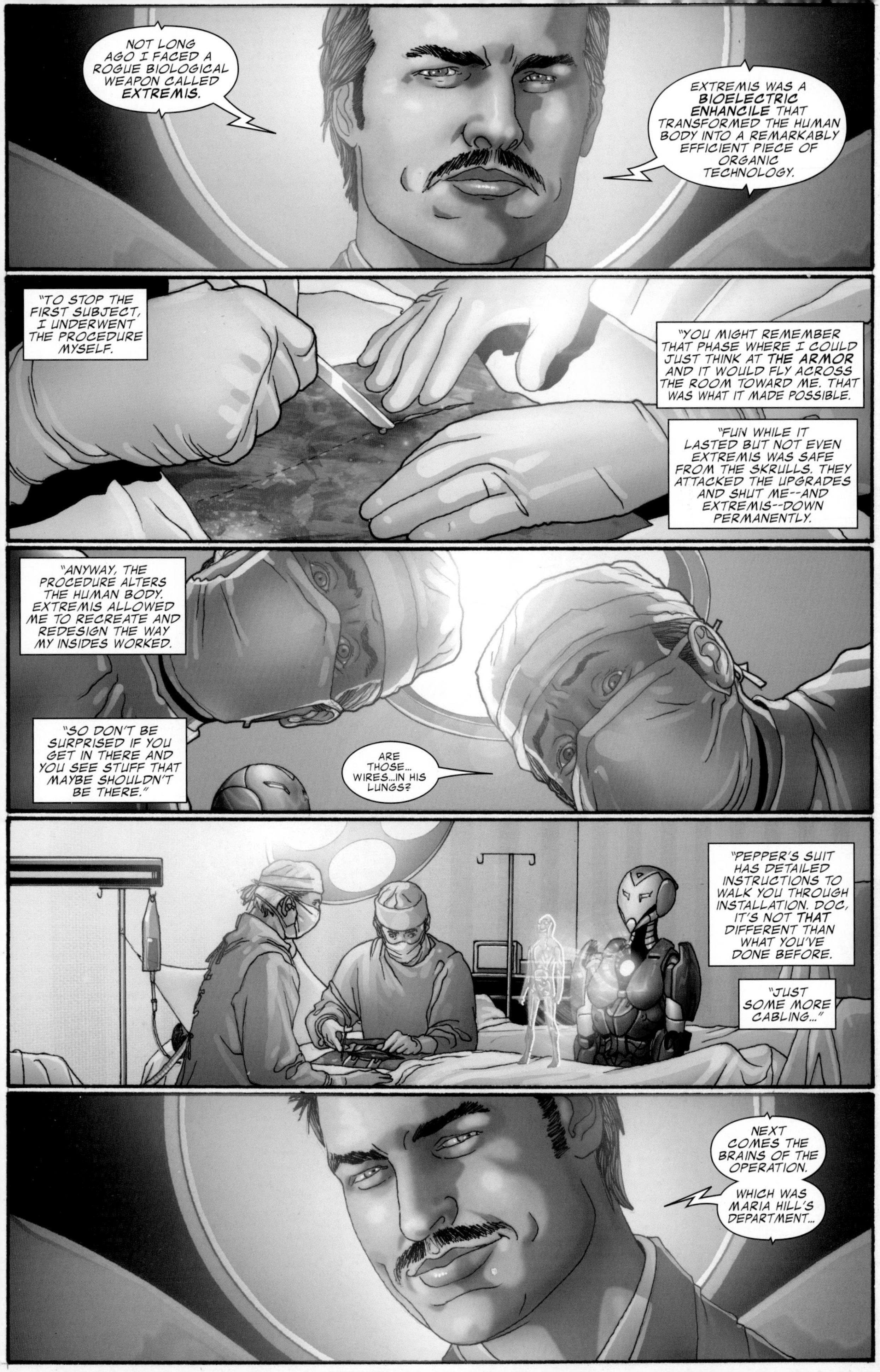
NOT LONG AGO I FACED A ROGUE BIOLOGICAL WEAPON CALLED EXTREMIS.
EXTREMIS WAS A BIOELECTRIC ENHANCILE THAT TRANSFORMED THE HUMAN BODY INTO A REMARKABLY EFFICIENT PIECE OF ORGANIC TECHNOLOGY.
"TO STOP THE FIRST SUBJECT, I UNDERWENT THE PROCEDURE MYSELF.
"YOU MIGHT REMEMBER THAT PHASE WHERE I COULD JUST THINK AT THE ARMOR AND IT WOULD FLY ACROSS THE ROOM TOWARD ME. THAT WAS WHAT IT MADE POSSIBLE.
"FUN WHILE IT LASTED BUT NOT EVEN EXTREMIS WAS SAFE FROM THE SKRULLS. THEY ATTACKED THE UPGRADES AND SHUT ME--AND EXTREMIS--DOWN PERMANENTLY.
"ANYWAY, THE PROCEDURE ALTERS THE HUMAN BODY. EXTREMIS ALLOWED ME TO RECREATE AND REDESIGN THE WAY MY INSIDES WORKED.
"SO DON'T BE SURPRISED IF YOU GET IN THERE AND YOU SEE STUFF THAT MAYBE SHOULDN'T BE THERE."
ARE THOSE... WIRES...IN HIS LUNGS?
"PEPPER'S SUIT HAS DETAILED INSTRUCTIONS TO WALK YOU THROUGH INSTALLATION. DOC, IT'S NOT THAT DIFFERENT THAN WHAT YOU'VE DONE BEFORE.
"JUST SOME MORE CABLING..."
NEXT COMES THE BRAINS OF THE OPERATION.
WHICH WAS MARIA HILL'S DEPARTMENT...

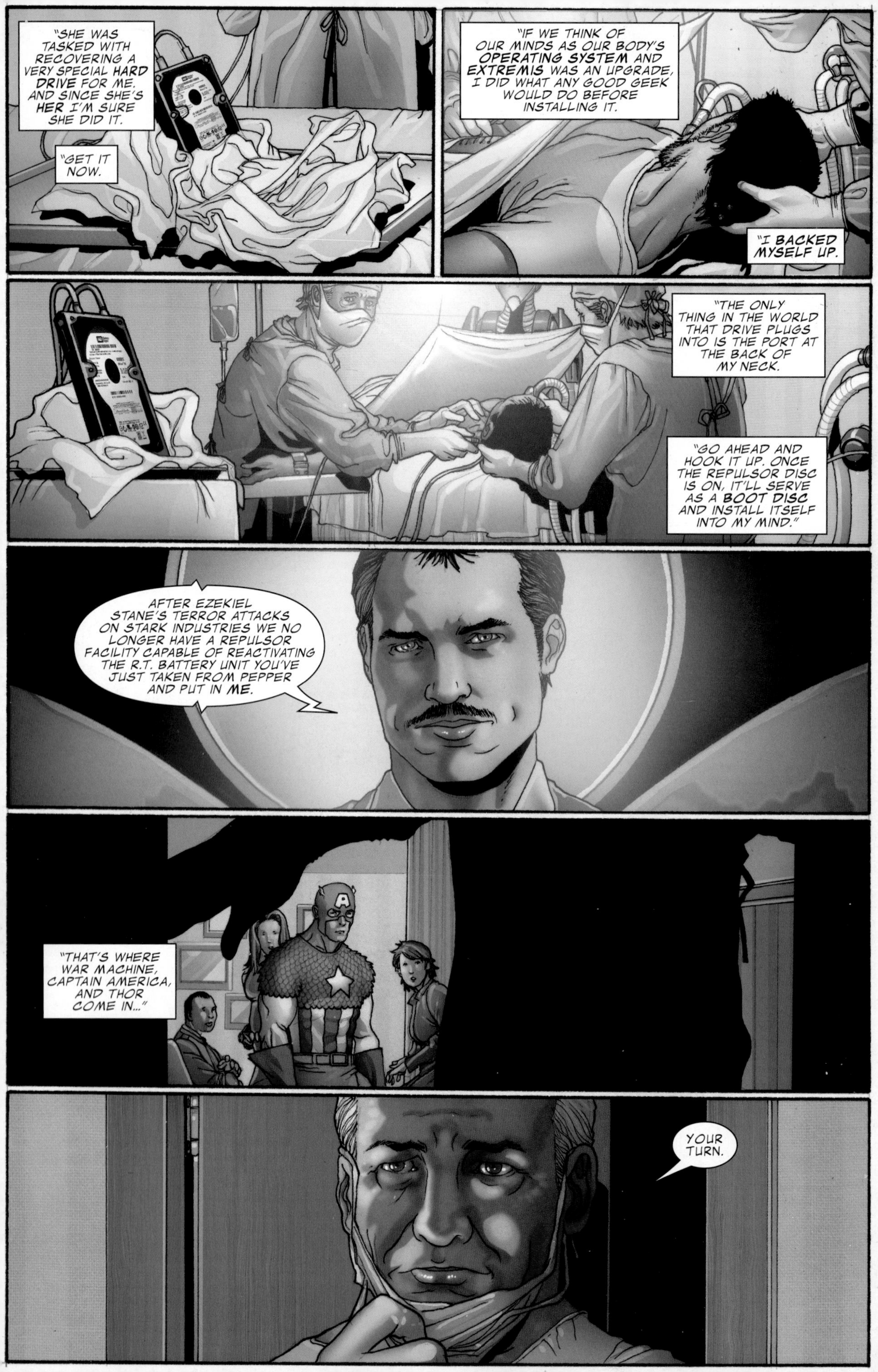
"SHE WAS TASKED WITH RECOVERING A VERY SPECIAL HARD DRIVE FOR ME. AND SINCE SHE'S HER I'M SURE SHE DID IT.
"GET IT NOW.
"IF WE THINK OF OUR MINDS AS OUR BODY'S OPERATING SYSTEM AND EXTREMIS WAS AN UPGRADE, I DID WHAT ANY GOOD GEEK WOULD DO BEFORE INSTALLING IT.
"I BACKED MYSELF UP.
"THE ONLY THING IN THE WORLD THAT DRIVE PLUGS INTO IS THE PORT AT THE BACK OF MY NECK.
"GO AHEAD AND HOOK IT UP. ONCE THE REPULSOR DISC IS ON, IT'LL SERVE AS A BOOT DISC AND INSTALL ITSELF INTO MY MIND."
AFTER EZEKIEL STANE'S TERROR ATTACKS ON STARK INDUSTRIES WE NO LONGER HAVE A REPULSOR FACILITY CAPABLE OF REACTIVATING THE R.T. BATTERY UNIT YOU'VE JUST TAKEN FROM PEPPER AND PUT IN ME.
"THAT'S WHERE WAR MACHINE, CAPTAIN AMERICA, AND THOR COME IN..."
YOUR TURN.

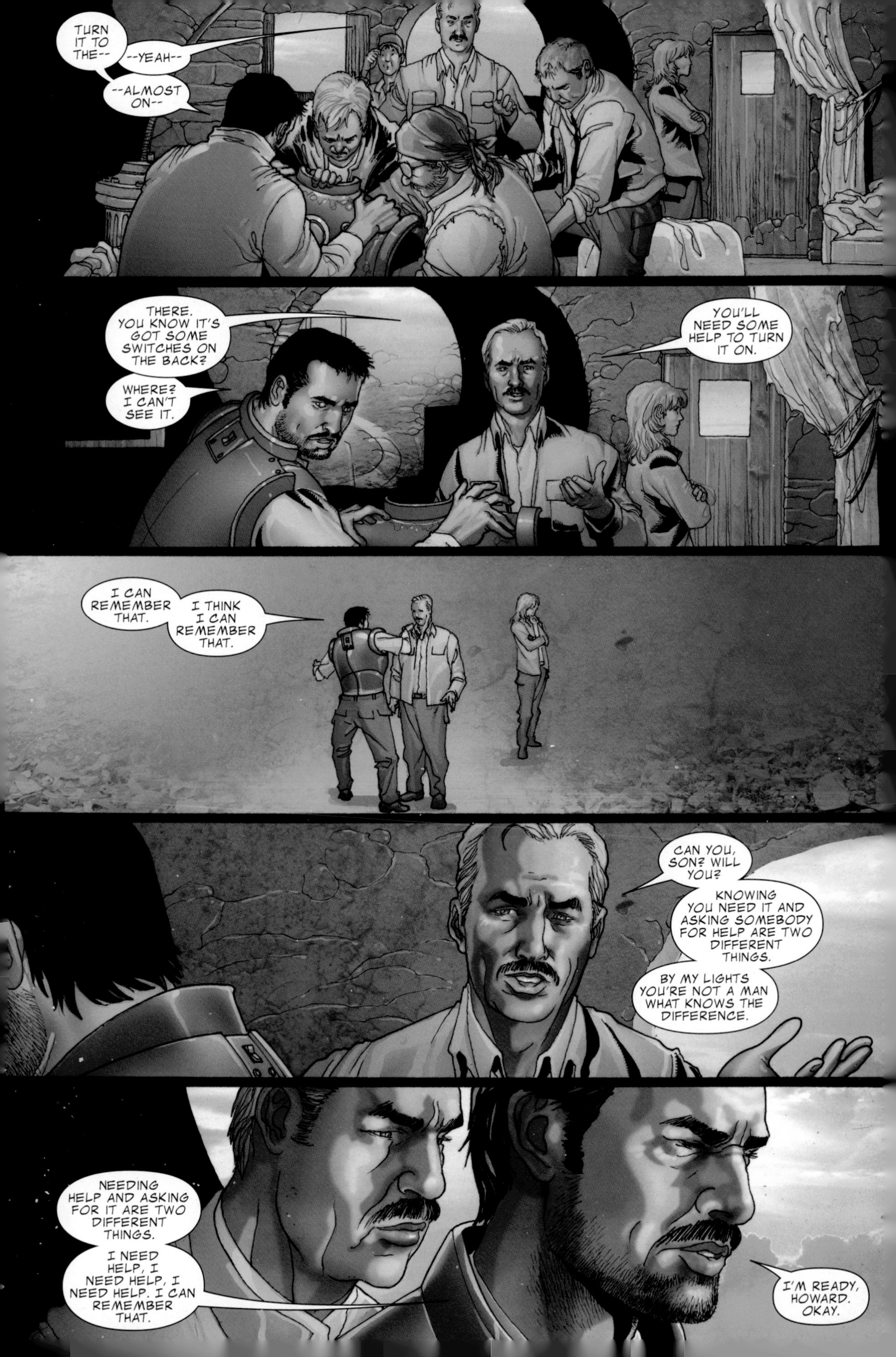
TURN IT TO THE--
--YEAH--
--ALMOST ON--
THERE. YOU KNOW IT'S GOT SOME SWITCHES ON THE BACK?
WHERE? I CAN'T SEE IT.
YOU'LL NEED SOME HELP TO TURN IT ON.
I CAN REMEMBER THAT.
I THINK I CAN REMEMBER THAT.
CAN YOU, SON? WILL YOU?
KNOWING YOU NEED IT AND ASKING SOMEBODY FOR HELP ARE TWO DIFFERENT THINGS.
BY MY LIGHTS YOU'RE NOT A MAN WHAT KNOWS THE DIFFERENCE.
NEEDING HELP AND ASKING FOR IT ARE TWO DIFFERENT THINGS.
I NEED HELP, I NEED HELP, I NEED HELP. I CAN REMEMBER THAT.
I'M READY, HOWARD. OKAY.

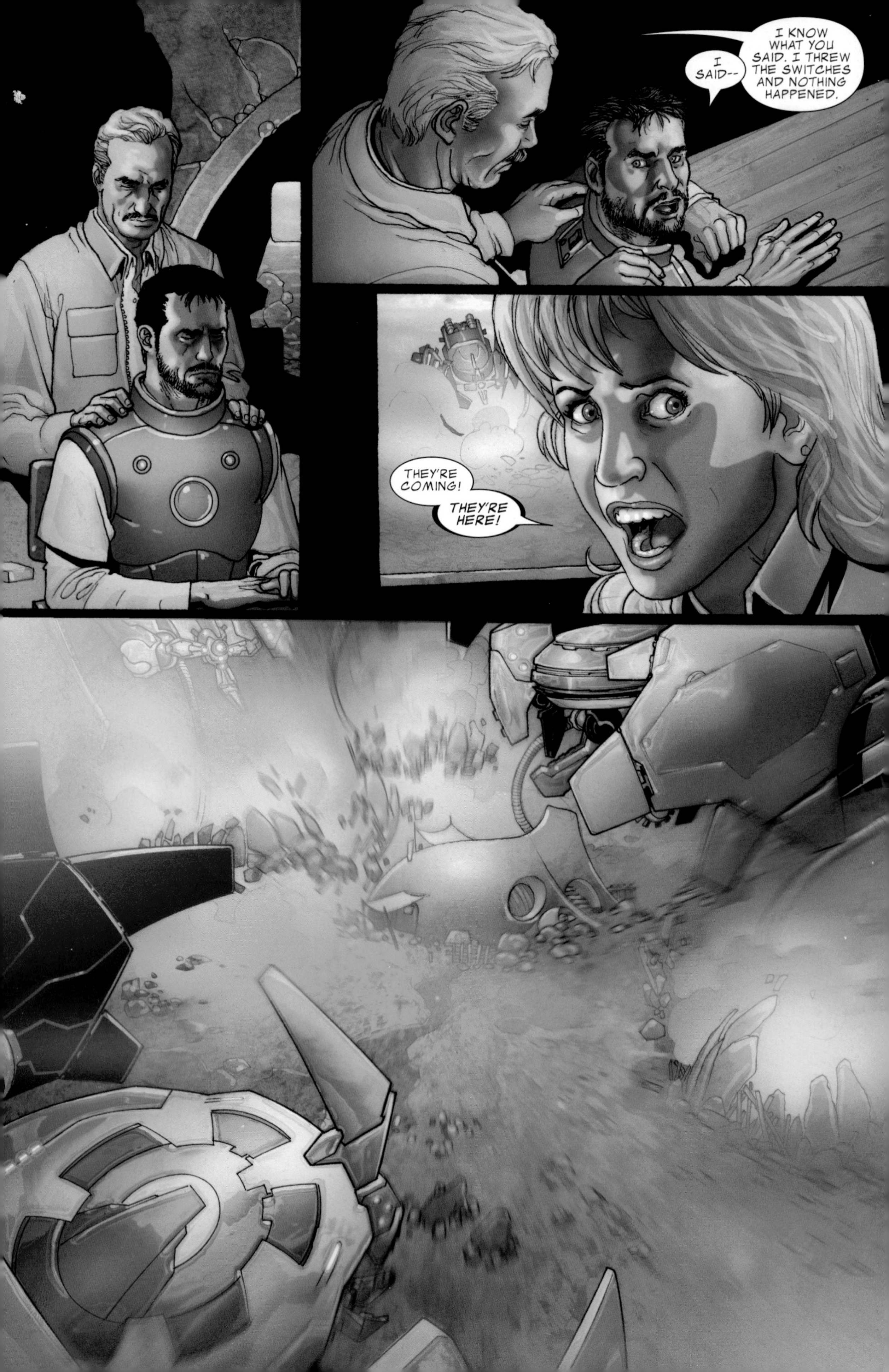
I SAID--
I KNOW WHAT YOU SAID. I THREW THE SWITCHES AND NOTHING HAPPENED.
THEY'RE COMING!
THEY'RE HERE!

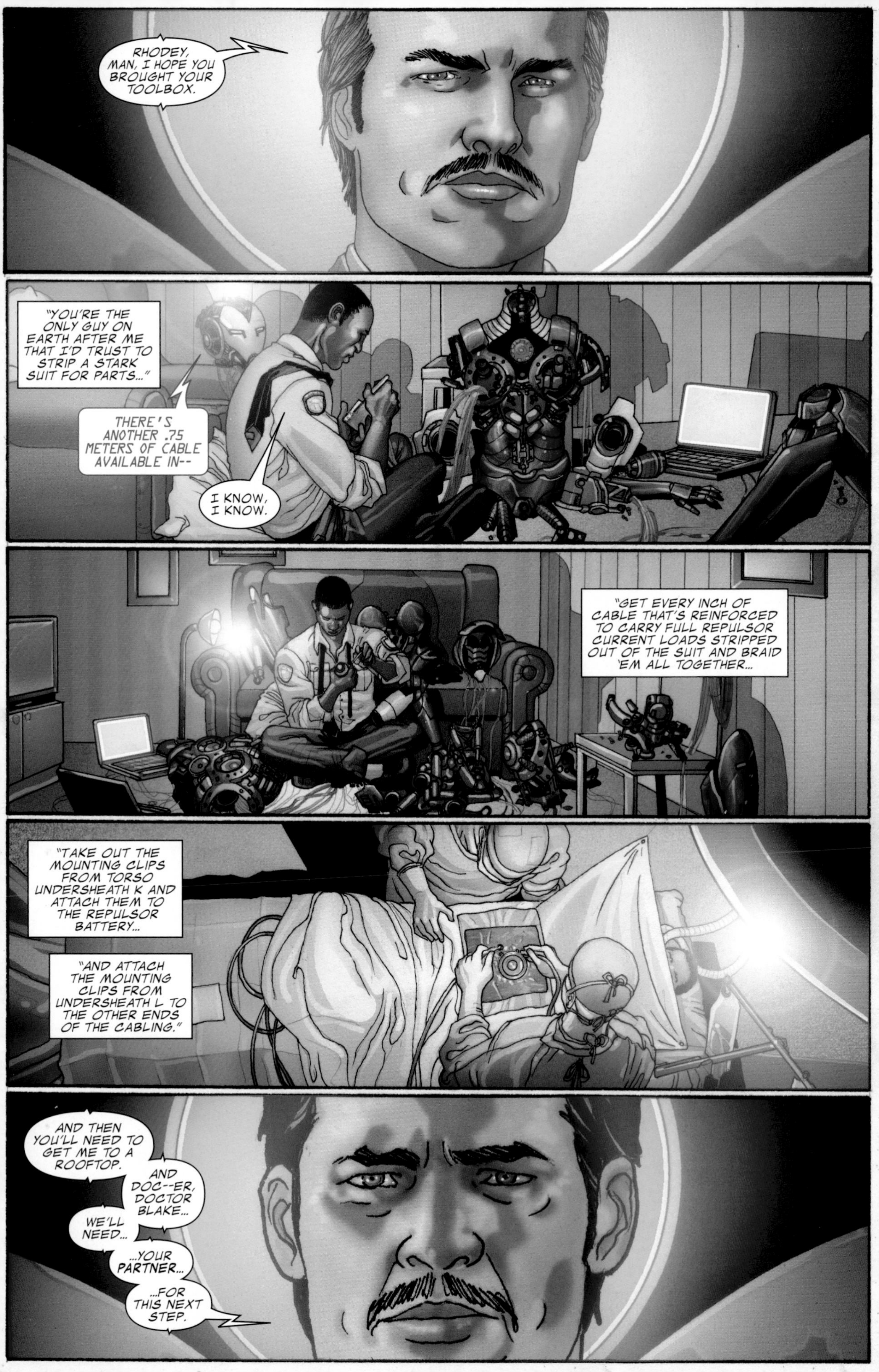
RHODEY, MAN, I HOPE YOU BROUGHT YOUR TOOLBOX.
"YOU'RE THE ONLY GUY ON EARTH AFTER ME THAT I'D TRUST TO STRIP A STARK SUIT FOR PARTS..."
THERE'S ANOTHER .75 METERS OF CABLE AVAILABLE IN--
I KNOW, I KNOW.
"GET EVERY INCH OF CABLE THAT'S REINFORCED TO CARRY FULL REPULSOR CURRENT LOADS STRIPPED OUT OF THE SUIT AND BRAID 'EM ALL TOGETHER...
"TAKE OUT THE MOUNTING CLIPS FROM TORSO UNDERSHEATH K AND ATTACH THEM TO THE REPULSOR BATTERY...
"AND ATTACH THE MOUNTING CLIPS FROM UNDERSHEATH L TO THE OTHER ENDS OF THE CABLING."
AND THEN YOU'LL NEED TO GET ME TO A ROOFTOP.
AND DOC--ER, DOCTOR BLAKE...
WE'LL NEED...
...YOUR PARTNER...
...FOR THIS NEXT STEP.

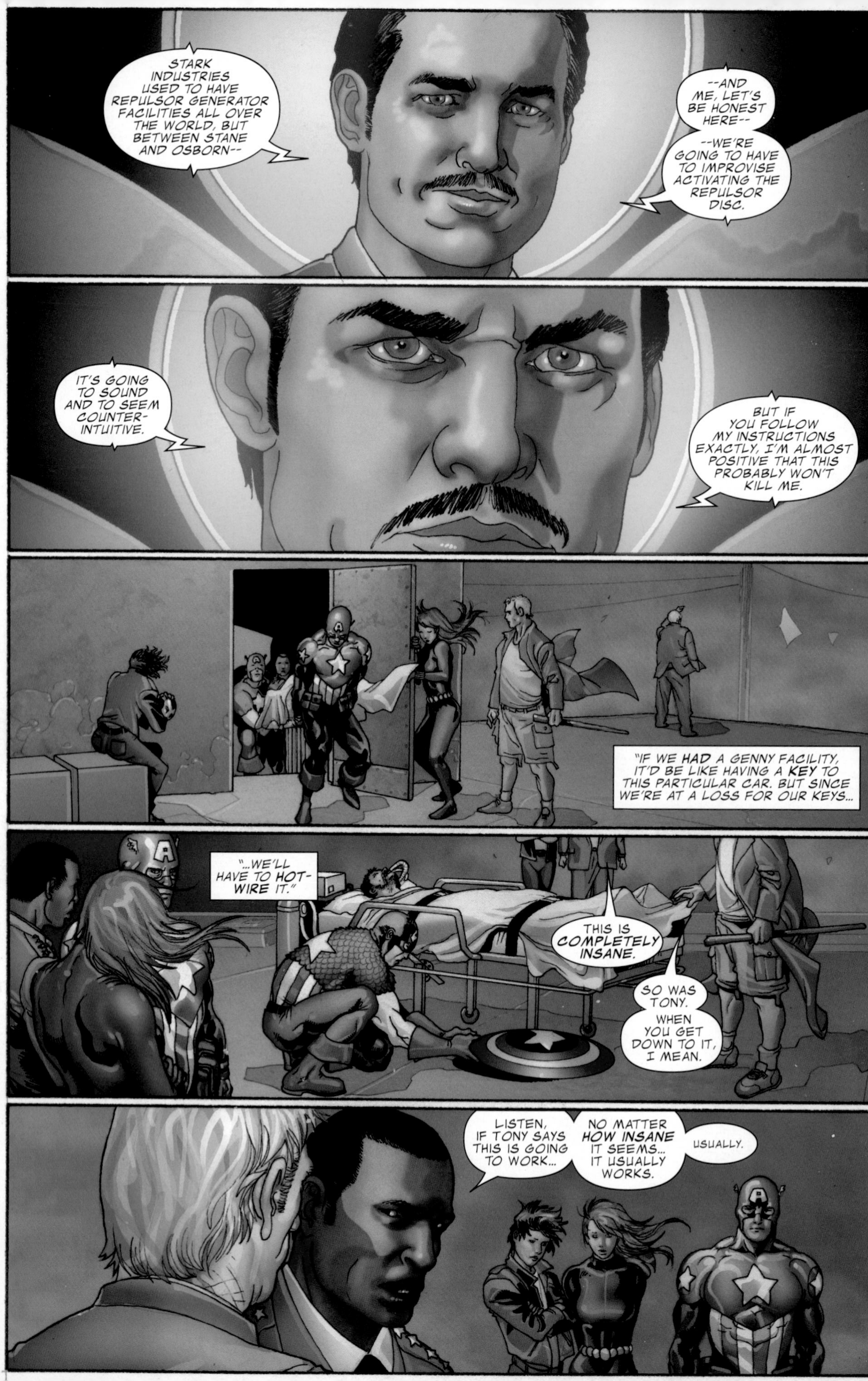
STARK INDUSTRIES USED TO HAVE REPULSOR GENERATOR FACILITIES ALL OVER THE WORLD, BUT BETWEEN STANE AND OSBORN--
--AND ME, LET'S BE HONEST HERE--
--WE'RE GOING TO HAVE TO IMPROVISE ACTIVATING THE REPULSOR DISC.
IT'S GOING TO SOUND AND TO SEEM COUNTER-INTUITIVE.
BUT IF YOU FOLLOW MY INSTRUCTIONS EXACTLY, I'M ALMOST POSITIVE THAT THIS PROBABLY WON'T KILL ME.
"IF WE HAD A GENNY FACILITY, IT'D BE LIKE HAVING A KEY TO THIS PARTICULAR CAR. BUT SINCE WE'RE AT A LOSS FOR OUR KEYS...
"...WE'LL HAVE TO HOT-WIRE IT."
THIS IS COMPLETELY INSANE.
SO WAS TONY.
WHEN YOU GET DOWN TO IT, I MEAN.
LISTEN, IF TONY SAYS THIS IS GOING TO WORK...
NO MATTER HOW INSANE IT SEEMS... IT USUALLY WORKS.
USUALLY.

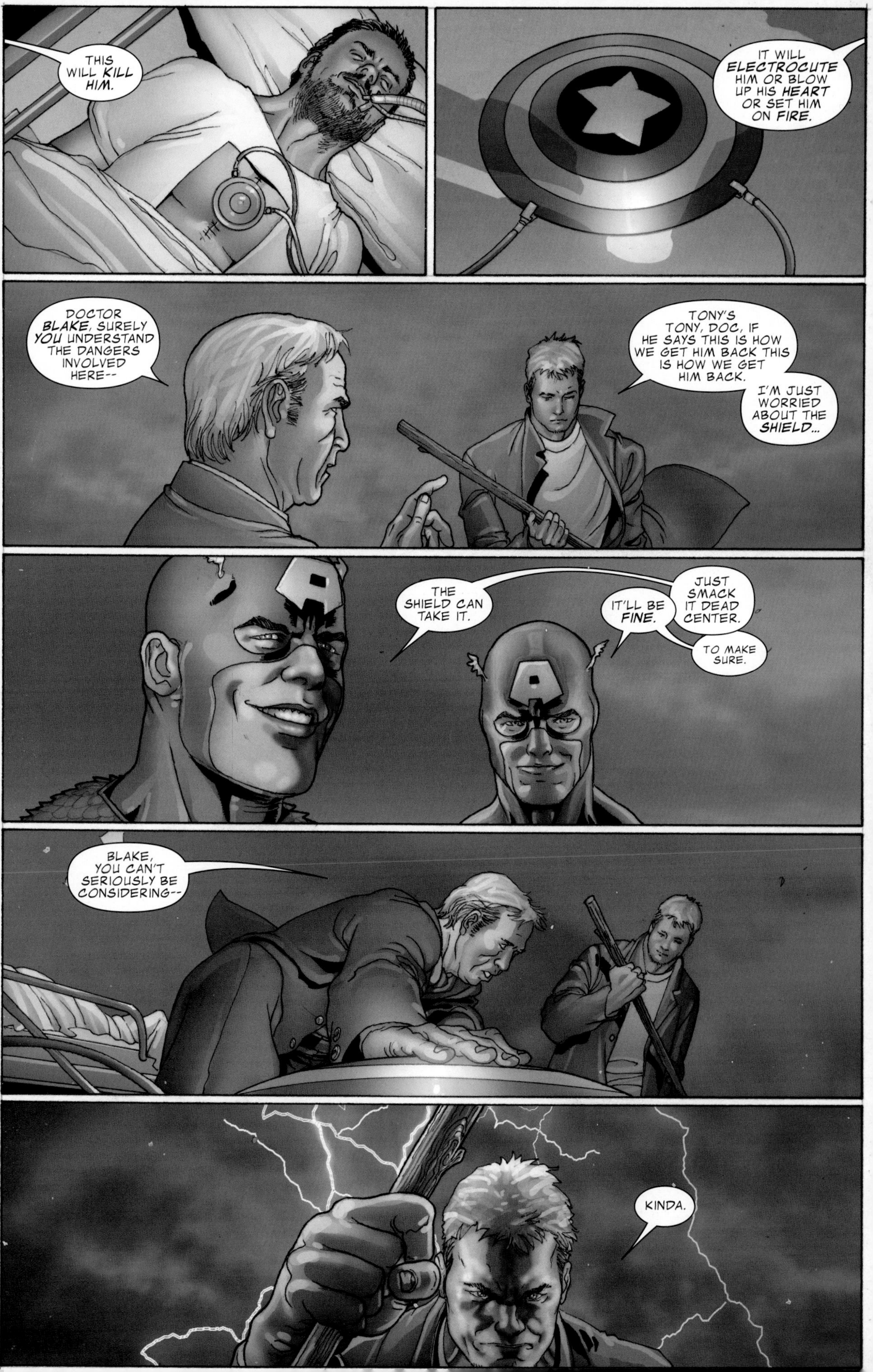
THIS WILL KILL HIM.
IT WILL ELECTROCUTE HIM OR BLOW UP HIS HEART OR SET HIM ON FIRE.
DOCTOR BLAKE, SURELY YOU UNDERSTAND THE DANGERS INVOLVED HERE--
TONY'S TONY, DOC, IF HE SAYS THIS IS HOW WE GET HIM BACK THIS IS HOW WE GET HIM BACK.
I'M JUST WORRIED ABOUT THE SHIELD...
THE SHIELD CAN TAKE IT.
JUST SMACK IT DEAD CENTER.
IT'LL BE FINE.
TO MAKE SURE.
BLAKE, YOU CAN'T SERIOUSLY BE CONSIDERING--
KINDA.

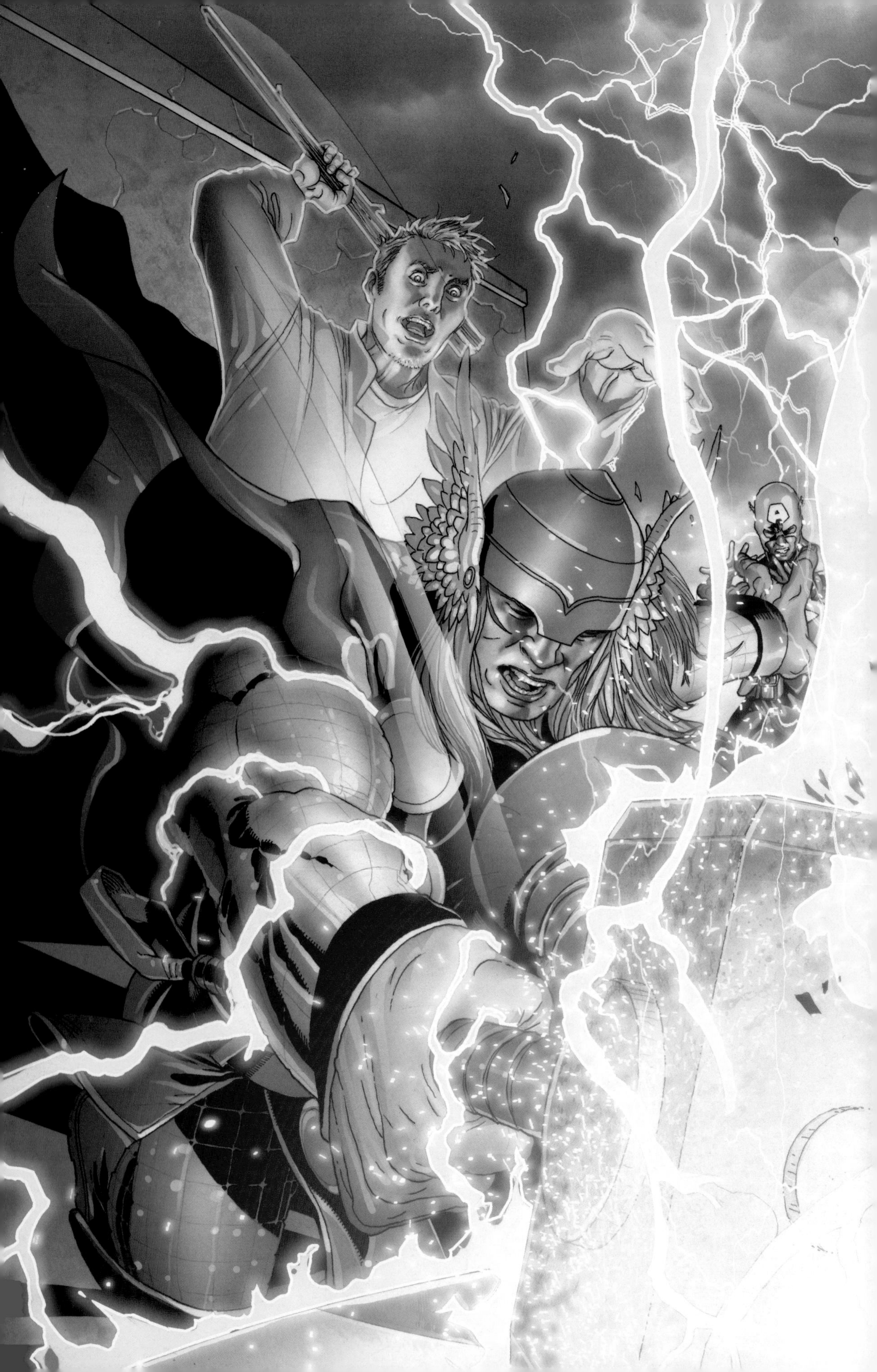

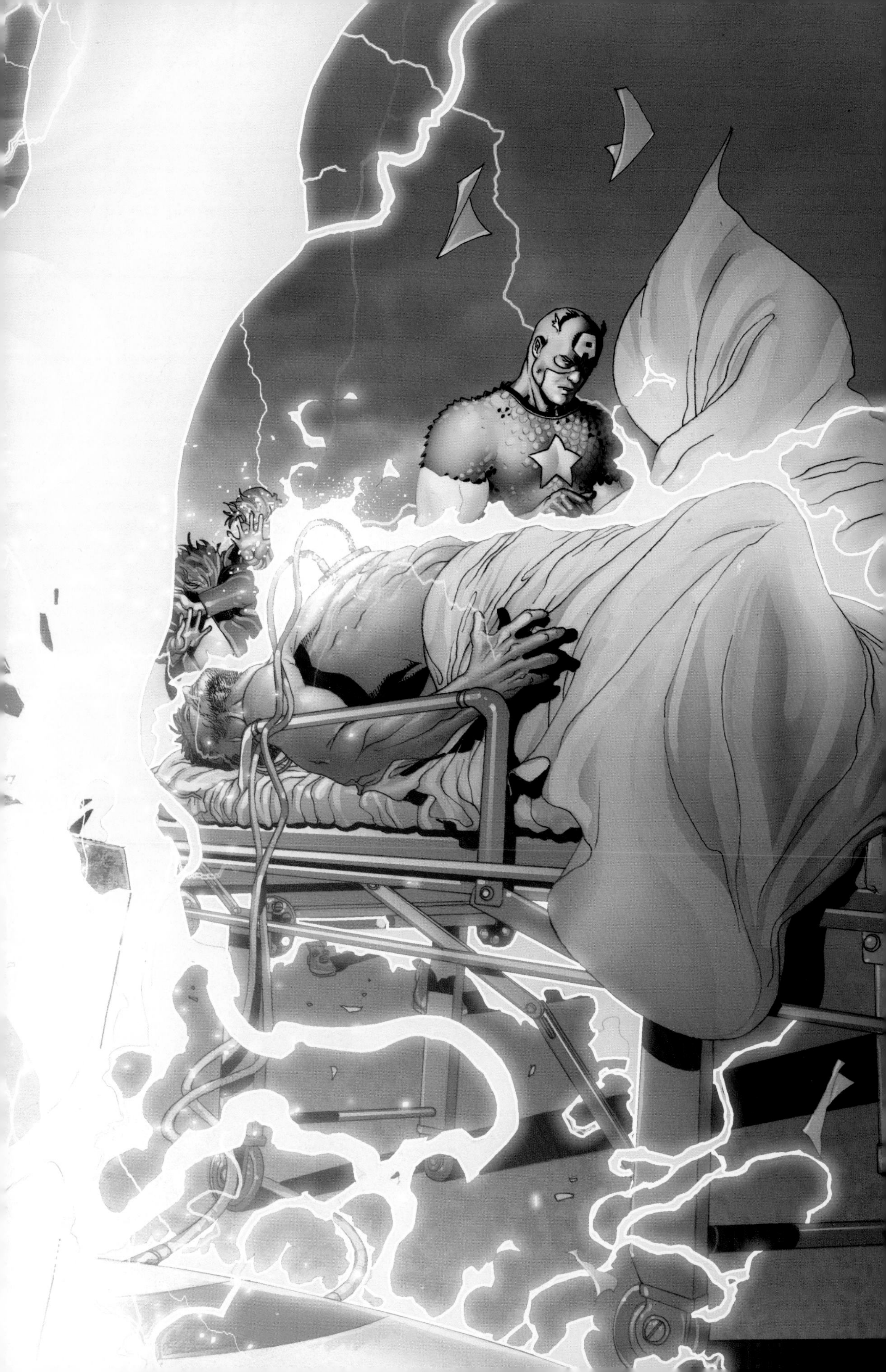

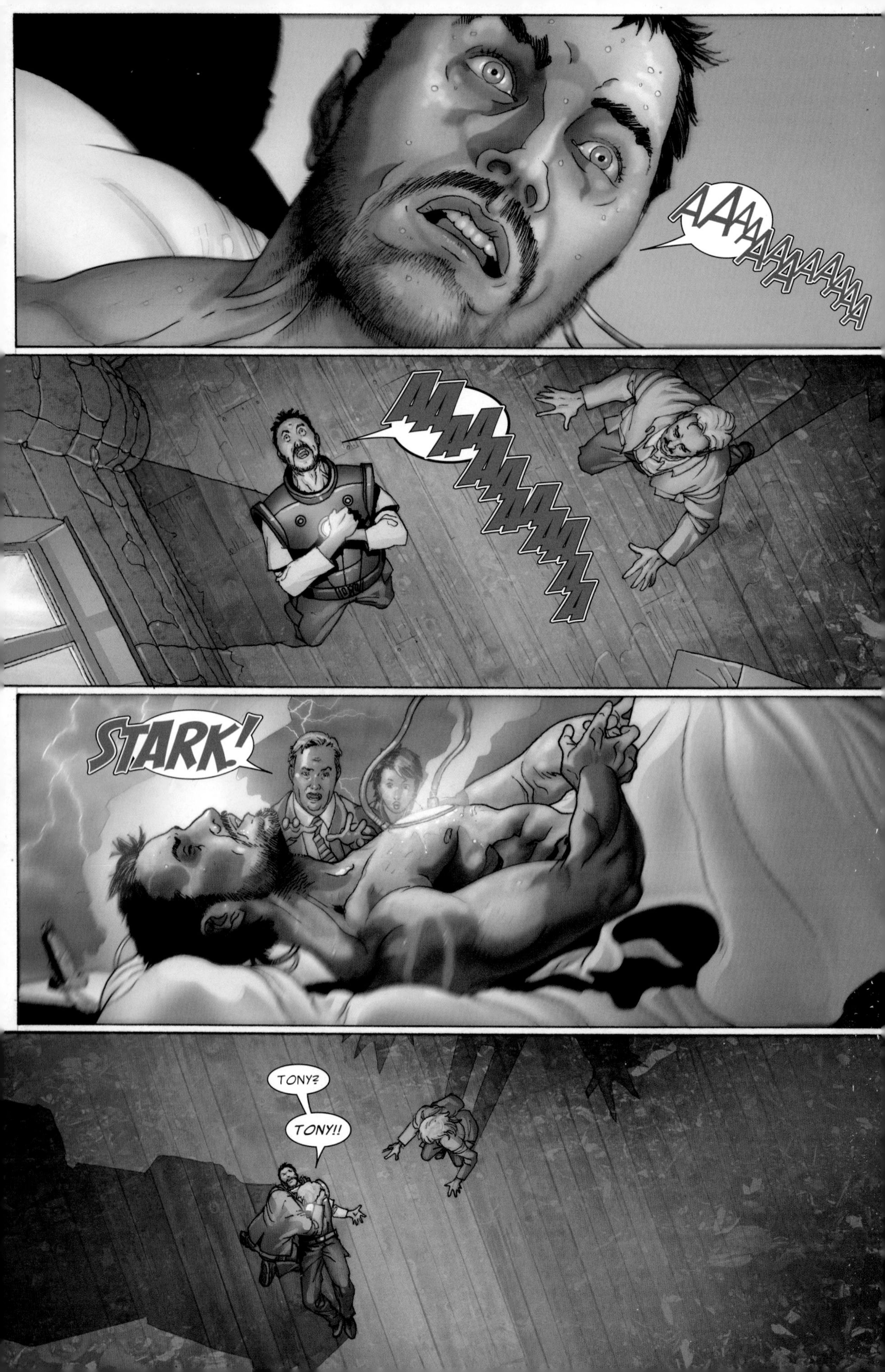
AAAAAAAAAAAAAA
AAAAAAAAAAAAA
STARK!
TONY?
TONY!!

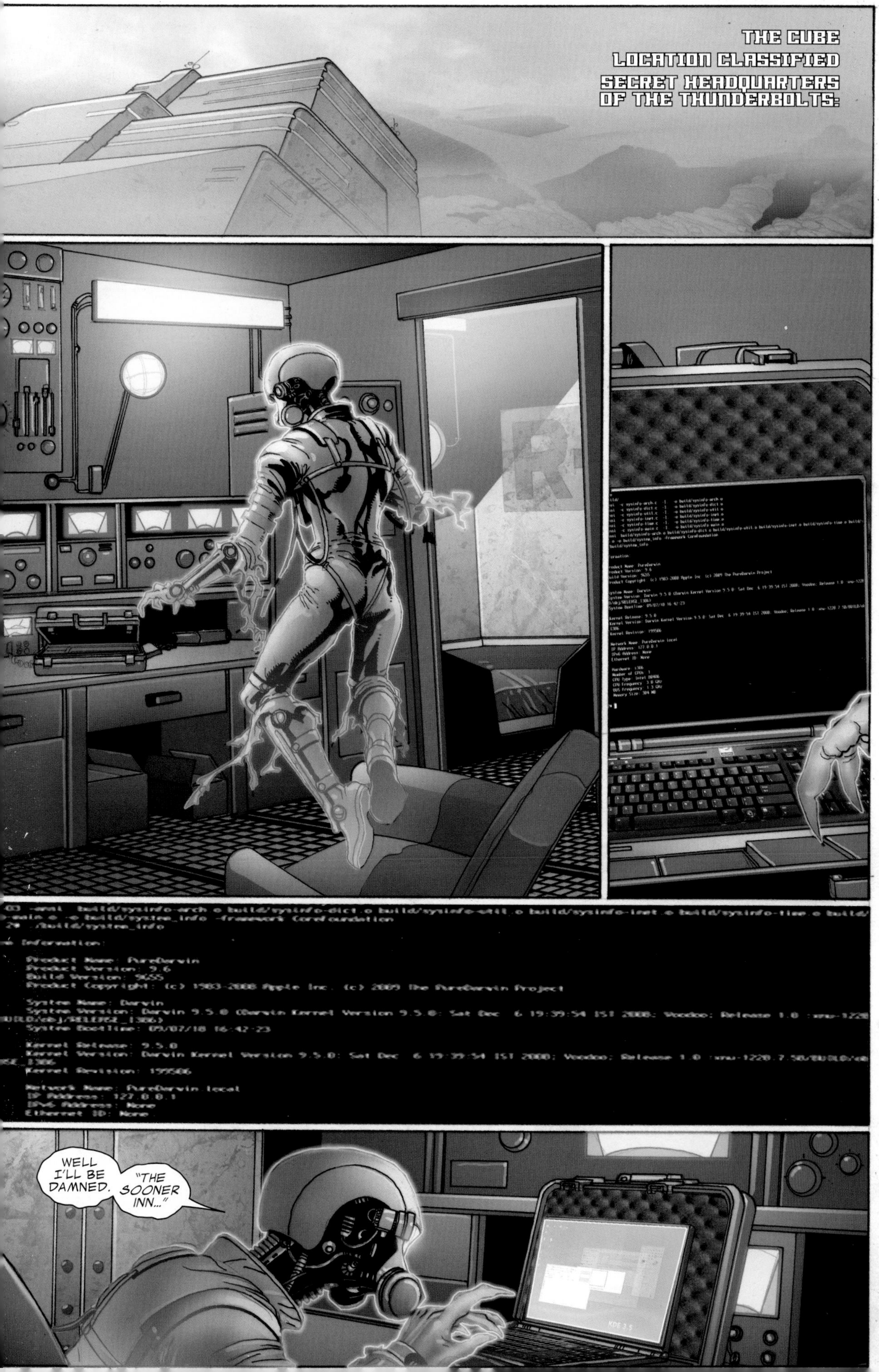
THE CUBE
LOCATION CLASSIFIED
SECRET HEADQUARTERS OF THE THUNDERBOLTS:
Product Name: PureDarwin
Product Version: 9.6
System Name: Darwin
Kernel Release: 9.5.0
Network Name: PureDarwin.local
IP Address: 127.0.0.1
IPv6 Address: None
Ethernet ID: None
WELL I'LL BE DAMNED.
"THE SOONER INN..."

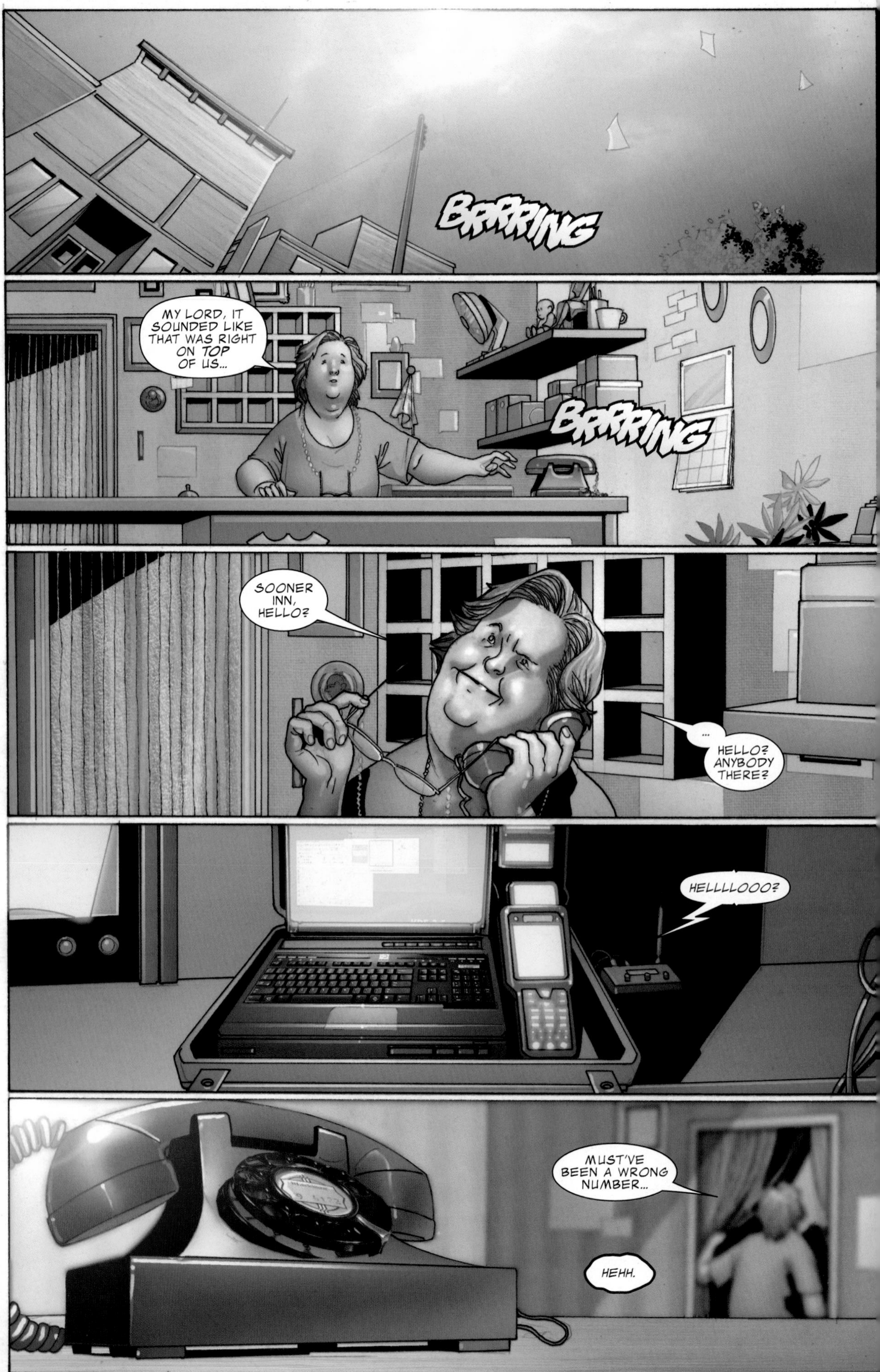
BRRRING
MY LORD, IT SOUNDED LIKE THAT WAS RIGHT ON *TOP* OF US...
BRRRING
SOONER INN, HELLO?
... HELLO? ANYBODY THERE?
HELLLLOOO?
MUST'VE BEEN A WRONG NUMBER...
HEHH.

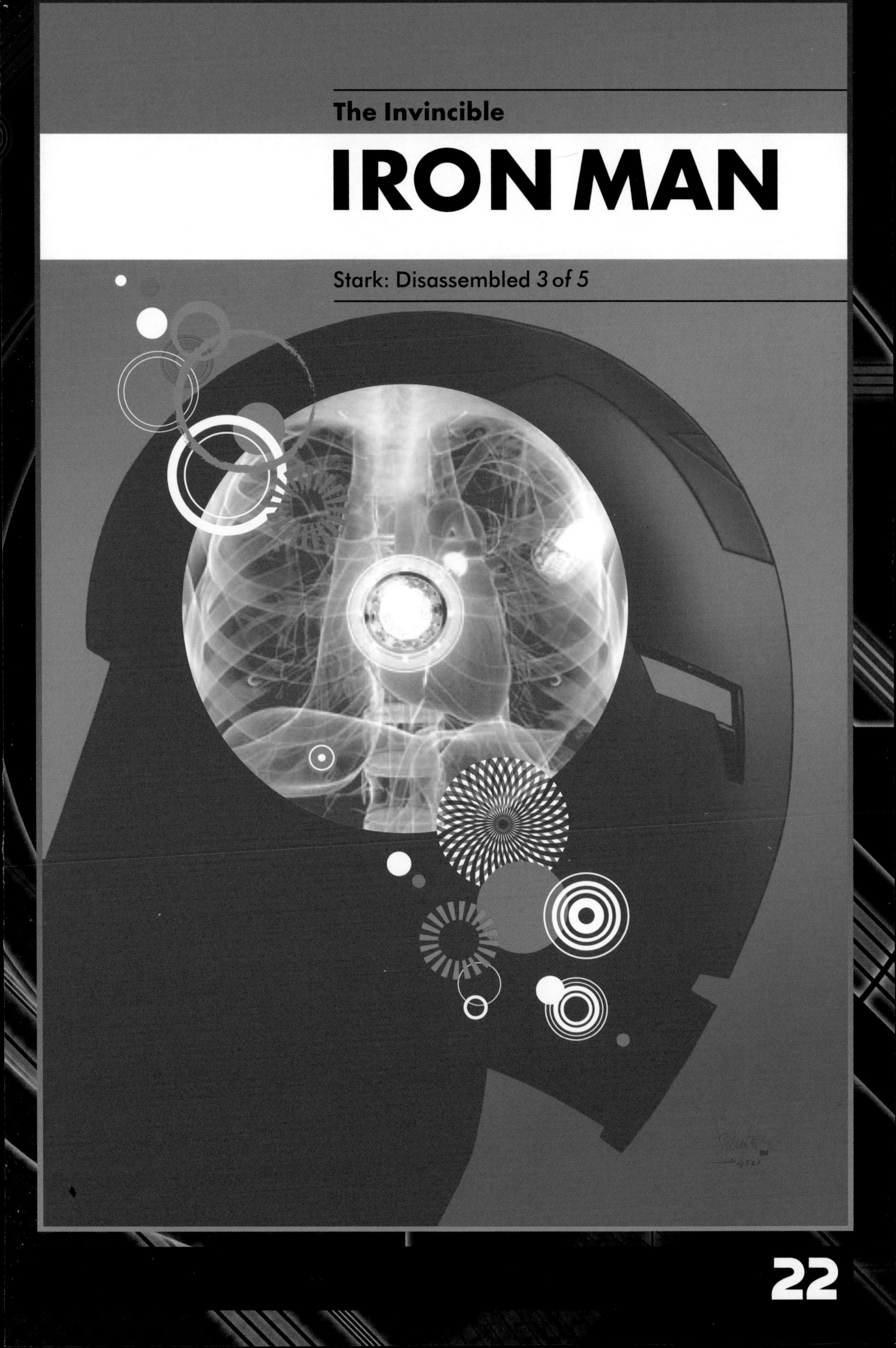

The Invincible
IRON MAN
Stark: Disassembled 3 of 5

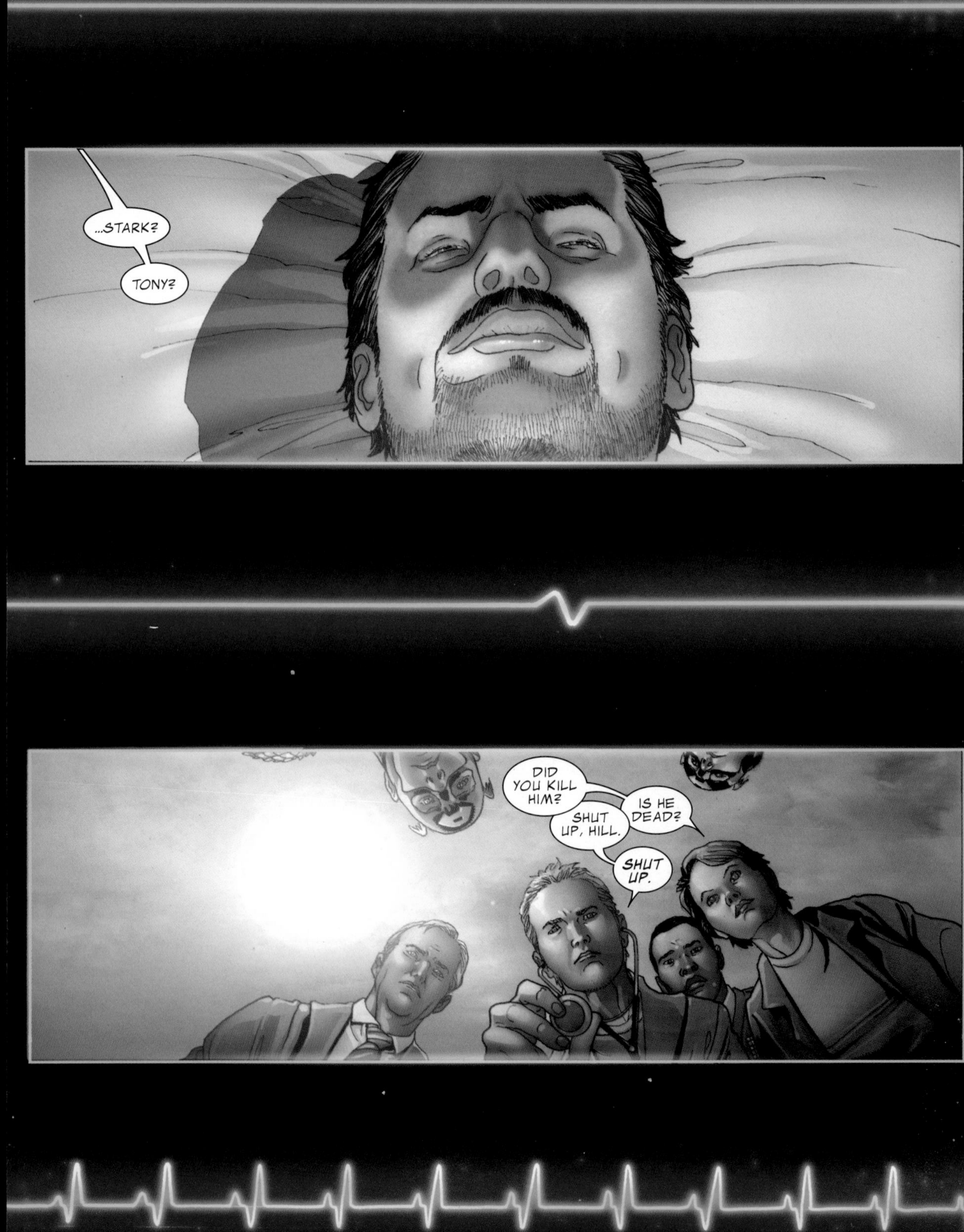
...STARK?
TONY?
DID YOU KILL HIM?
IS HE DEAD?
SHUT UP, HILL.
SHUT UP.

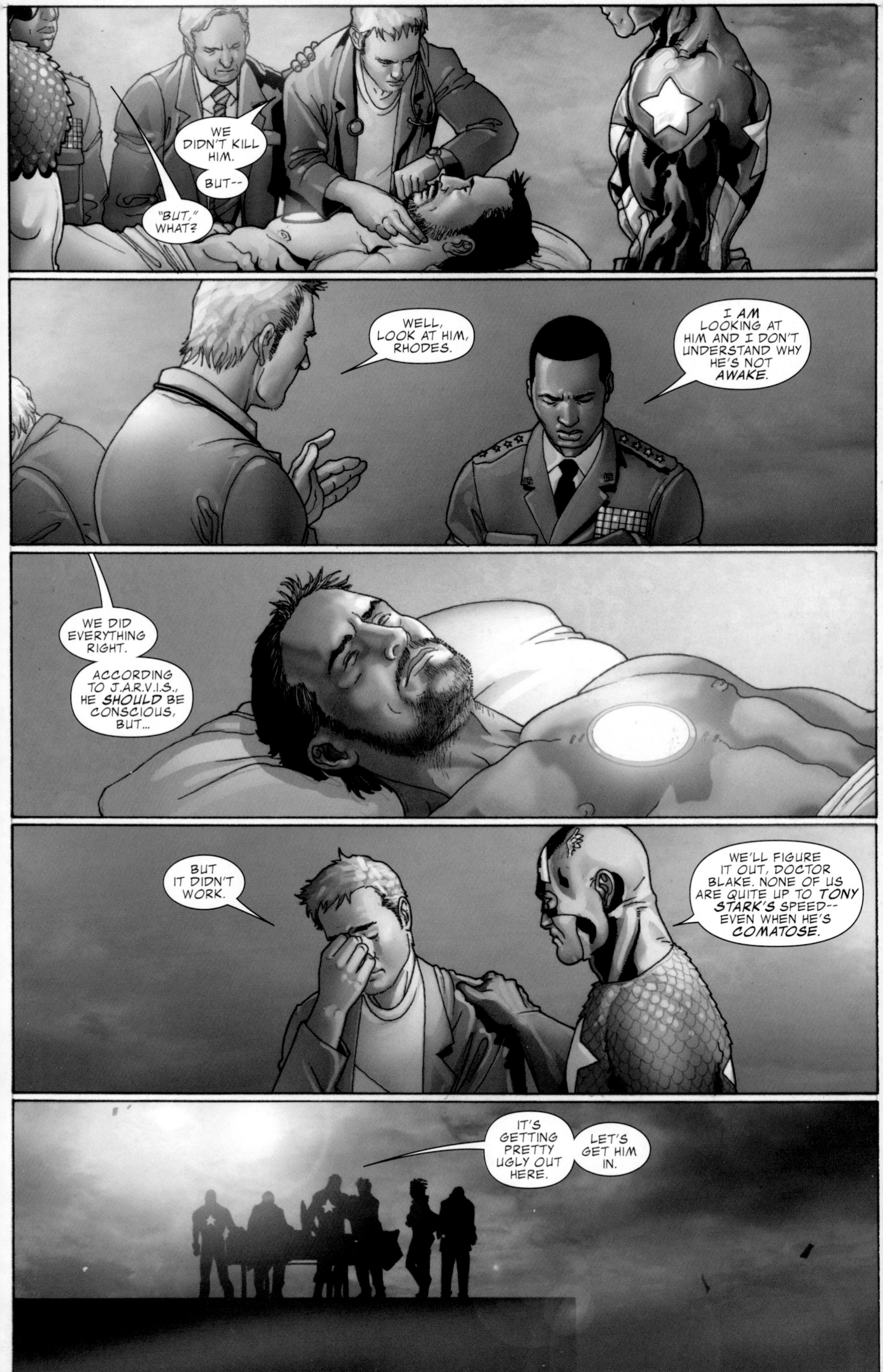

WE DIDN'T KILL HIM.
BUT--
"BUT," WHAT?
WELL, LOOK AT HIM, RHODES.
I AM LOOKING AT HIM AND I DON'T UNDERSTAND WHY HE'S NOT AWAKE.
WE DID EVERYTHING RIGHT.
ACCORDING TO J.A.R.V.I.S., HE SHOULD BE CONSCIOUS, BUT...
BUT IT DIDN'T WORK.
WE'LL FIGURE IT OUT, DOCTOR BLAKE. NONE OF US ARE QUITE UP TO TONY STARK'S SPEED-- EVEN WHEN HE'S COMATOSE.
IT'S GETTING PRETTY UGLY OUT HERE.
LET'S GET HIM IN.

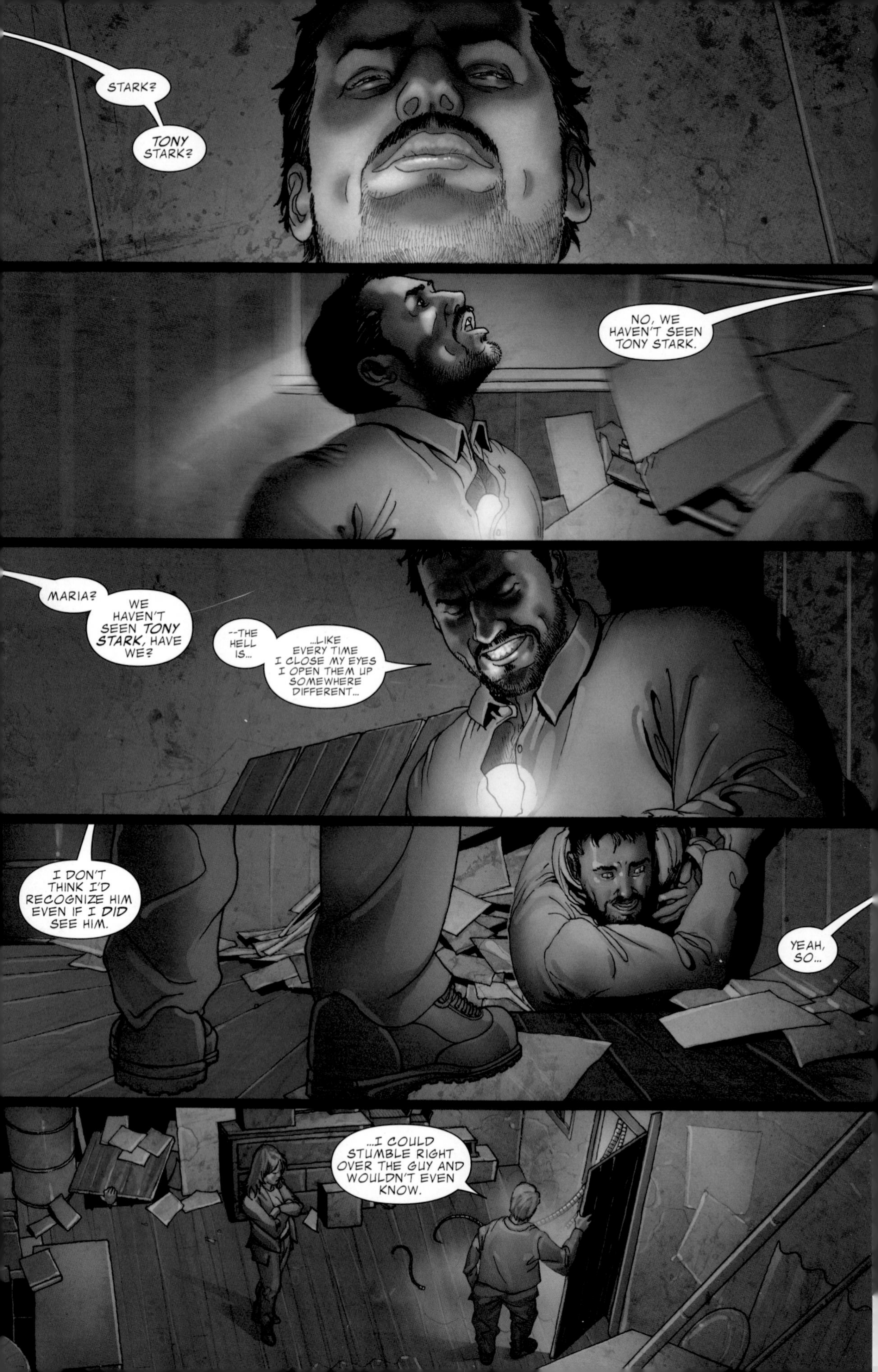
STARK?
TONY STARK?
NO, WE HAVEN'T SEEN TONY STARK.
MARIA? WE HAVEN'T SEEN TONY STARK, HAVE WE?
--THE HELL IS...
...LIKE EVERY TIME I CLOSE MY EYES I OPEN THEM UP SOMEWHERE DIFFERENT...
I DON'T THINK I'D RECOGNIZE HIM EVEN IF I DID SEE HIM.
YEAH, SO...
...I COULD STUMBLE RIGHT OVER THE GUY AND WOULDN'T EVEN KNOW.

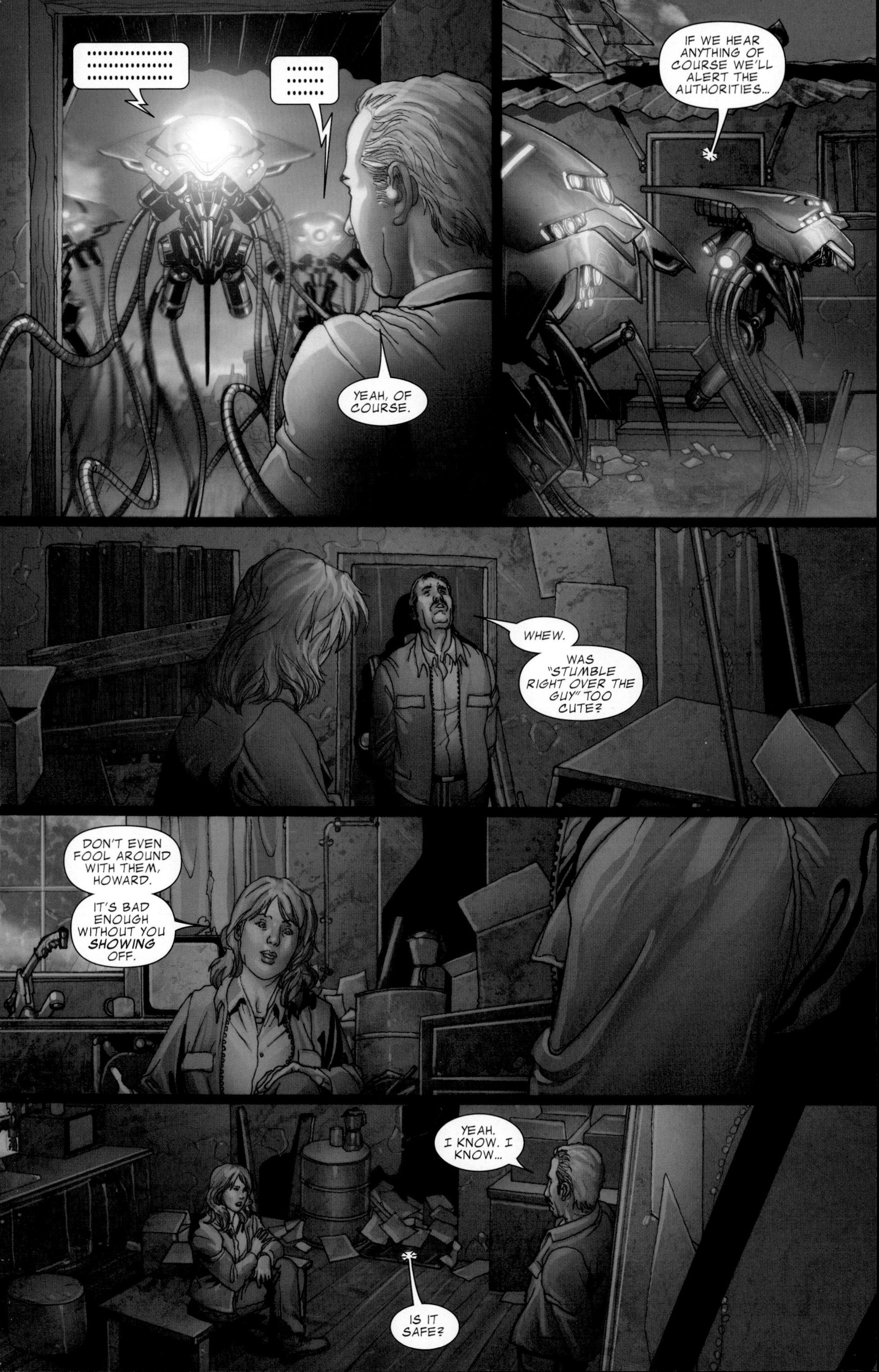
……………………
……………………
……………………
………
………
………
YEAH, OF COURSE.
IF WE HEAR ANYTHING OF COURSE WE'LL ALERT THE AUTHORITIES...
WHEW.
WAS "STUMBLE RIGHT OVER THE GUY" TOO CUTE?
DON'T EVEN FOOL AROUND WITH THEM, HOWARD.
IT'S BAD ENOUGH WITHOUT YOU *SHOWING* OFF.
YEAH. I KNOW. I KNOW...
IS IT SAFE?

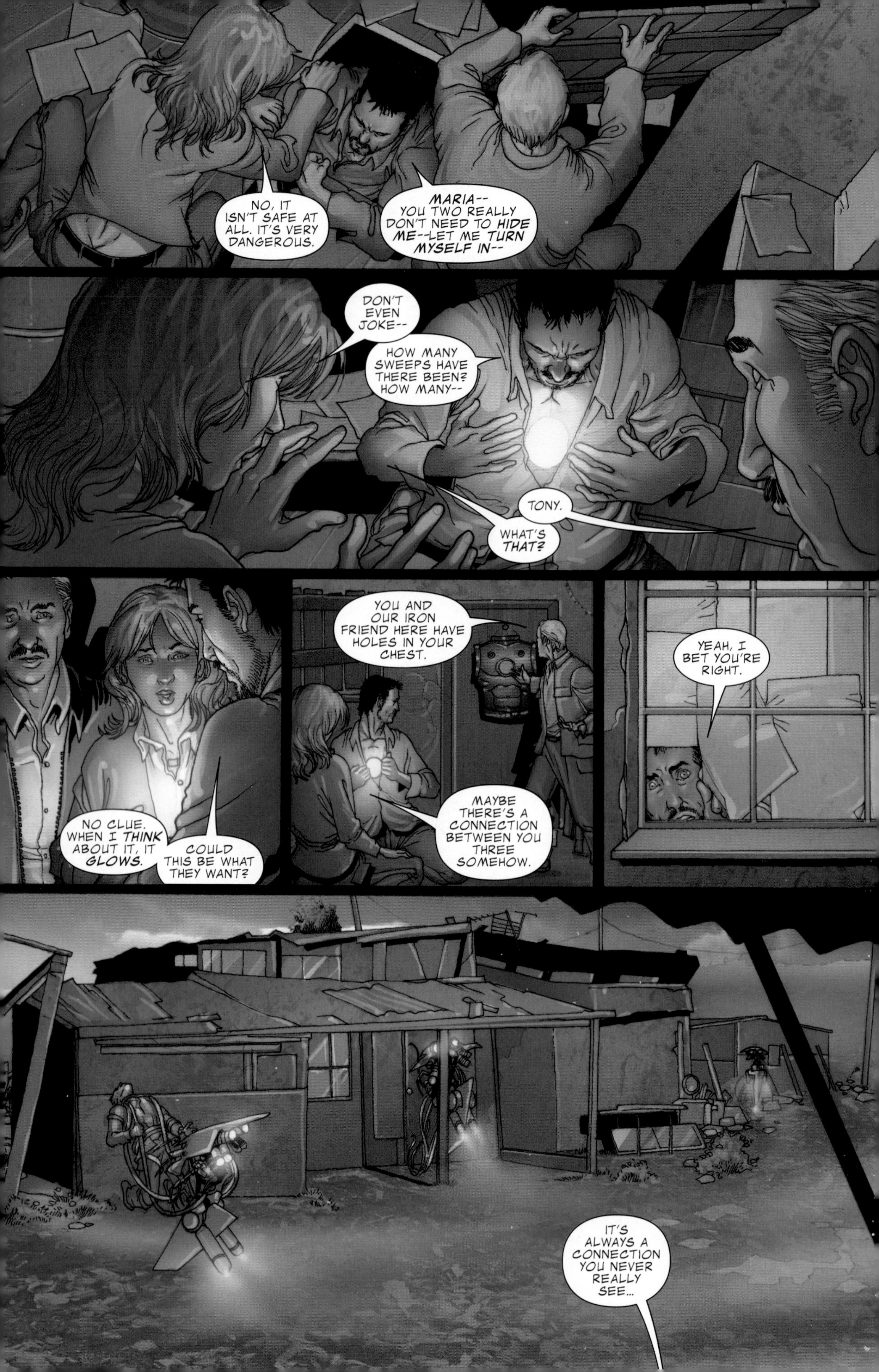
NO, IT ISN'T SAFE AT ALL. IT'S VERY DANGEROUS.
MARIA-- YOU TWO REALLY DON'T NEED TO HIDE ME--LET ME TURN MYSELF IN--
DON'T EVEN JOKE--
HOW MANY SWEEPS HAVE THERE BEEN? HOW MANY--
TONY.
WHAT'S THAT?
NO CLUE. WHEN I THINK ABOUT IT, IT GLOWS.
COULD THIS BE WHAT THEY WANT?
YOU AND OUR IRON FRIEND HERE HAVE HOLES IN YOUR CHEST.
MAYBE THERE'S A CONNECTION BETWEEN YOU THREE SOMEHOW.
YEAH, I BET YOU'RE RIGHT.
IT'S ALWAYS A CONNECTION YOU NEVER REALLY SEE...

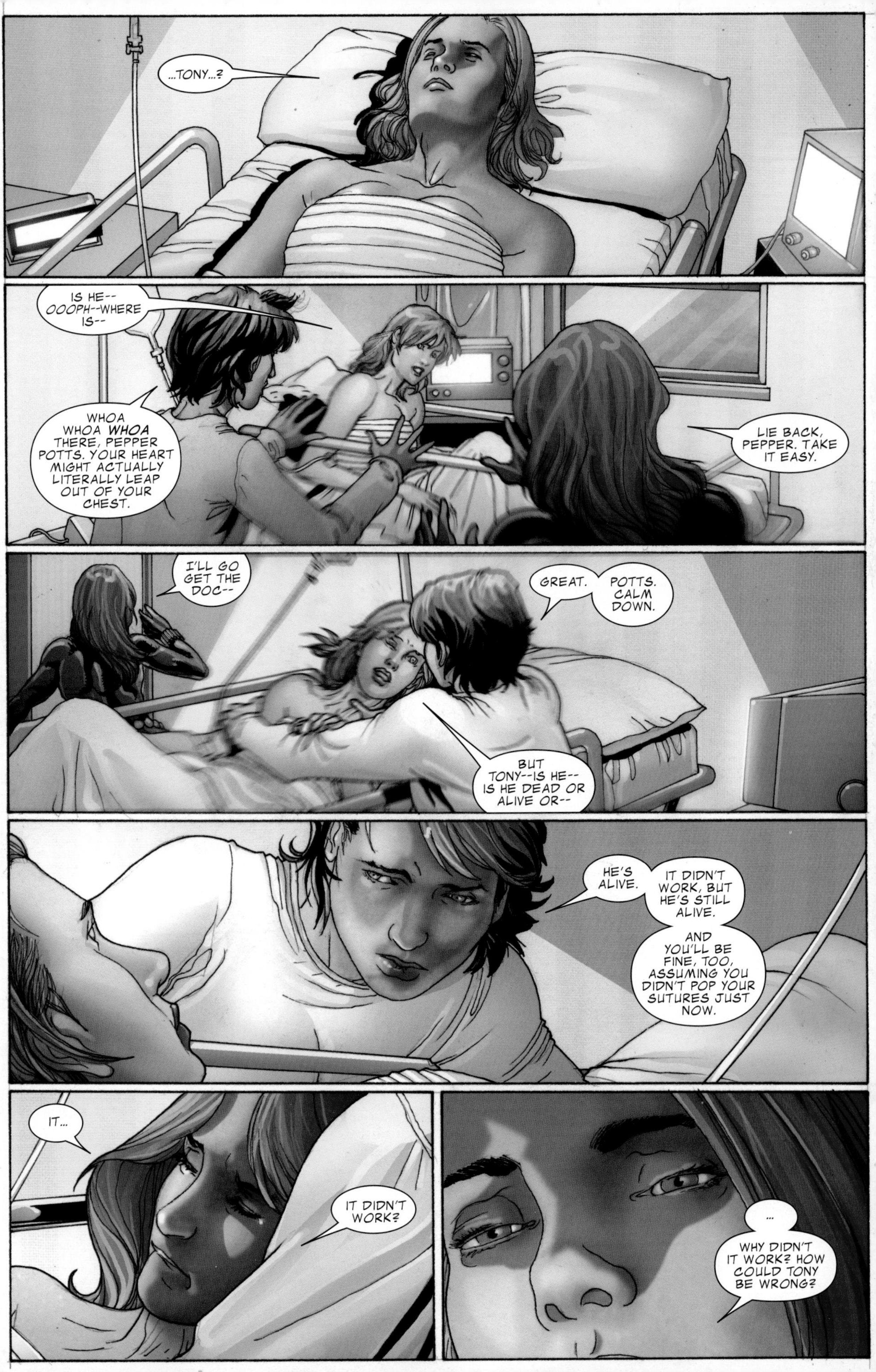
...TONY...?
IS HE--OOOPH--WHERE IS--
WHOA WHOA *WHOA* THERE, PEPPER POTTS. YOUR HEART MIGHT ACTUALLY LITERALLY LEAP OUT OF YOUR CHEST.
LIE BACK, PEPPER. TAKE IT EASY.
I'LL GO GET THE DOC--
GREAT.
POTTS. CALM DOWN.
BUT TONY--IS HE--IS HE DEAD OR ALIVE OR--
HE'S ALIVE.
IT DIDN'T WORK, BUT HE'S STILL ALIVE.
AND YOU'LL BE FINE, TOO, ASSUMING YOU DIDN'T POP YOUR SUTURES JUST NOW.
IT...
IT DIDN'T WORK?
...
WHY DIDN'T IT WORK? HOW COULD TONY BE WRONG?

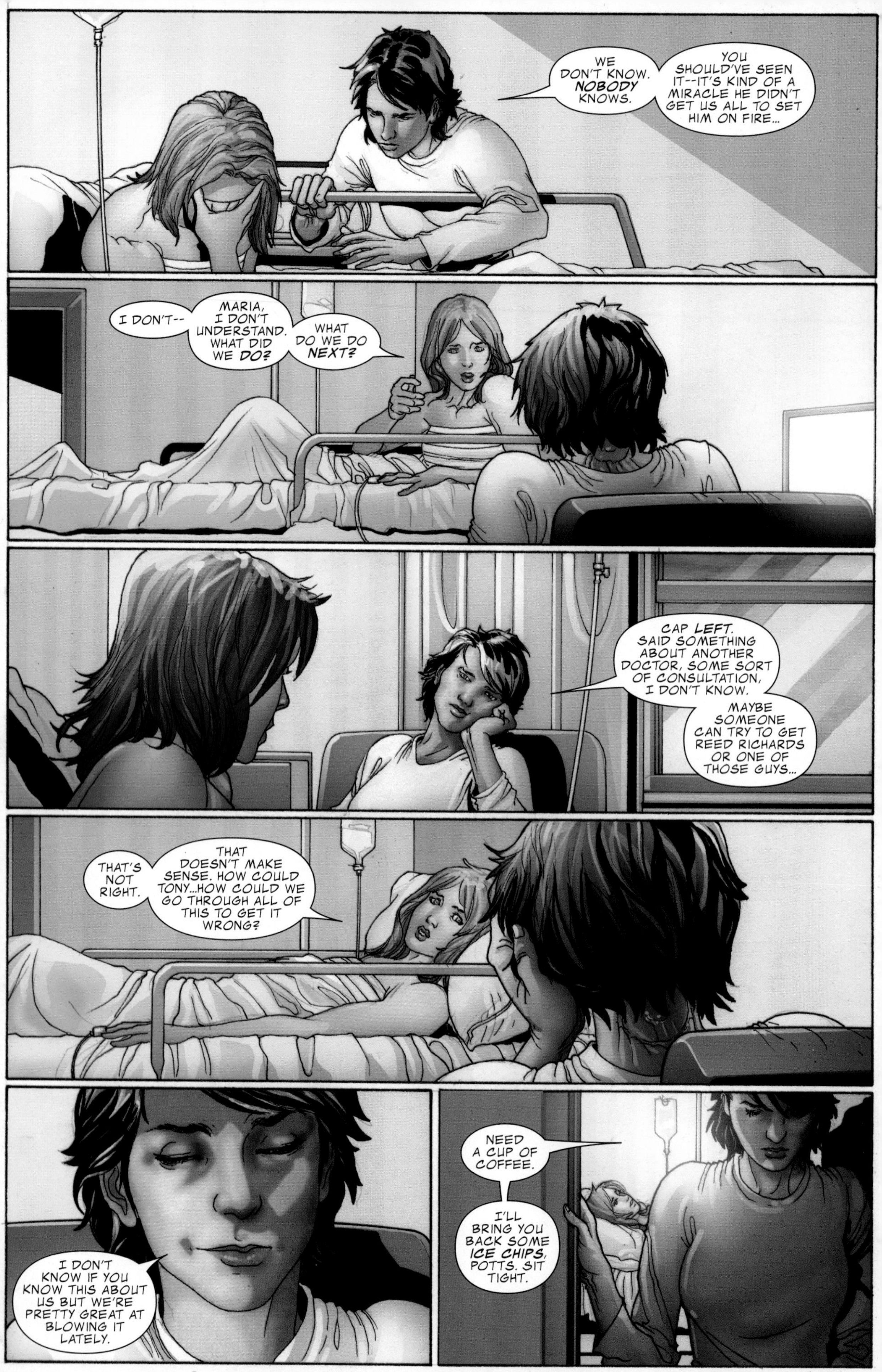
WE DON'T KNOW. NOBODY KNOWS.
YOU SHOULD'VE SEEN IT--IT'S KIND OF A MIRACLE HE DIDN'T GET US ALL TO SET HIM ON FIRE...
I DON'T--
MARIA, I DON'T UNDERSTAND. WHAT DID WE DO?
WHAT DO WE DO NEXT?
CAP LEFT. SAID SOMETHING ABOUT ANOTHER DOCTOR, SOME SORT OF CONSULTATION, I DON'T KNOW.
MAYBE SOMEONE CAN TRY TO GET REED RICHARDS OR ONE OF THOSE GUYS...
THAT'S NOT RIGHT.
THAT DOESN'T MAKE SENSE. HOW COULD TONY...HOW COULD WE GO THROUGH ALL OF THIS TO GET IT WRONG?
I DON'T KNOW IF YOU KNOW THIS ABOUT US BUT WE'RE PRETTY GREAT AT BLOWING IT LATELY.
NEED A CUP OF COFFEE.
I'LL BRING YOU BACK SOME ICE CHIPS, POTTS. SIT TIGHT.

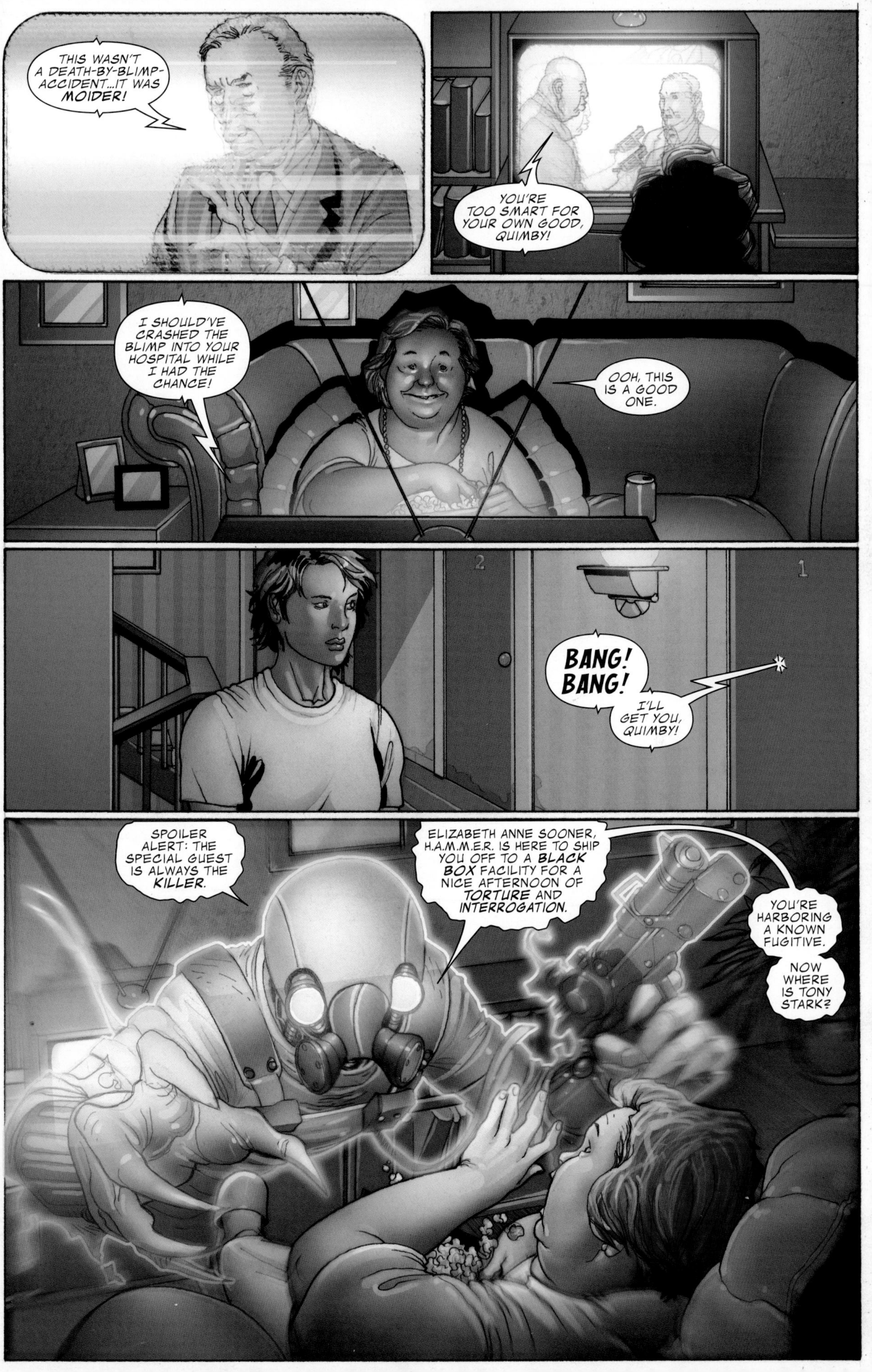
THIS WASN'T A DEATH-BY-BLIMP-ACCIDENT...IT WAS MOIDER!
YOU'RE TOO SMART FOR YOUR OWN GOOD, QUIMBY!
I SHOULD'VE CRASHED THE BLIMP INTO YOUR HOSPITAL WHILE I HAD THE CHANCE!
OOH, THIS IS A GOOD ONE.
BANG! BANG!
I'LL GET YOU, QUIMBY!
SPOILER ALERT: THE SPECIAL GUEST IS ALWAYS THE KILLER.
ELIZABETH ANNE SOONER, H.A.M.M.E.R. IS HERE TO SHIP YOU OFF TO A BLACK BOX FACILITY FOR A NICE AFTERNOON OF TORTURE AND INTERROGATION.
YOU'RE HARBORING A KNOWN FUGITIVE.
NOW WHERE IS TONY STARK?

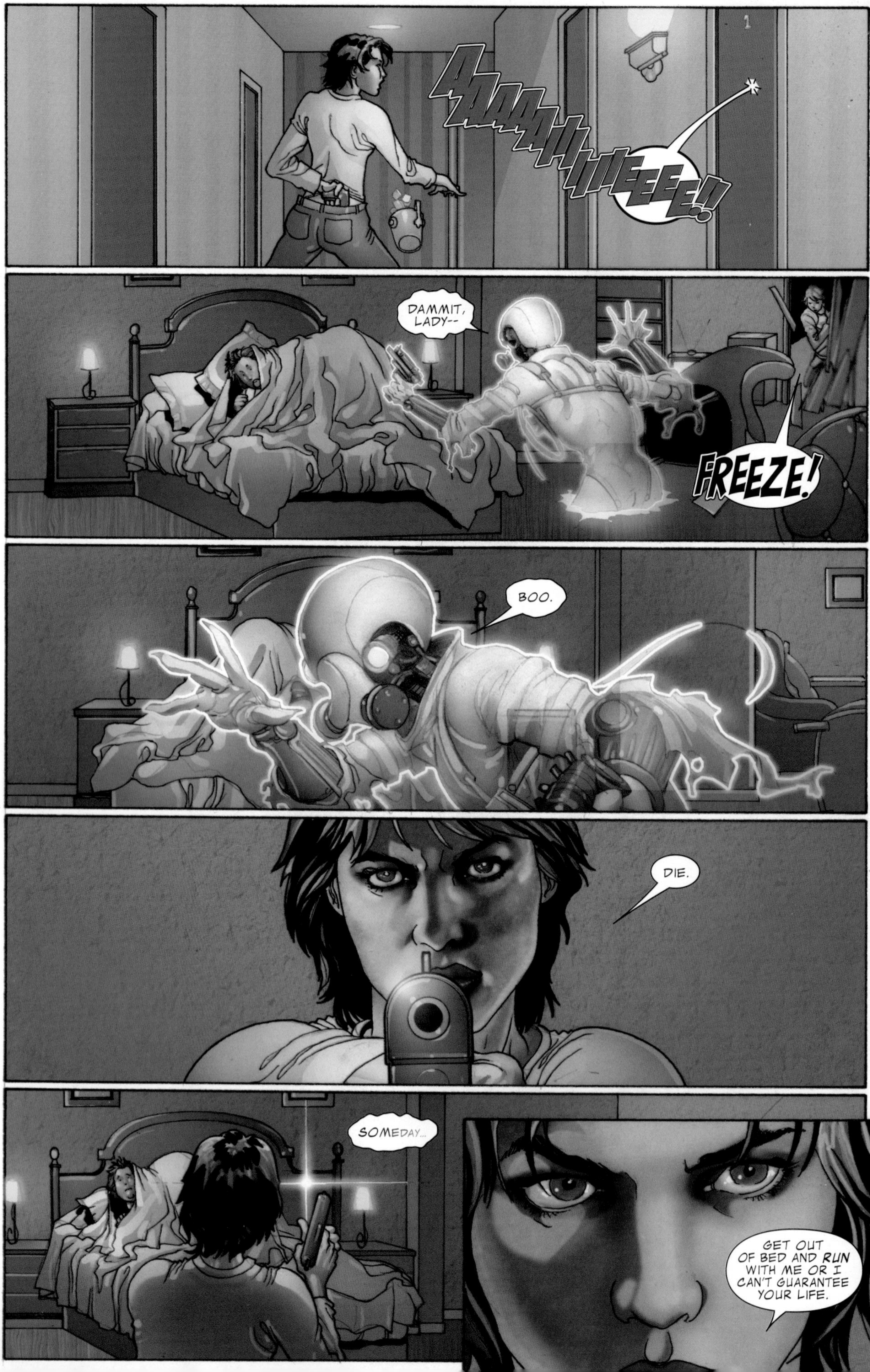
AAAAAIIIIIEEEEE!!
DAMMIT, LADY--
FREEZE!
BOO.
DIE.
SOMEDAY...
GET OUT OF BED AND RUN WITH ME OR I CAN'T GUARANTEE YOUR LIFE.

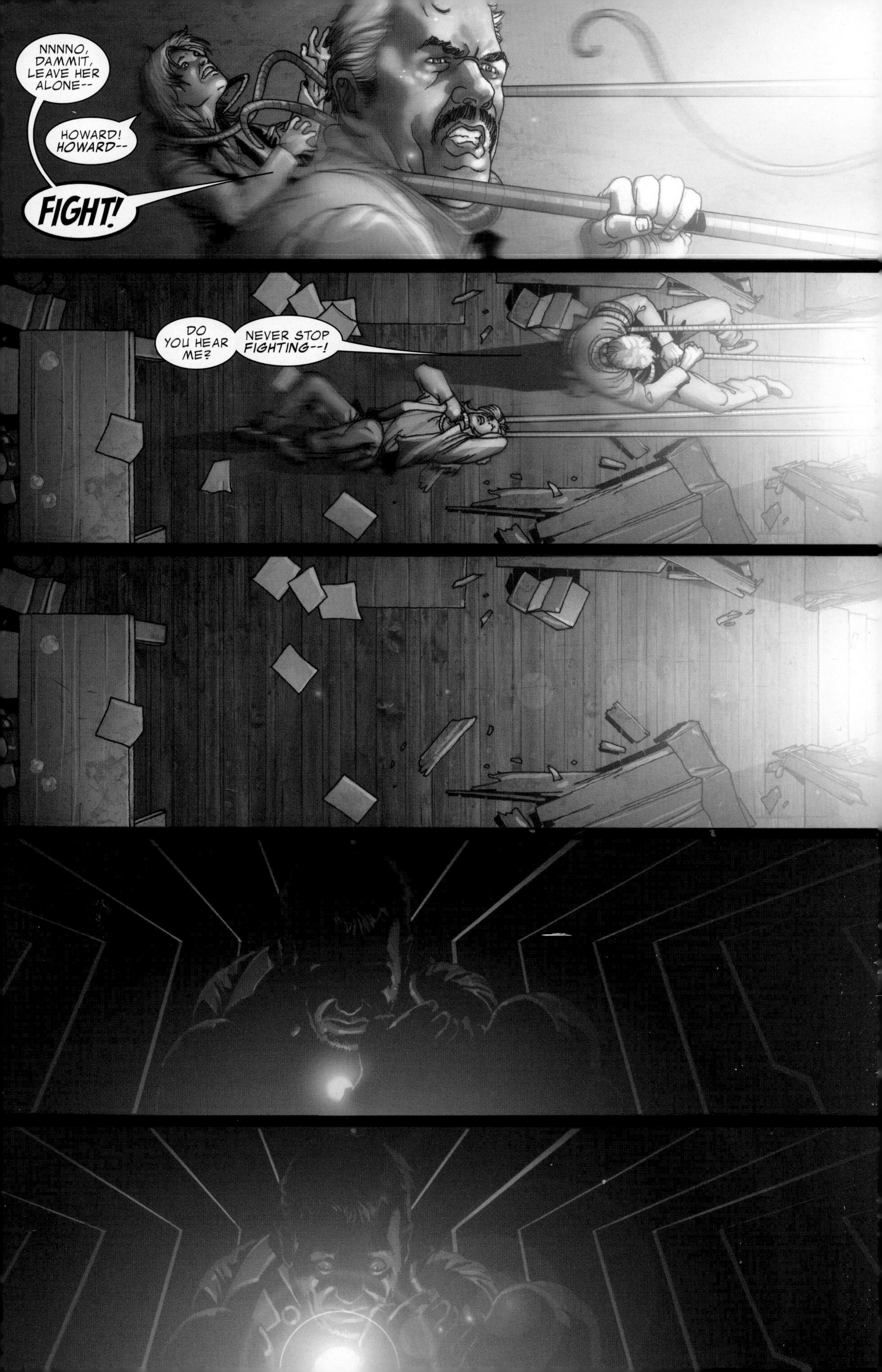
NNNNO, DAMMIT, LEAVE HER ALONE--
HOWARD! HOWARD--
FIGHT!
DO YOU HEAR ME?
NEVER STOP FIGHTING--!

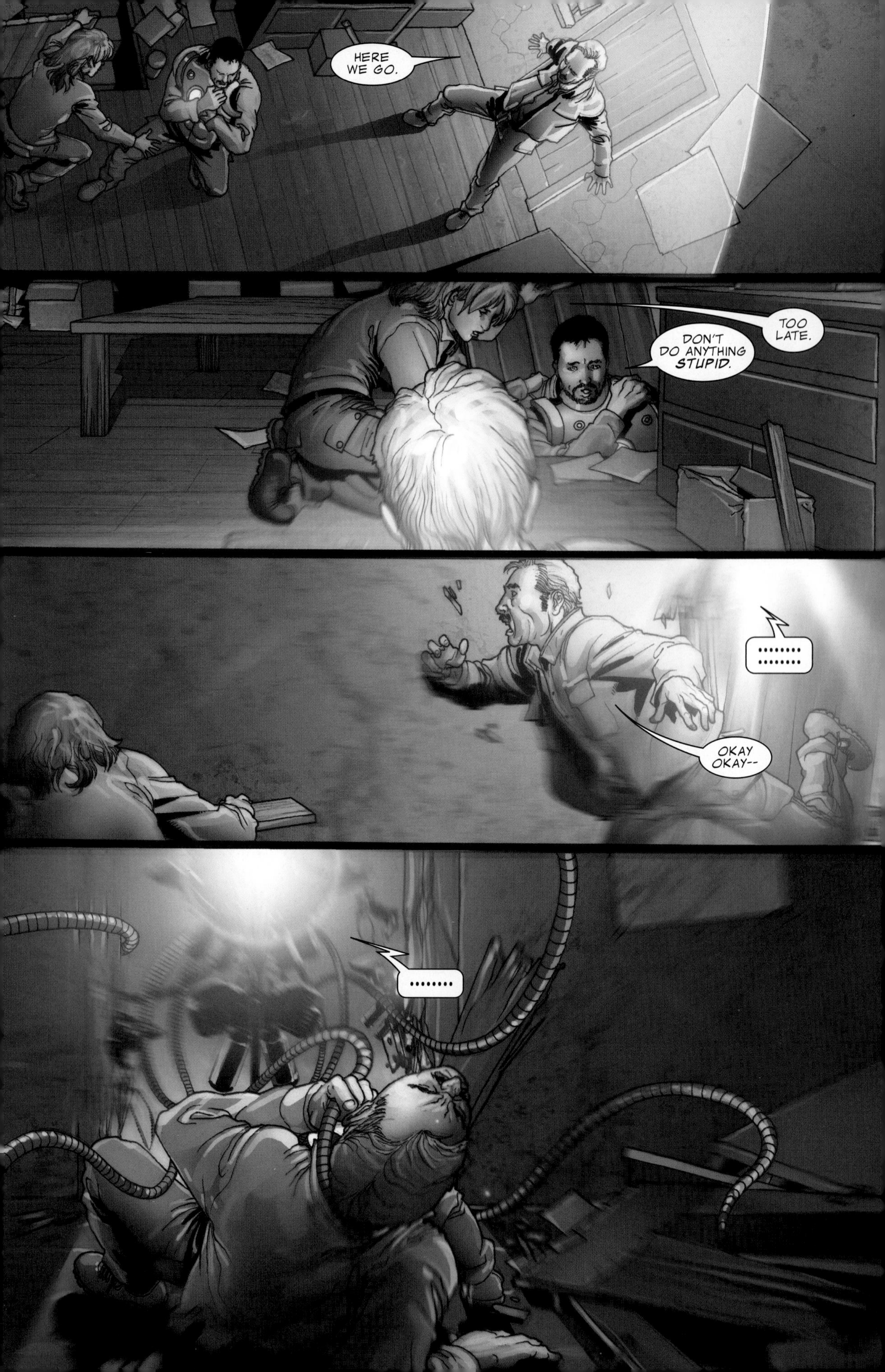
HERE WE GO.
TOO LATE.
DON'T DO ANYTHING STUPID.
....
....
OKAY OKAY--
....

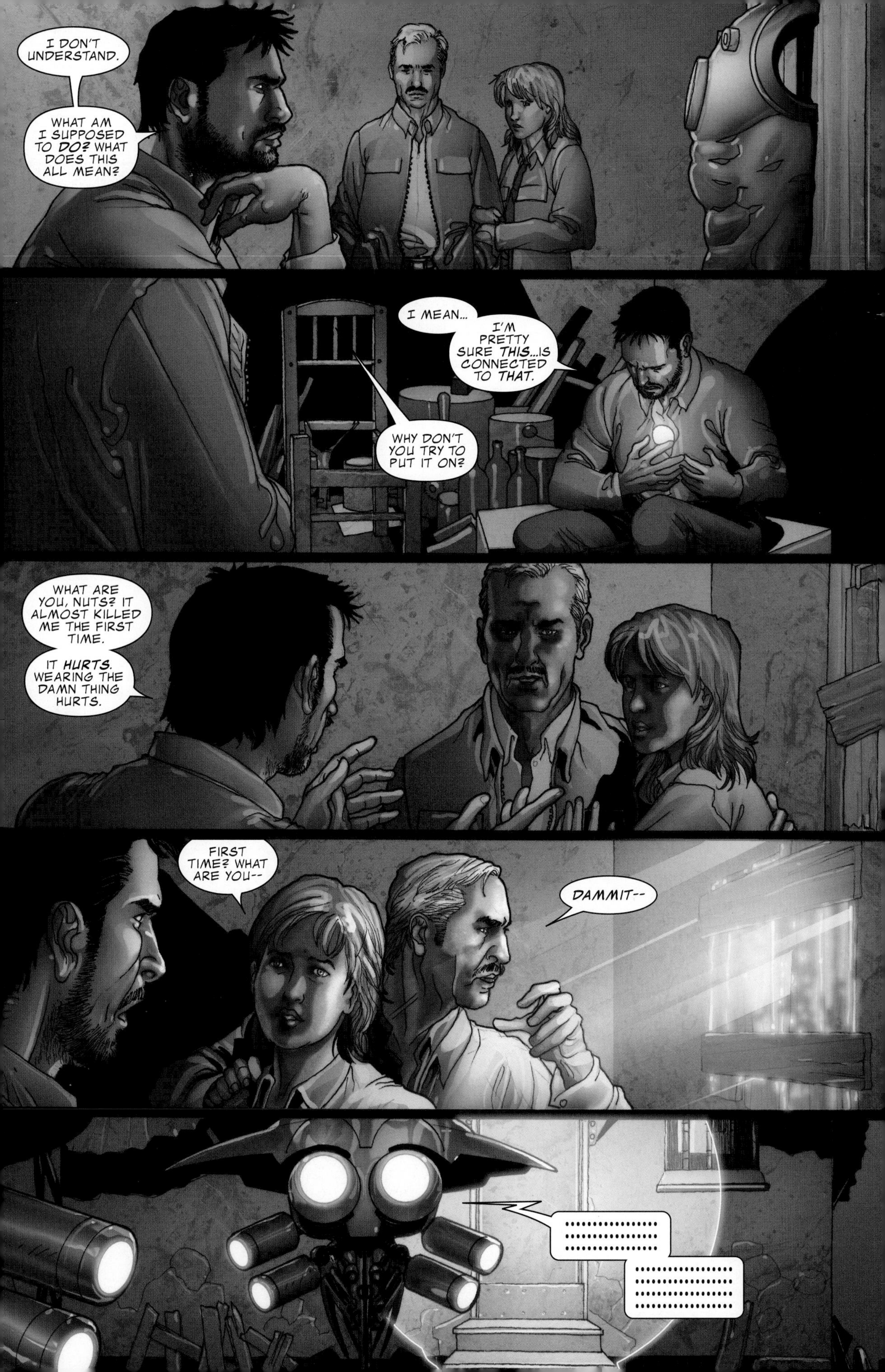
I DON'T UNDERSTAND.
WHAT AM I SUPPOSED TO DO? WHAT DOES THIS ALL MEAN?
I MEAN... I'M PRETTY SURE THIS...IS CONNECTED TO THAT.
WHY DON'T YOU TRY TO PUT IT ON?
WHAT ARE YOU, NUTS? IT ALMOST KILLED ME THE FIRST TIME.
IT HURTS. WEARING THE DAMN THING HURTS.
FIRST TIME? WHAT ARE YOU--
DAMMIT--

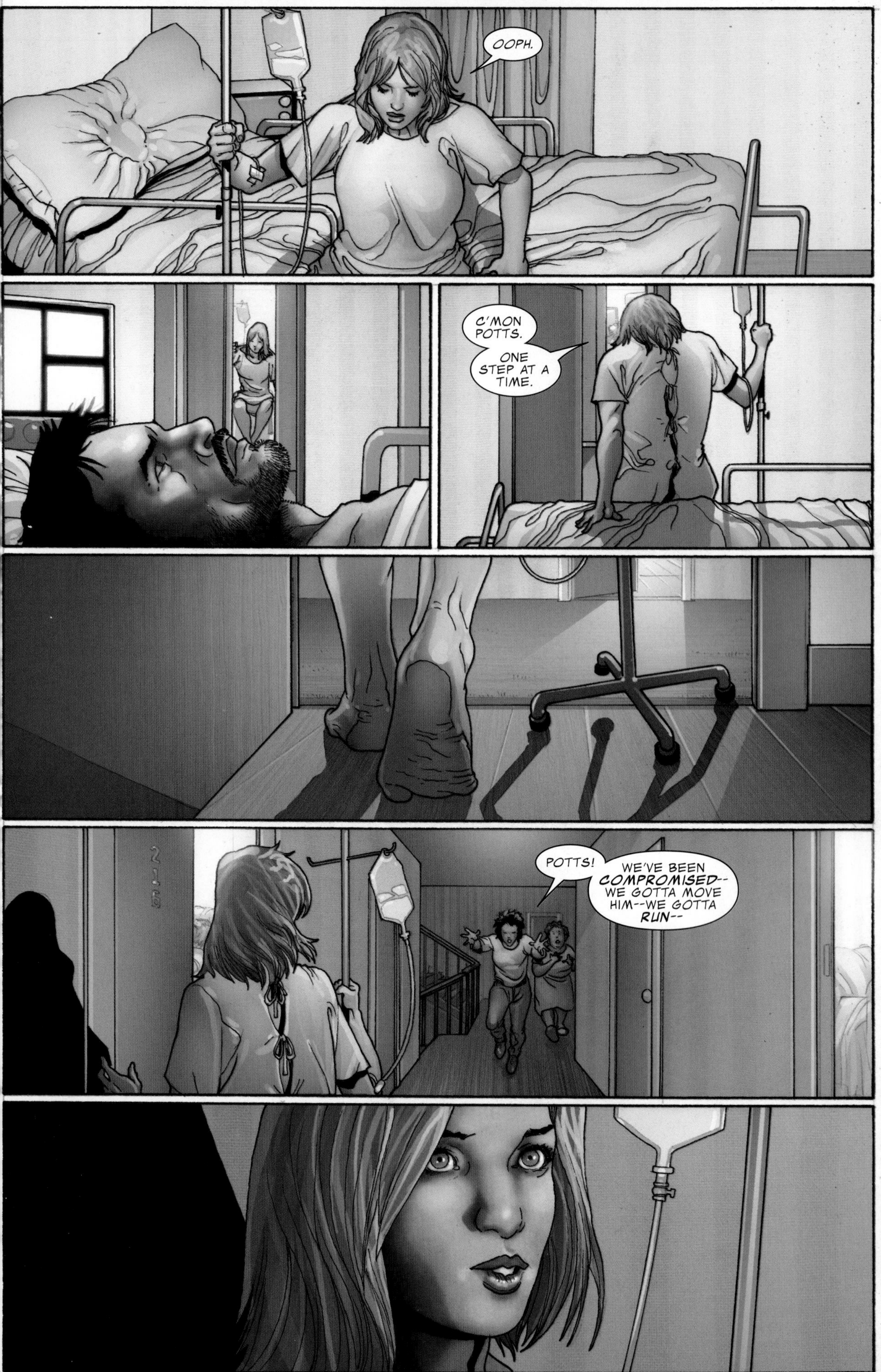
OOPH.
C'MON POTTS.
ONE STEP AT A TIME.
POTTS!
WE'VE BEEN COMPROMISED-- WE GOTTA MOVE HIM--WE GOTTA RUN--

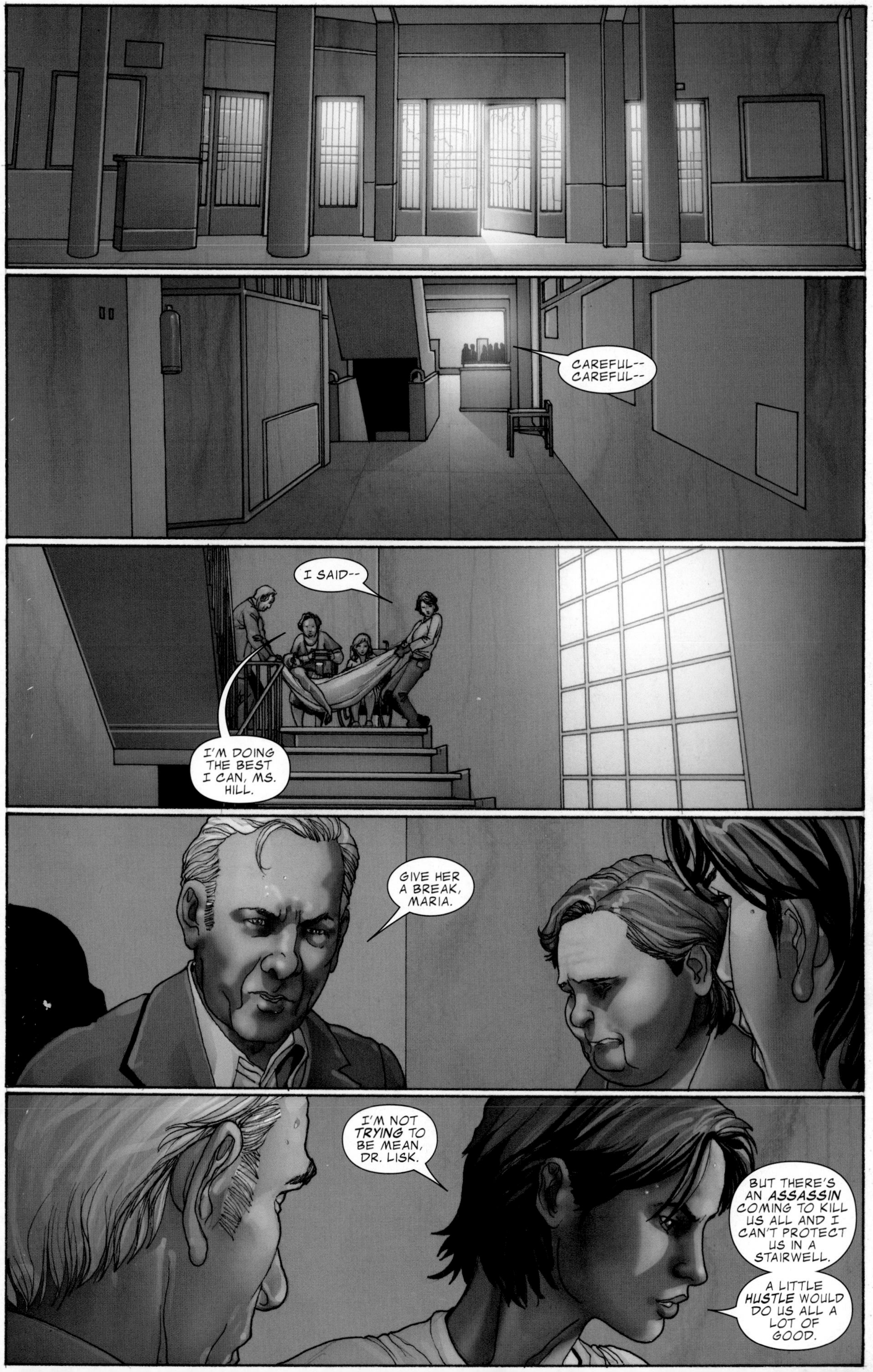
CAREFUL--
CAREFUL--
I SAID--
I'M DOING THE BEST I CAN, MS. HILL.
GIVE HER A BREAK, MARIA.
I'M NOT TRYING TO BE MEAN, DR. LISK.
BUT THERE'S AN ASSASSIN COMING TO KILL US ALL AND I CAN'T PROTECT US IN A STAIRWELL.
A LITTLE HUSTLE WOULD DO US ALL A LOT OF GOOD.

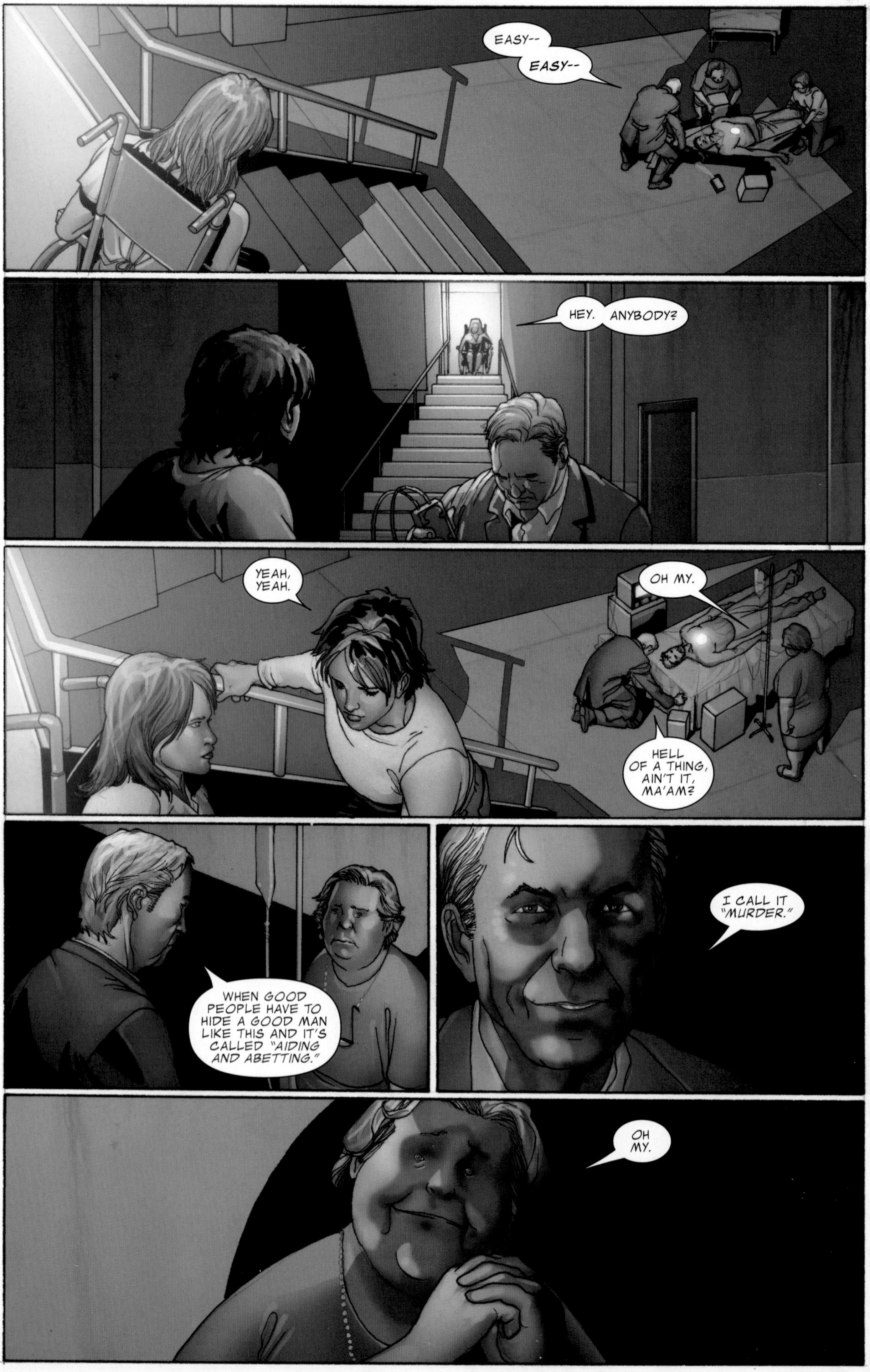
EASY--
EASY--
HEY. ANYBODY?
YEAH, YEAH.
OH MY.
HELL OF A THING, AIN'T IT, MA'AM?
WHEN GOOD PEOPLE HAVE TO HIDE A GOOD MAN LIKE THIS AND IT'S CALLED "AIDING AND ABETTING."
I CALL IT "MURDER."
OH MY.

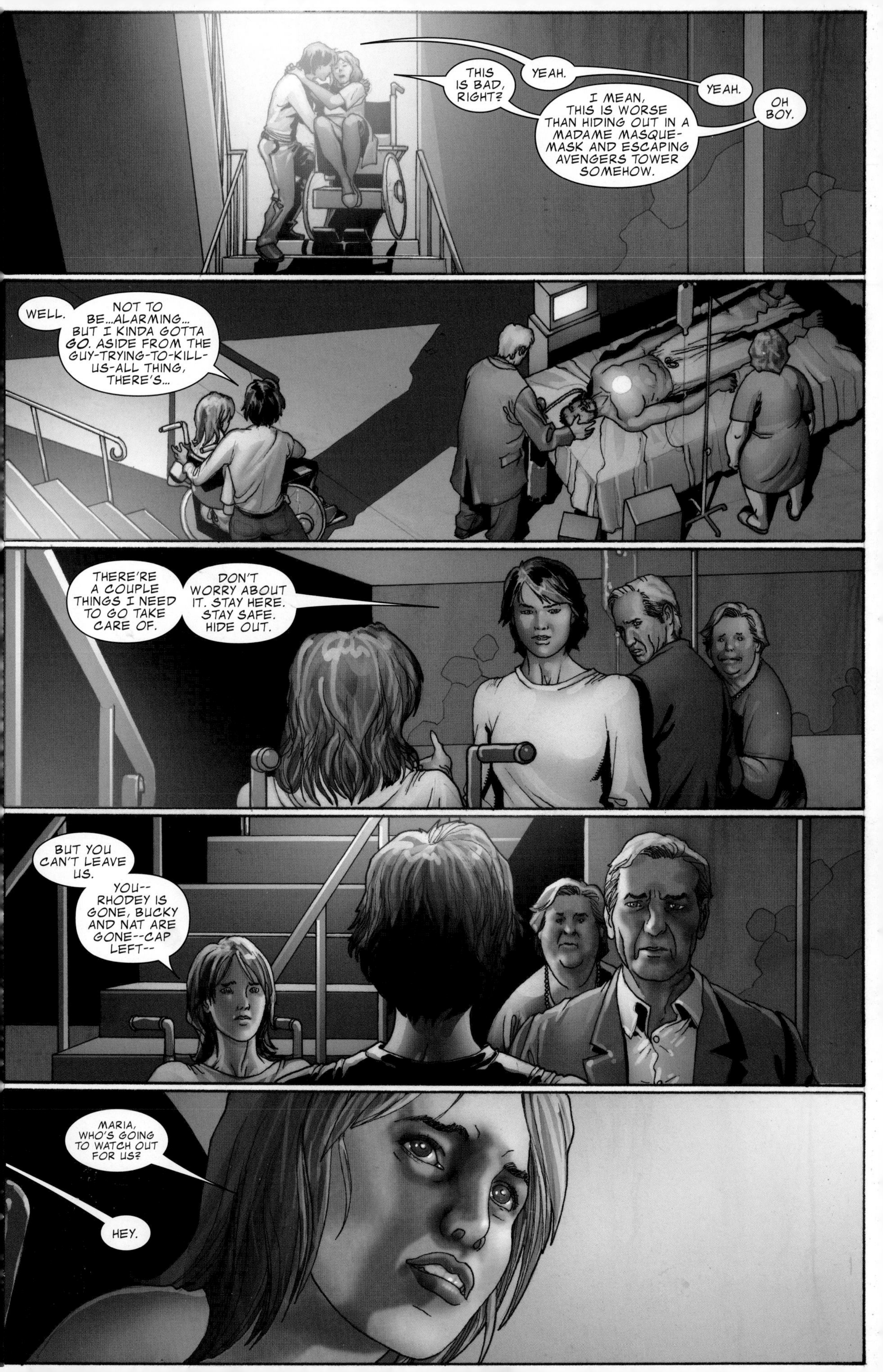
THIS IS BAD, RIGHT?
YEAH.
YEAH.
I MEAN, THIS IS WORSE THAN HIDING OUT IN A MADAME MASQUE-MASK AND ESCAPING AVENGERS TOWER SOMEHOW.
OH BOY.
WELL.
NOT TO BE...ALARMING... BUT I KINDA GOTTA GO. ASIDE FROM THE GUY-TRYING-TO-KILL-US-ALL THING, THERE'S...
THERE'RE A COUPLE THINGS I NEED TO GO TAKE CARE OF.
DON'T WORRY ABOUT IT. STAY HERE. STAY SAFE. HIDE OUT.
BUT YOU CAN'T LEAVE US.
YOU-- RHODEY IS GONE, BUCKY AND NAT ARE GONE--CAP LEFT--
MARIA, WHO'S GOING TO WATCH OUT FOR US?
HEY.

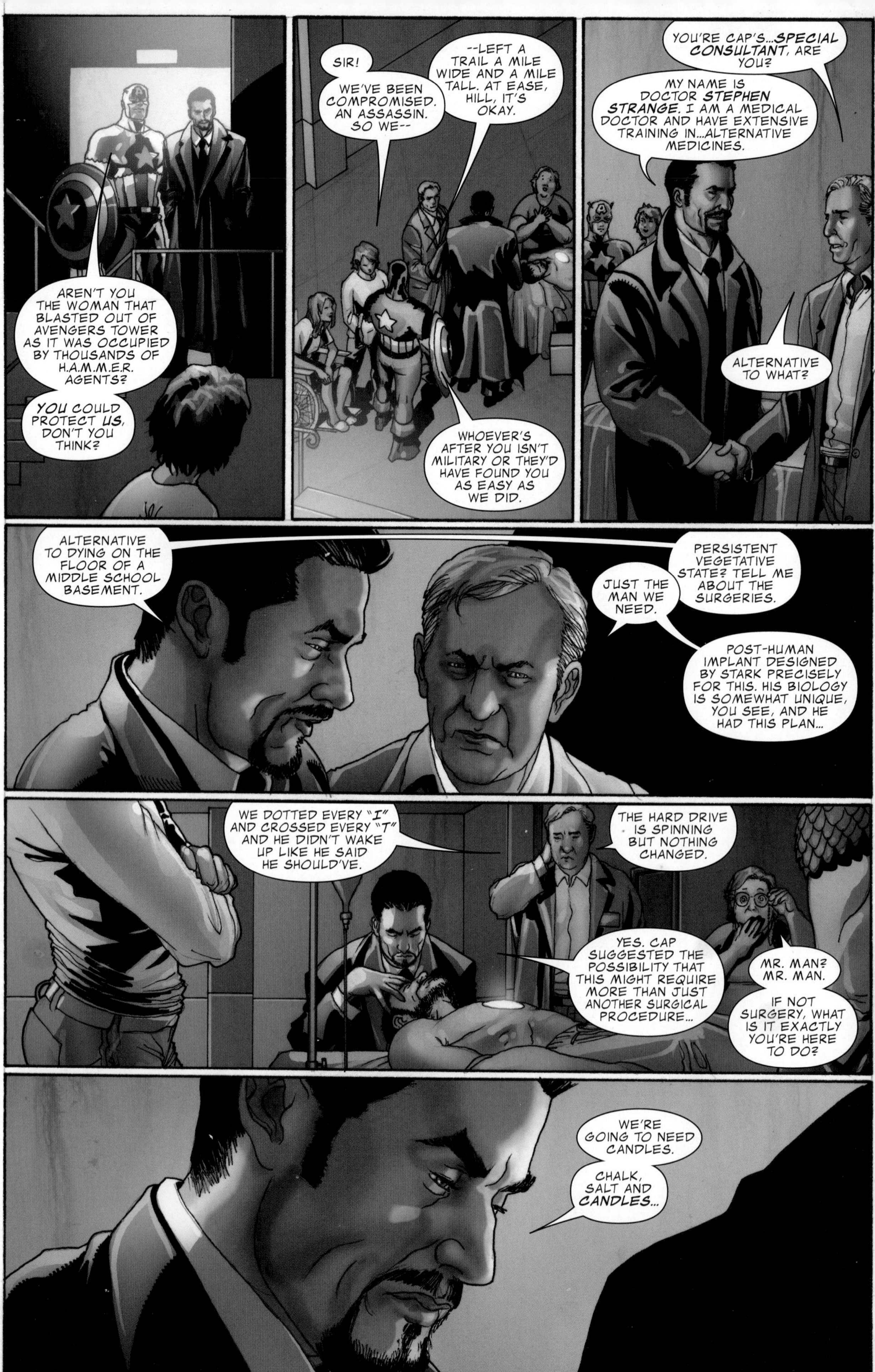
AREN'T YOU THE WOMAN THAT BLASTED OUT OF AVENGERS TOWER AS IT WAS OCCUPIED BY THOUSANDS OF H.A.M.M.E.R. AGENTS?
YOU COULD PROTECT US, DON'T YOU THINK?
SIR!
WE'VE BEEN COMPROMISED. AN ASSASSIN. SO WE--
--LEFT A TRAIL A MILE WIDE AND A MILE TALL. AT EASE, HILL, IT'S OKAY.
WHOEVER'S AFTER YOU ISN'T MILITARY OR THEY'D HAVE FOUND YOU AS EASY AS WE DID.
YOU'RE CAP'S...SPECIAL CONSULTANT, ARE YOU?
MY NAME IS DOCTOR STEPHEN STRANGE. I AM A MEDICAL DOCTOR AND HAVE EXTENSIVE TRAINING IN...ALTERNATIVE MEDICINES.
ALTERNATIVE TO WHAT?
ALTERNATIVE TO DYING ON THE FLOOR OF A MIDDLE SCHOOL BASEMENT.
PERSISTENT VEGETATIVE STATE? TELL ME ABOUT THE SURGERIES.
JUST THE MAN WE NEED.
POST-HUMAN IMPLANT DESIGNED BY STARK PRECISELY FOR THIS. HIS BIOLOGY IS SOMEWHAT UNIQUE, YOU SEE, AND HE HAD THIS PLAN...
WE DOTTED EVERY "I" AND CROSSED EVERY "T" AND HE DIDN'T WAKE UP LIKE HE SAID HE SHOULD'VE.
THE HARD DRIVE IS SPINNING BUT NOTHING CHANGED.
YES. CAP SUGGESTED THE POSSIBILITY THAT THIS MIGHT REQUIRE MORE THAN JUST ANOTHER SURGICAL PROCEDURE...
MR. MAN? MR. MAN.
IF NOT SURGERY, WHAT IS IT EXACTLY YOU'RE HERE TO DO?
WE'RE GOING TO NEED CANDLES.
CHALK, SALT AND CANDLES...

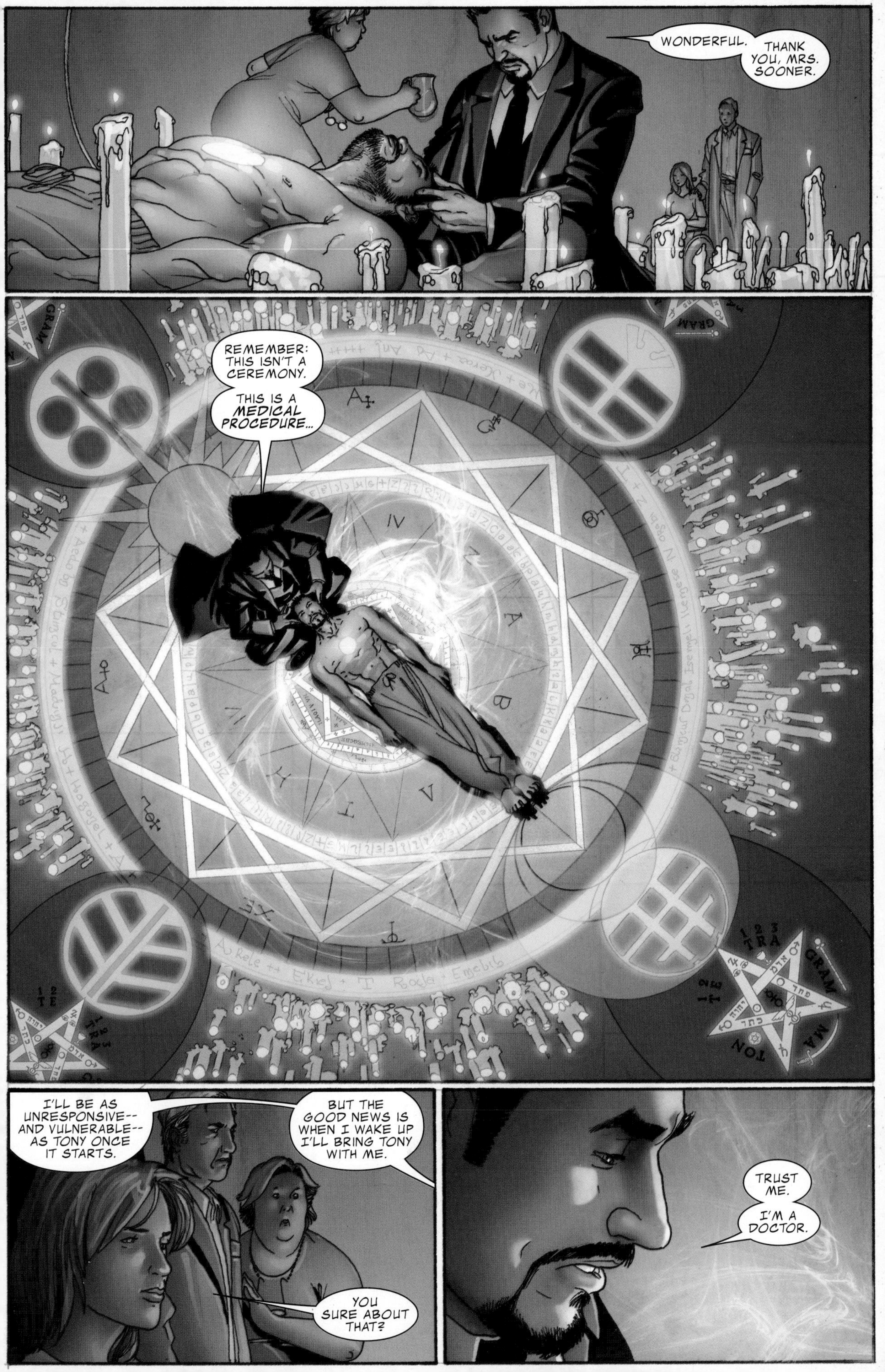
WONDERFUL.
THANK YOU, MRS. SOONER.
REMEMBER: THIS ISN'T A CEREMONY.
THIS IS A MEDICAL PROCEDURE...
I'LL BE AS UNRESPONSIVE-- AND VULNERABLE-- AS TONY ONCE IT STARTS.
BUT THE GOOD NEWS IS WHEN I WAKE UP I'LL BRING TONY WITH ME.
YOU SURE ABOUT THAT?
TRUST ME.
I'M A DOCTOR.

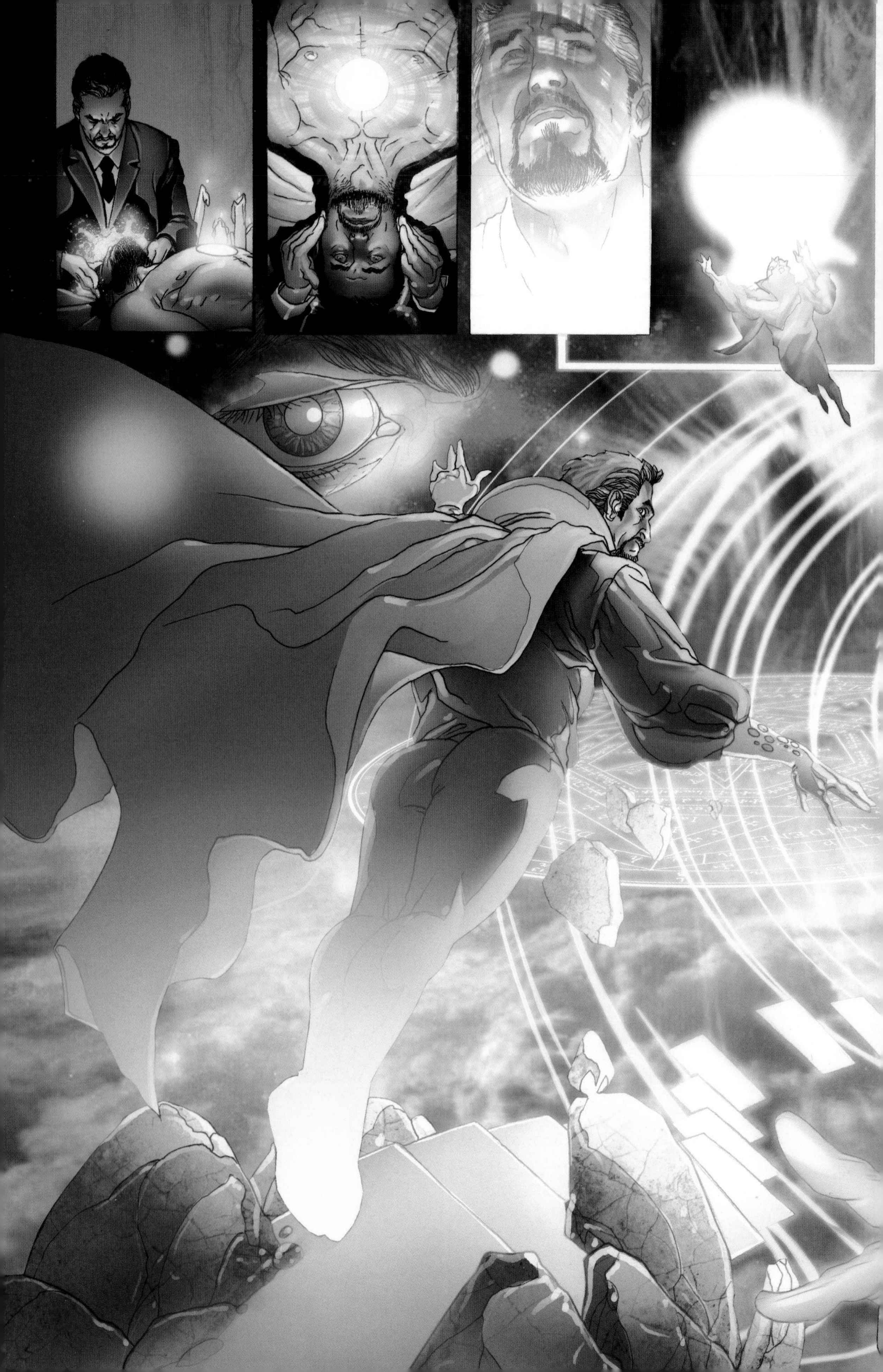

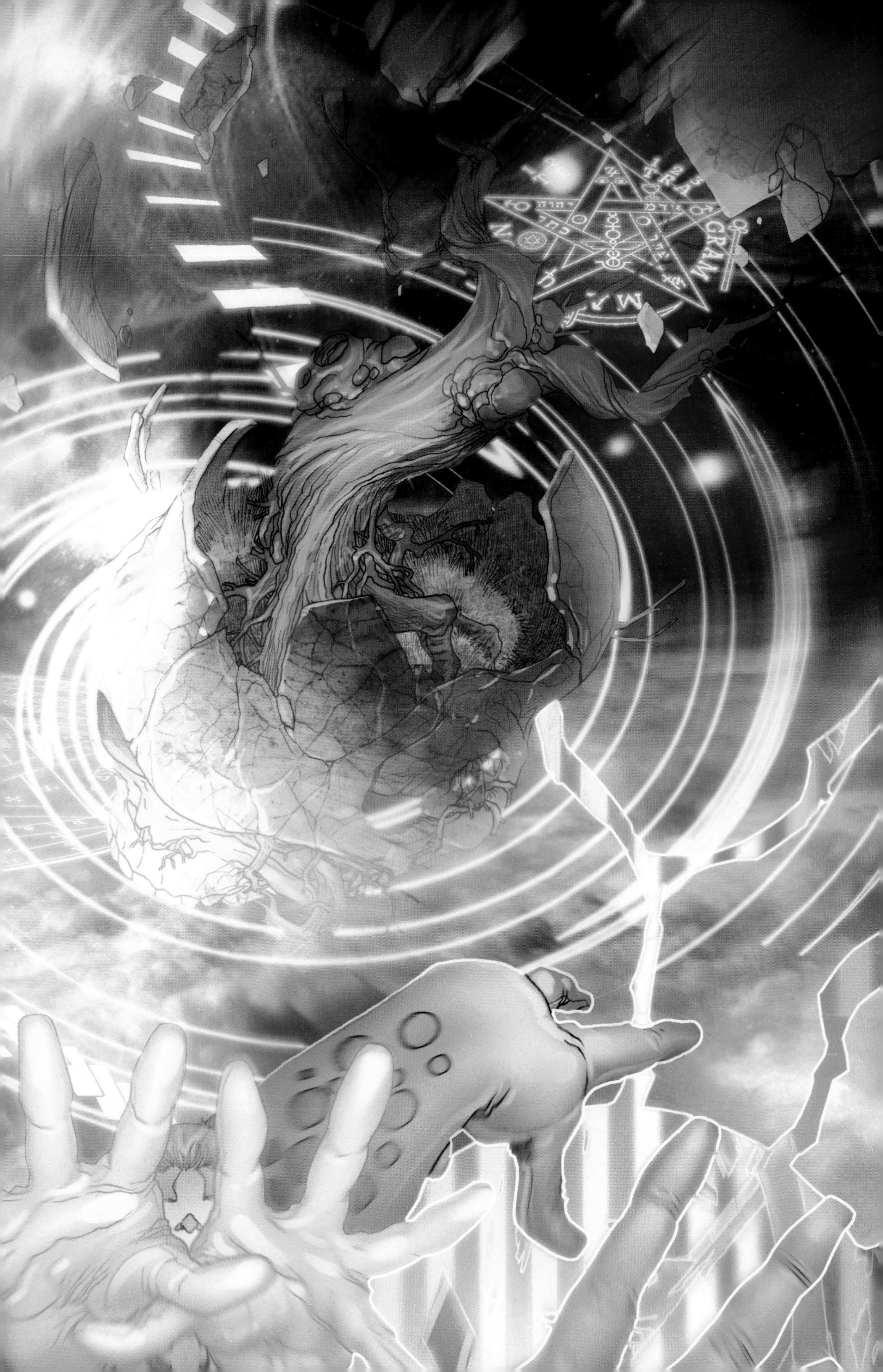

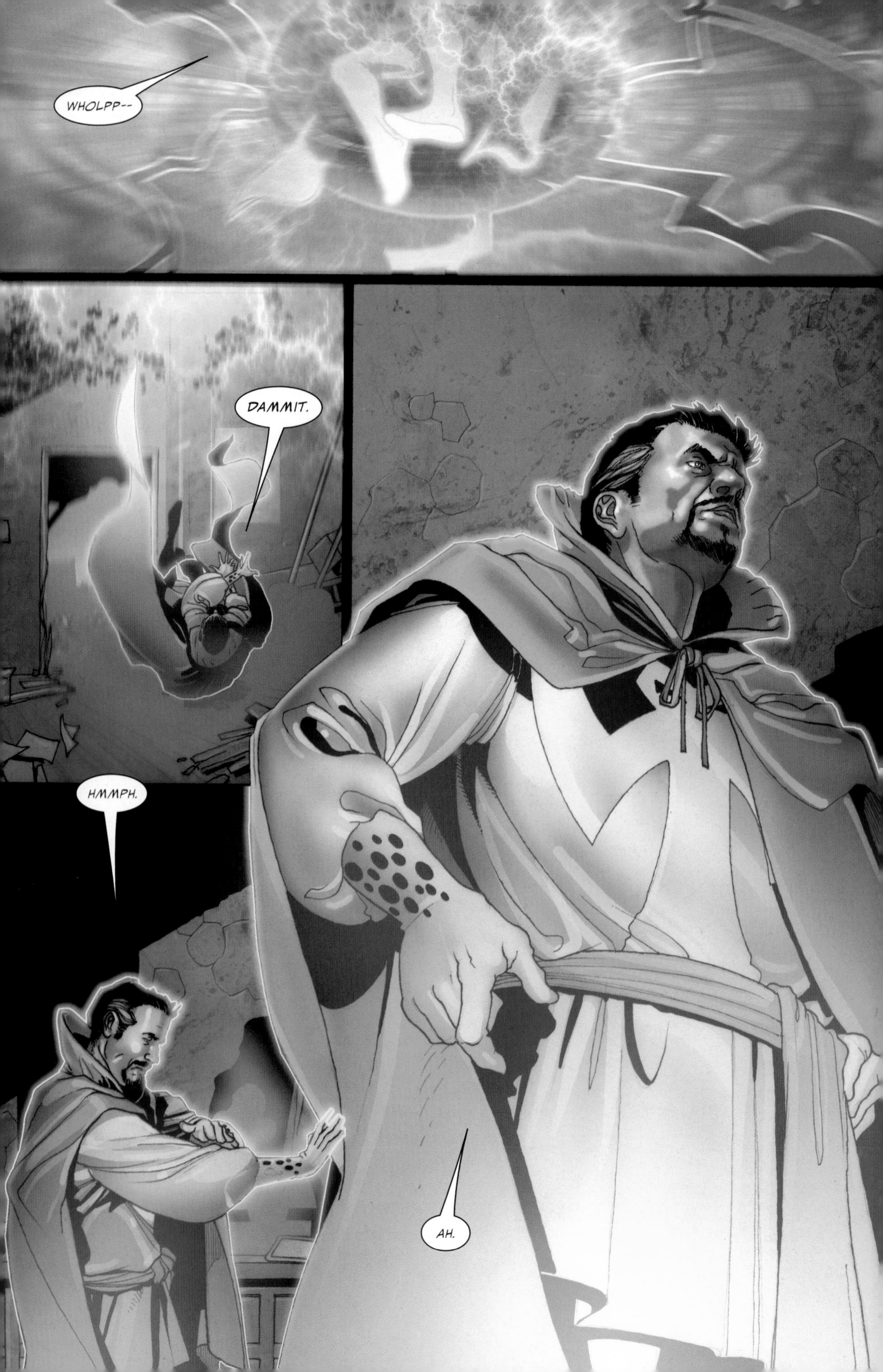
WHOLPP--
DAMMIT.
HMMPH.
AH.

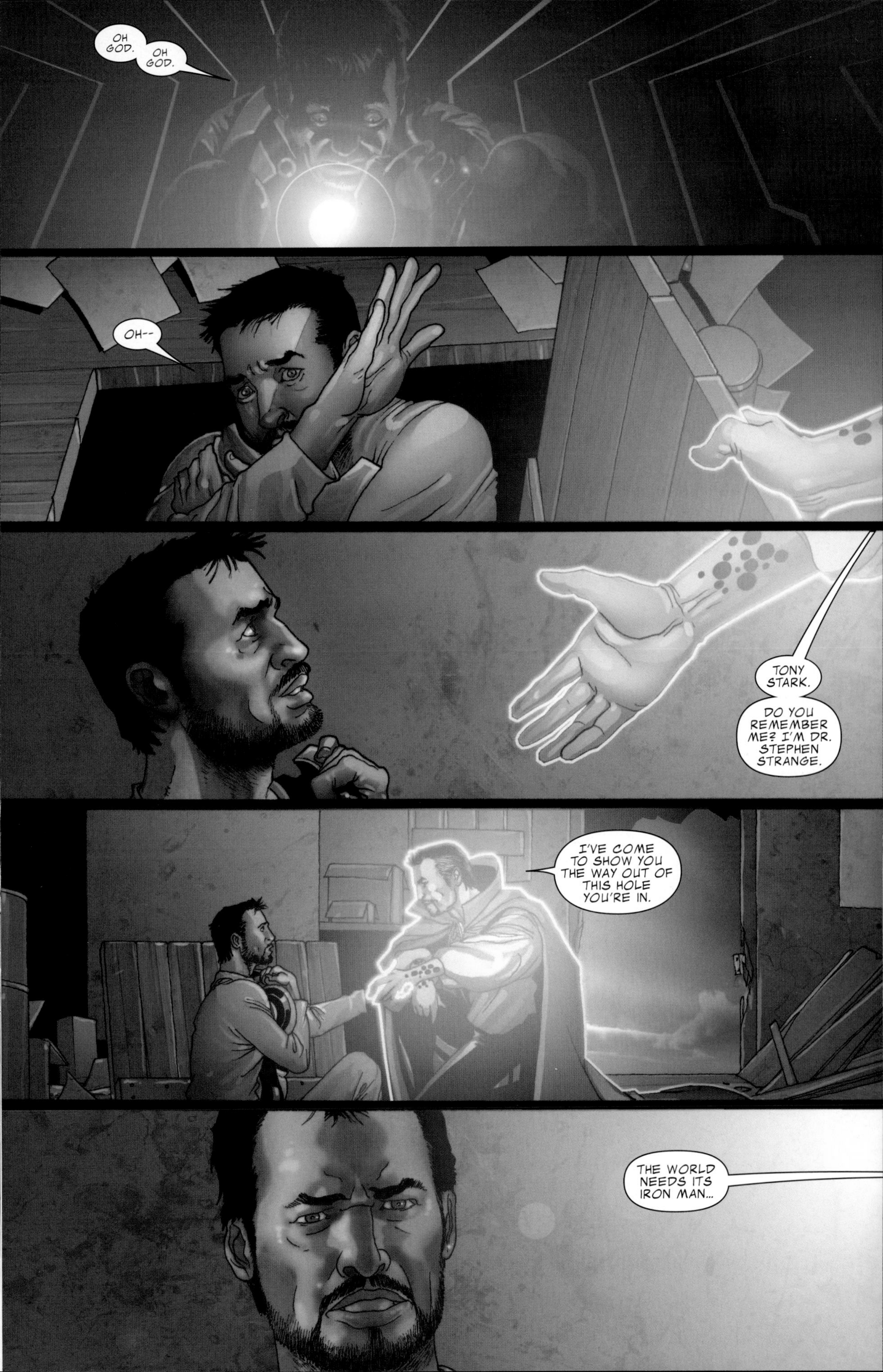
OH GOD.
OH GOD.
OH--
TONY STARK.
DO YOU REMEMBER ME? I'M DR. STEPHEN STRANGE.
I'VE COME TO SHOW YOU THE WAY OUT OF THIS HOLE YOU'RE IN.
THE WORLD NEEDS ITS IRON MAN...

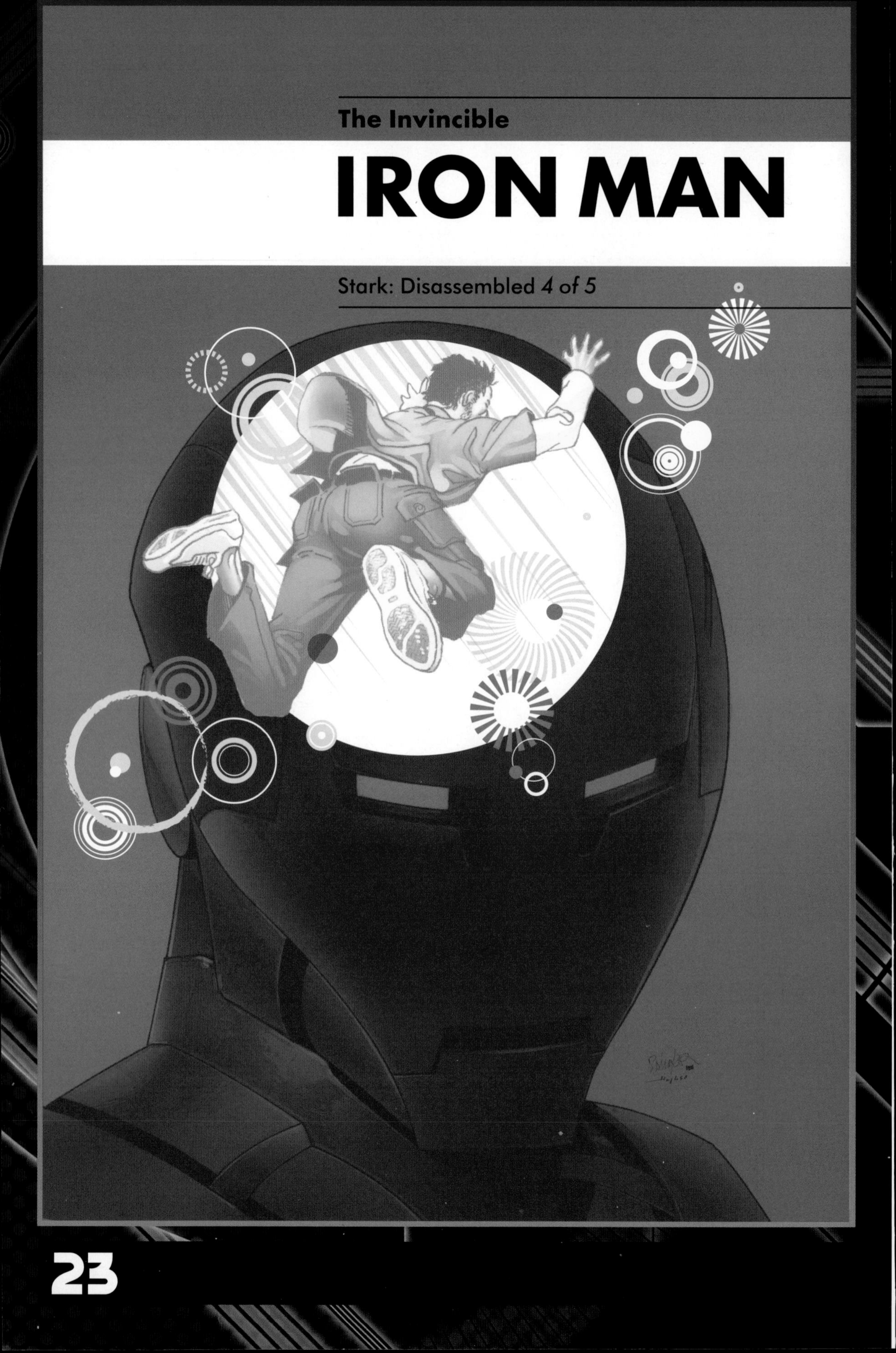
The Invincible
IRON MAN
Stark: Disassembled 4 of 5

23

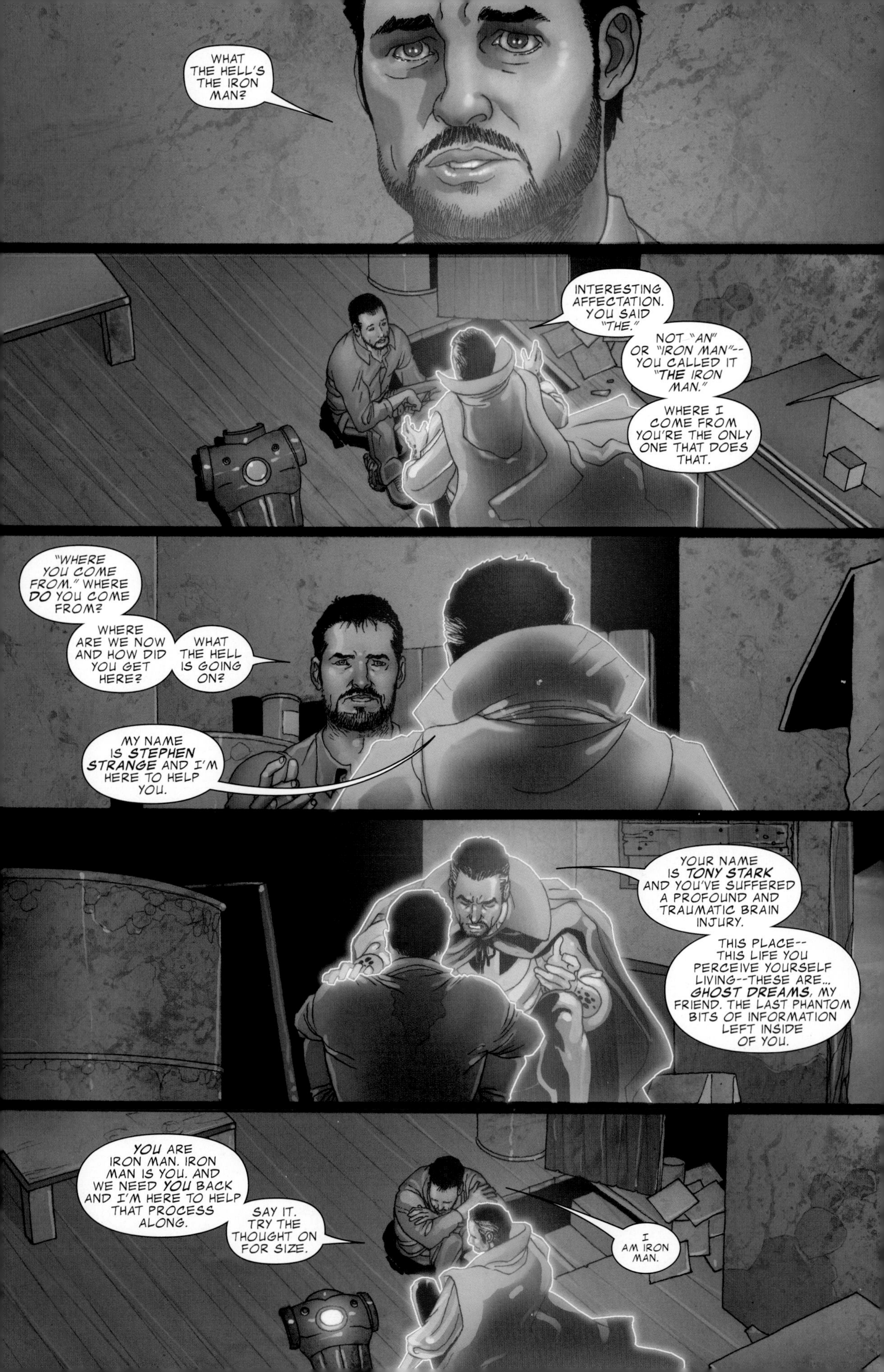
WHAT THE HELL'S THE IRON MAN?
INTERESTING AFFECTATION. YOU SAID "THE."
NOT "AN" OR "IRON MAN"-- YOU CALLED IT "THE IRON MAN."
WHERE I COME FROM YOU'RE THE ONLY ONE THAT DOES THAT.
"WHERE YOU COME FROM." WHERE DO YOU COME FROM?
WHERE ARE WE NOW AND HOW DID YOU GET HERE?
WHAT THE HELL IS GOING ON?
MY NAME IS STEPHEN STRANGE AND I'M HERE TO HELP YOU.
YOUR NAME IS TONY STARK AND YOU'VE SUFFERED A PROFOUND AND TRAUMATIC BRAIN INJURY.
THIS PLACE-- THIS LIFE YOU PERCEIVE YOURSELF LIVING--THESE ARE... GHOST DREAMS, MY FRIEND. THE LAST PHANTOM BITS OF INFORMATION LEFT INSIDE OF YOU.
YOU ARE IRON MAN. IRON MAN IS YOU. AND WE NEED YOU BACK AND I'M HERE TO HELP THAT PROCESS ALONG.
SAY IT. TRY THE THOUGHT ON FOR SIZE.
I AM IRON MAN.

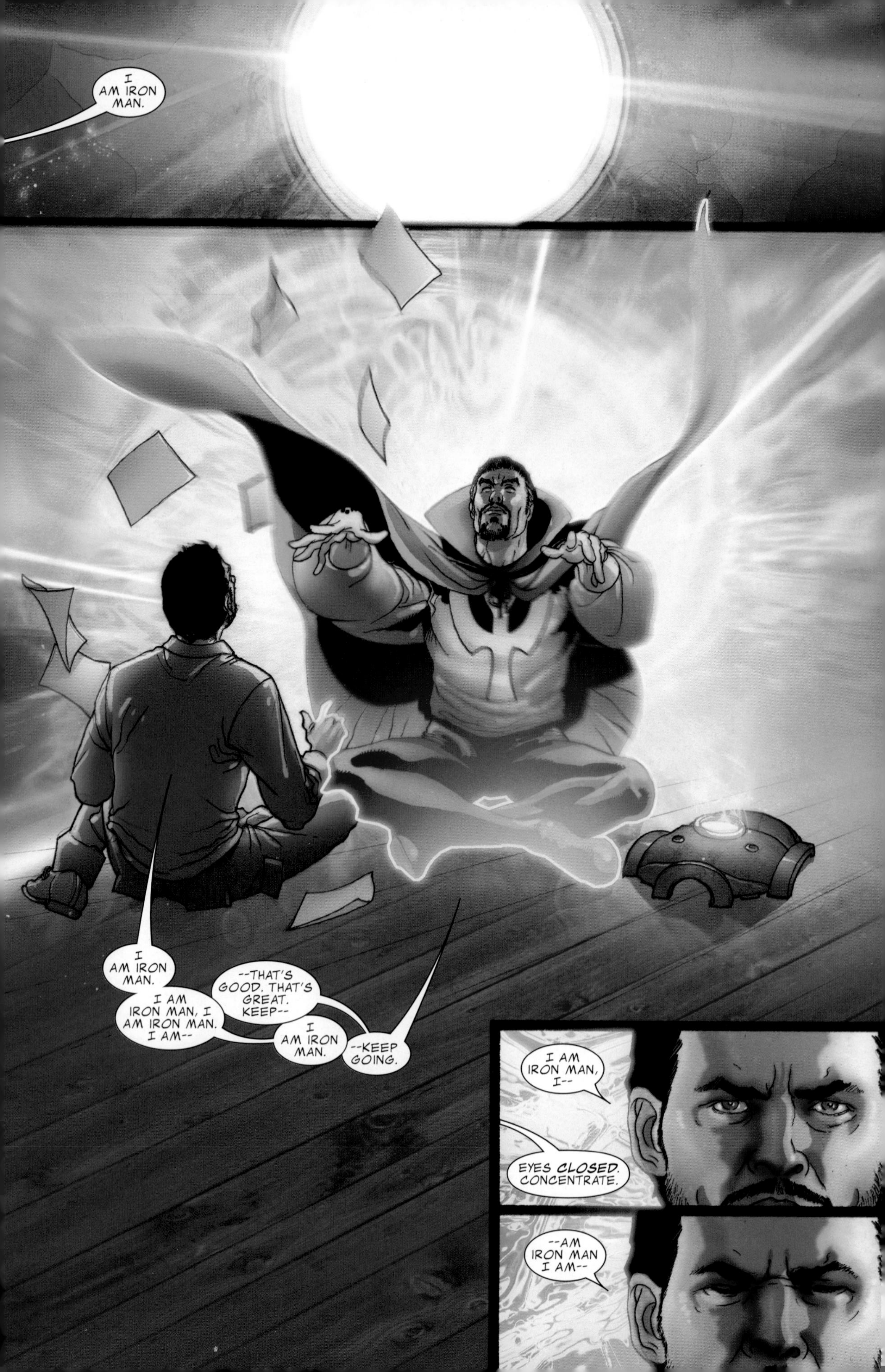

I AM IRON MAN.
I AM IRON MAN.
I AM IRON MAN, I AM IRON MAN. I AM--
--THAT'S GOOD. THAT'S GREAT. KEEP--
I AM IRON MAN.
--KEEP GOING.
I AM IRON MAN, I--
EYES CLOSED. CONCENTRATE.
--AM IRON MAN I AM--

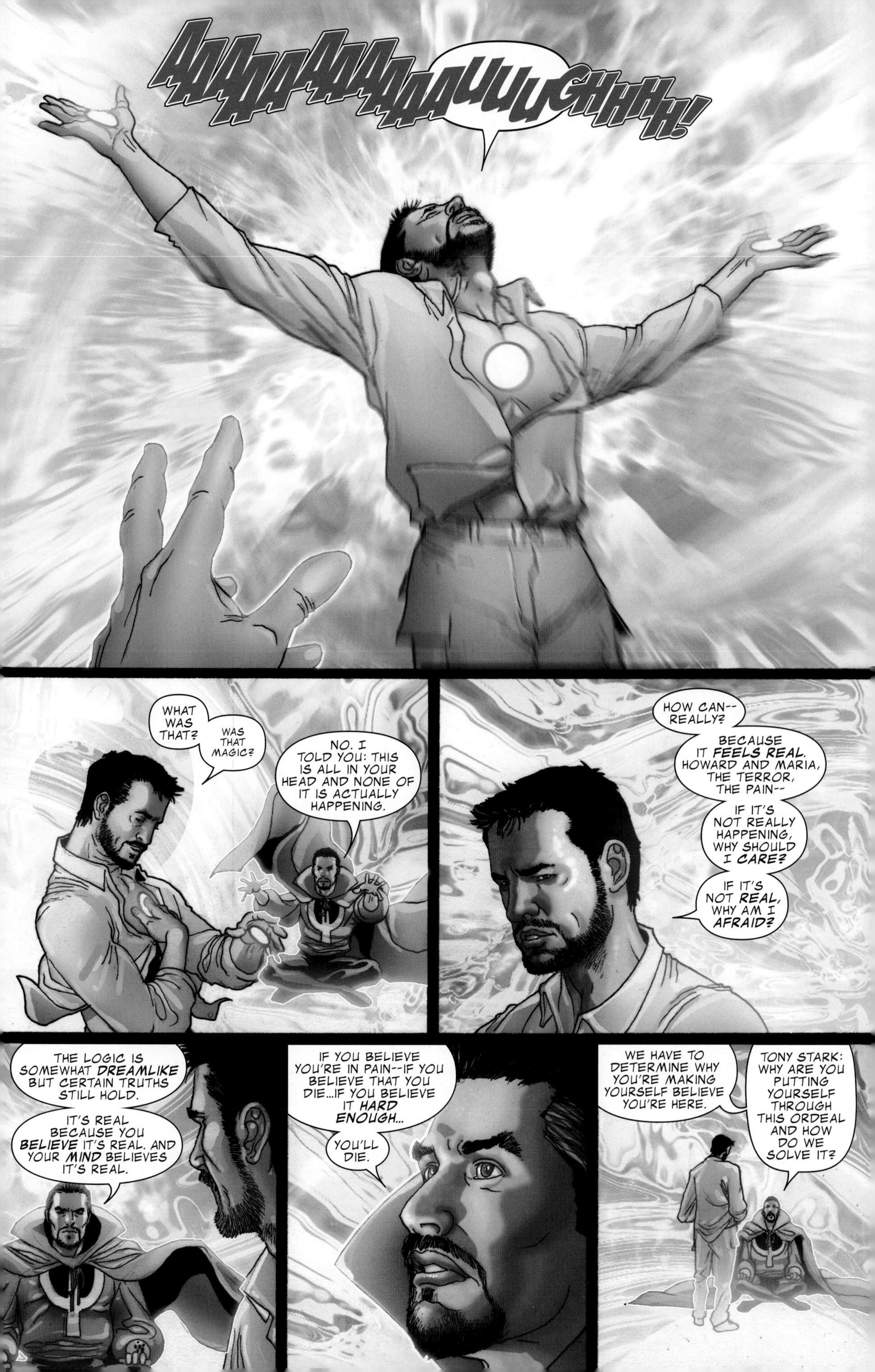
AAAAAAAAAAAAAUUUUGHHHH!
WHAT WAS THAT?
WAS THAT MAGIC?
NO. I TOLD YOU: THIS IS ALL IN YOUR HEAD AND NONE OF IT IS ACTUALLY HAPPENING.
HOW CAN-- REALLY?
BECAUSE IT FEELS REAL. HOWARD AND MARIA, THE TERROR, THE PAIN--
IF IT'S NOT REALLY HAPPENING, WHY SHOULD I CARE?
IF IT'S NOT REAL, WHY AM I AFRAID?
THE LOGIC IS SOMEWHAT DREAMLIKE BUT CERTAIN TRUTHS STILL HOLD.
IT'S REAL BECAUSE YOU BELIEVE IT'S REAL. AND YOUR MIND BELIEVES IT'S REAL.
IF YOU BELIEVE YOU'RE IN PAIN--IF YOU BELIEVE THAT YOU DIE...IF YOU BELIEVE IT HARD ENOUGH...
YOU'LL DIE.
WE HAVE TO DETERMINE WHY YOU'RE MAKING YOURSELF BELIEVE YOU'RE HERE.
TONY STARK: WHY ARE YOU PUTTING YOURSELF THROUGH THIS ORDEAL AND HOW DO WE SOLVE IT?

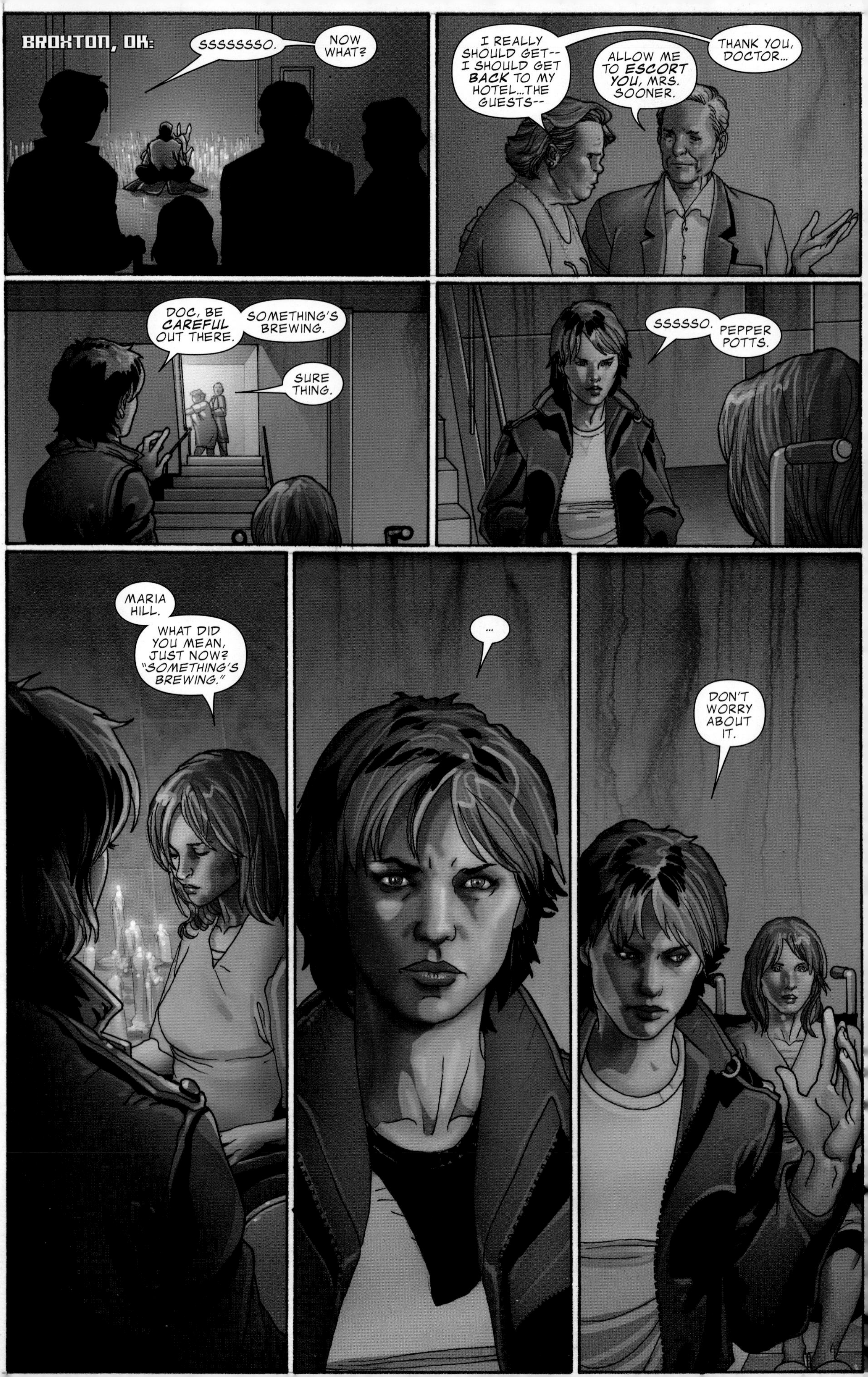
BROXTON, OK:
SSSSSSSO.
NOW WHAT?
I REALLY SHOULD GET-- I SHOULD GET BACK TO MY HOTEL...THE GUESTS--
THANK YOU, DOCTOR...
ALLOW ME TO ESCORT YOU, MRS. SOONER.
DOC, BE CAREFUL OUT THERE.
SOMETHING'S BREWING.
SURE THING.
SSSSSO.
PEPPER POTTS.
MARIA HILL.
WHAT DID YOU MEAN, JUST NOW? "SOMETHING'S BREWING."
...
DON'T WORRY ABOUT IT.

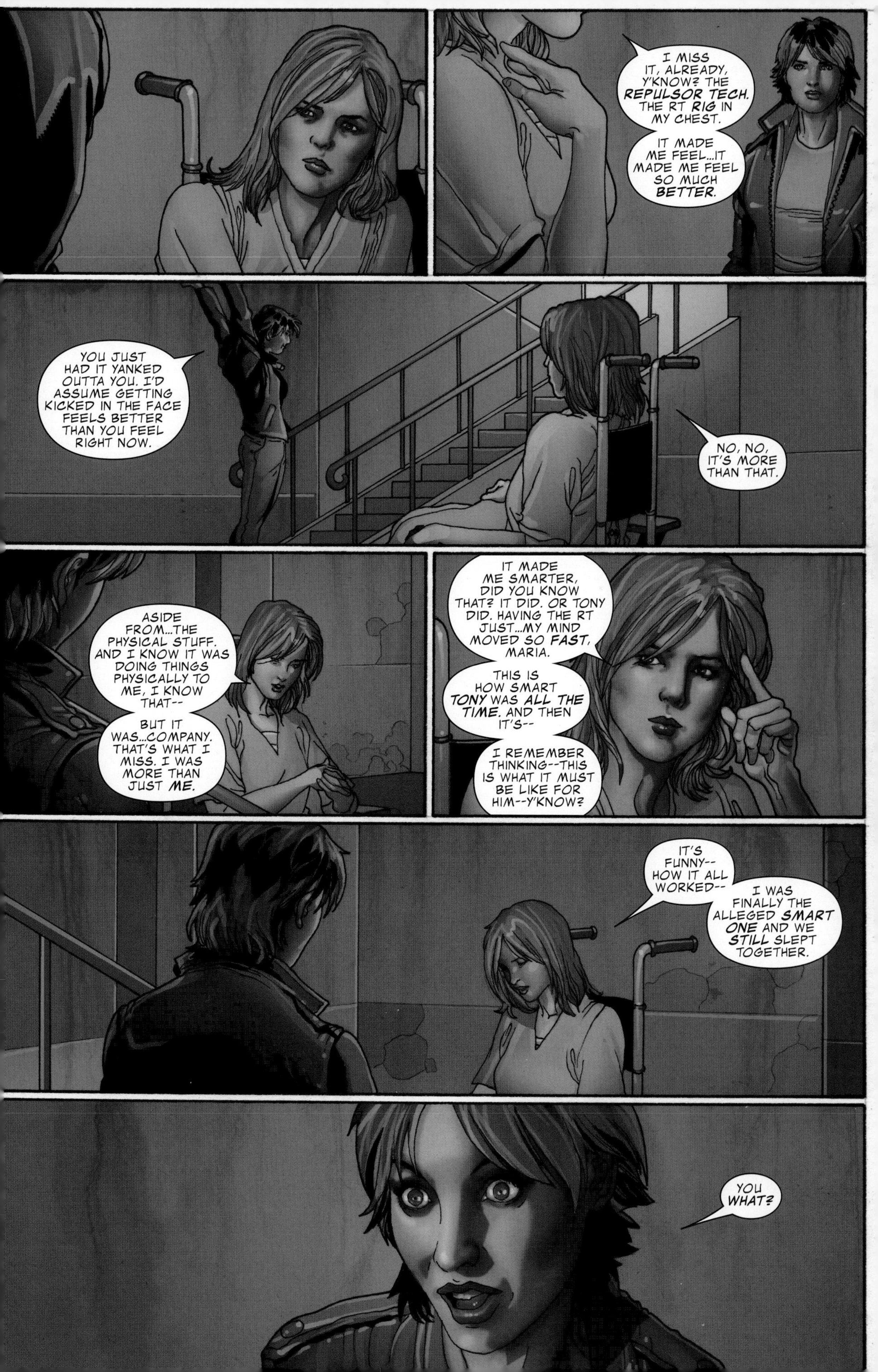
I MISS IT, ALREADY, Y'KNOW? THE REPULSOR TECH. THE RT RIG IN MY CHEST.
IT MADE ME FEEL...IT MADE ME FEEL SO MUCH BETTER.
YOU JUST HAD IT YANKED OUTTA YOU. I'D ASSUME GETTING KICKED IN THE FACE FEELS BETTER THAN YOU FEEL RIGHT NOW.
NO, NO, IT'S MORE THAN THAT.
ASIDE FROM...THE PHYSICAL STUFF. AND I KNOW IT WAS DOING THINGS PHYSICALLY TO ME, I KNOW THAT--
BUT IT WAS...COMPANY. THAT'S WHAT I MISS. I WAS MORE THAN JUST ME.
IT MADE ME SMARTER, DID YOU KNOW THAT? IT DID. OR TONY DID. HAVING THE RT JUST...MY MIND MOVED SO FAST, MARIA.
THIS IS HOW SMART TONY WAS ALL THE TIME. AND THEN IT'S--
I REMEMBER THINKING--THIS IS WHAT IT MUST BE LIKE FOR HIM--Y'KNOW?
IT'S FUNNY-- HOW IT ALL WORKED--
I WAS FINALLY THE ALLEGED SMART ONE AND WE STILL SLEPT TOGETHER.
YOU WHAT?

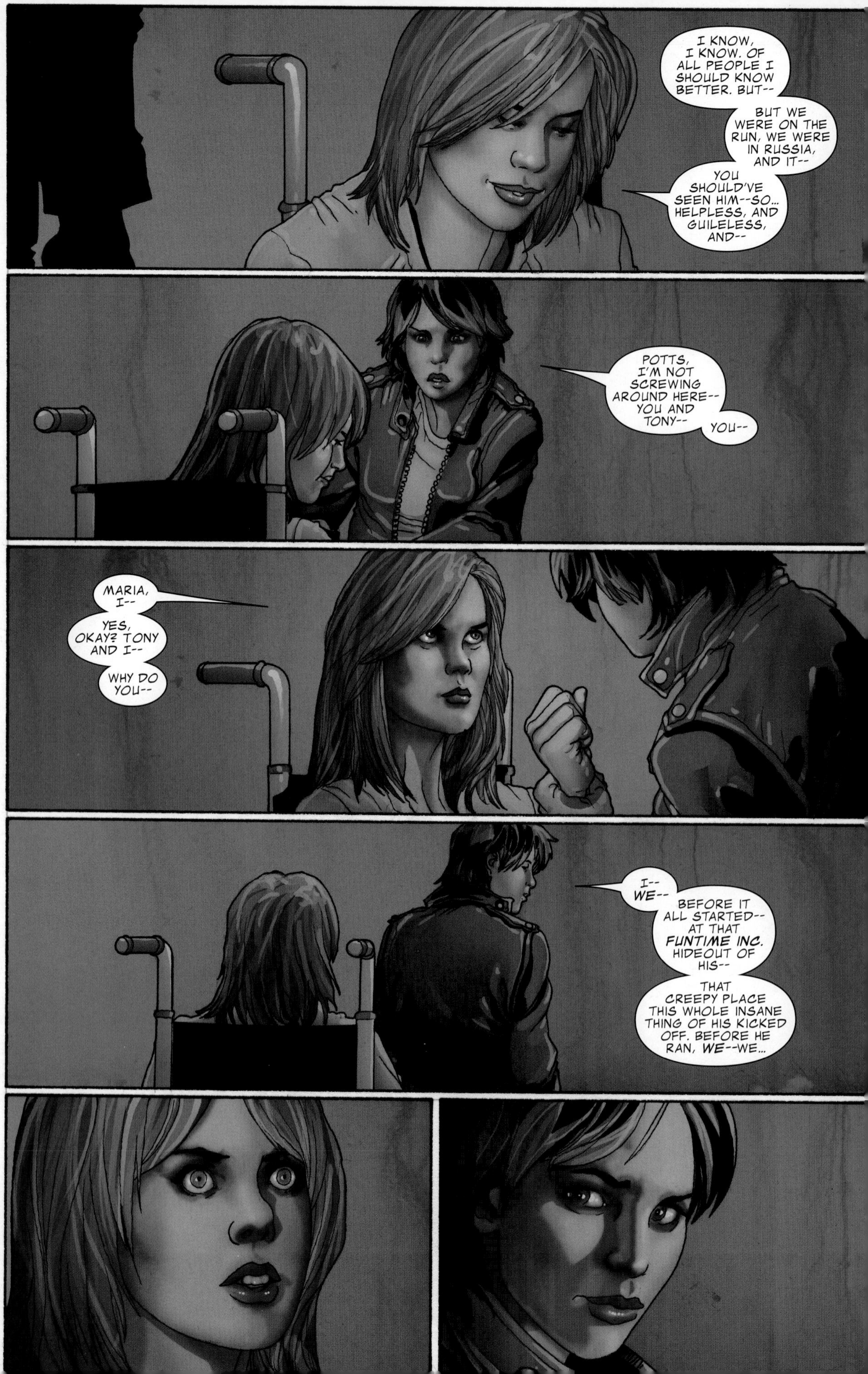
I KNOW, I KNOW. OF ALL PEOPLE I SHOULD KNOW BETTER. BUT--
BUT WE WERE ON THE RUN, WE WERE IN RUSSIA, AND IT--
YOU SHOULD'VE SEEN HIM--SO... HELPLESS, AND GUILELESS, AND--
POTTS, I'M NOT SCREWING AROUND HERE-- YOU AND TONY--
YOU--
MARIA, I--
YES, OKAY? TONY AND I--
WHY DO YOU--
I-- WE--
BEFORE IT ALL STARTED-- AT THAT FUNTIME INC. HIDEOUT OF HIS--
THAT CREEPY PLACE THIS WHOLE INSANE THING OF HIS KICKED OFF. BEFORE HE RAN, WE--WE...

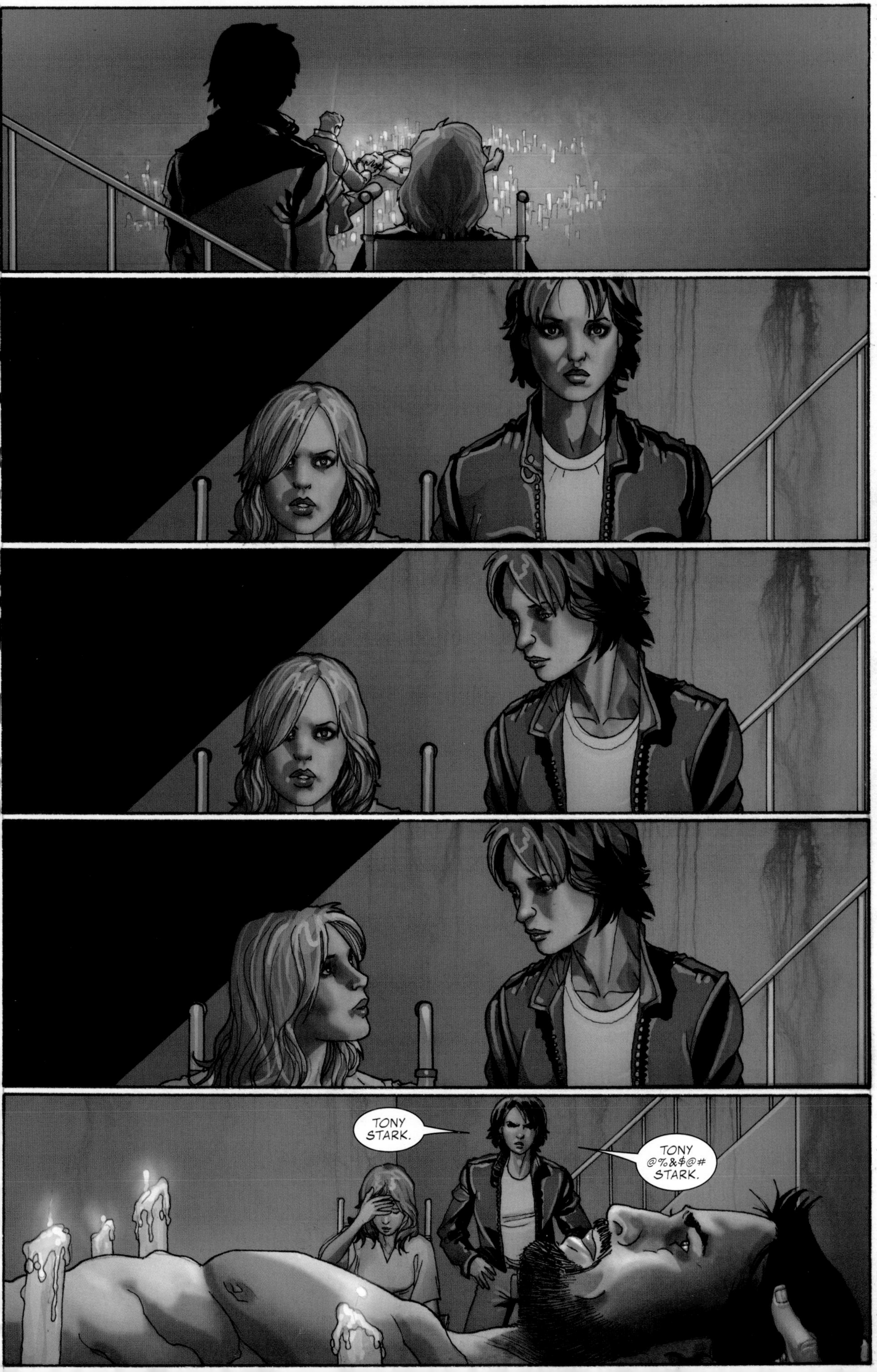
TONY
STARK.
TONY
@%&$@#
STARK.

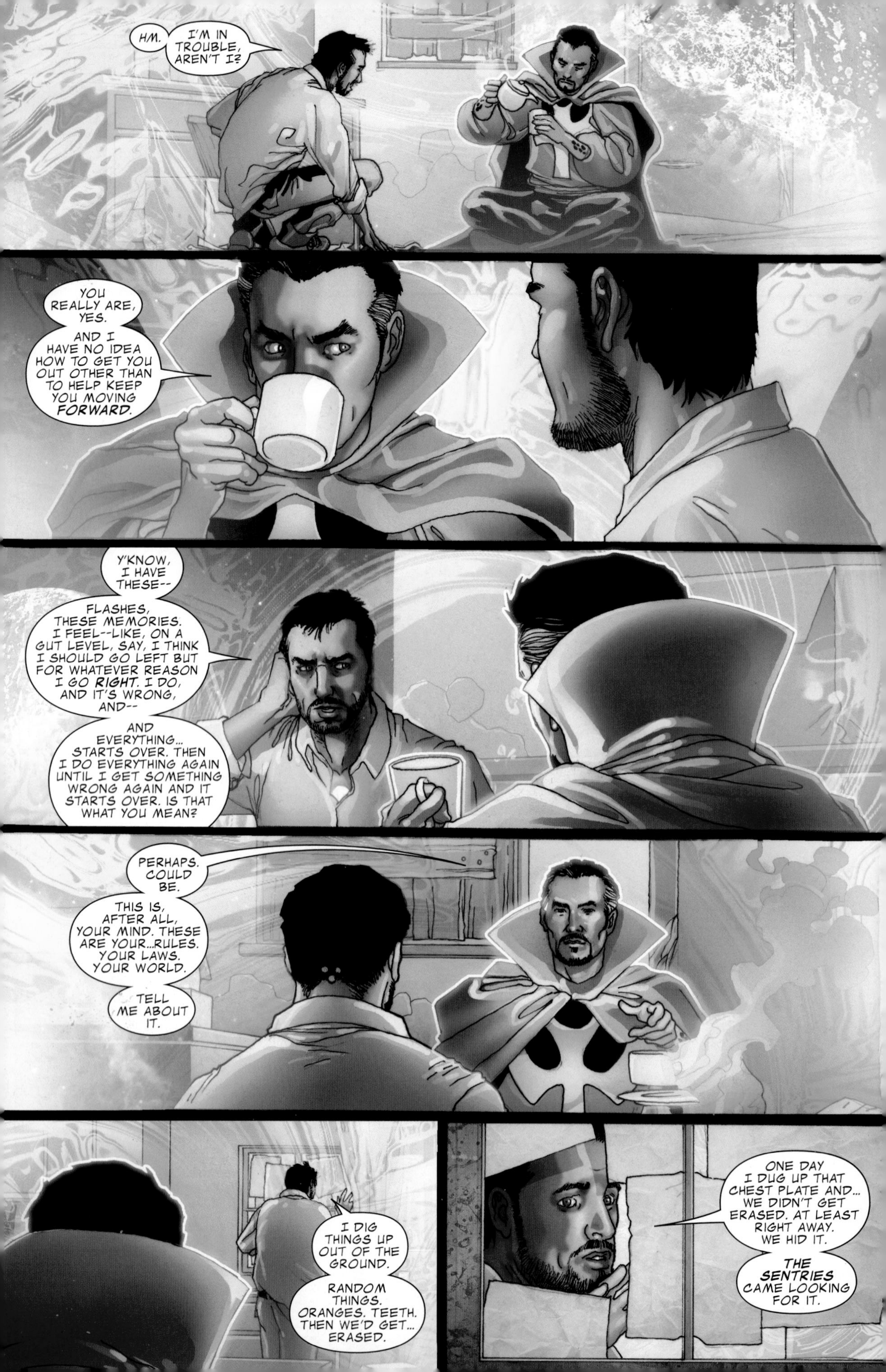
HM.
I'M IN TROUBLE, AREN'T I?
YOU REALLY ARE, YES.
AND I HAVE NO IDEA HOW TO GET YOU OUT OTHER THAN TO HELP KEEP YOU MOVING **FORWARD**.
Y'KNOW, I HAVE THESE--
FLASHES, THESE MEMORIES. I FEEL--LIKE, ON A GUT LEVEL, SAY, I THINK I SHOULD GO LEFT BUT FOR WHATEVER REASON I GO **RIGHT**. I DO, AND IT'S WRONG, AND--
AND EVERYTHING... STARTS OVER. THEN I DO EVERYTHING AGAIN UNTIL I GET SOMETHING WRONG AGAIN AND IT STARTS OVER. IS THAT WHAT YOU MEAN?
PERHAPS. COULD BE.
THIS IS, AFTER ALL, YOUR MIND. THESE ARE YOUR...RULES. YOUR LAWS. YOUR WORLD.
TELL ME ABOUT IT.
I DIG THINGS UP OUT OF THE GROUND.
RANDOM THINGS. ORANGES. TEETH. THEN WE'D GET... ERASED.
ONE DAY I DUG UP THAT CHEST PLATE AND... WE DIDN'T GET ERASED. AT LEAST RIGHT AWAY. WE HID IT.
THE SENTRIES CAME LOOKING FOR IT.

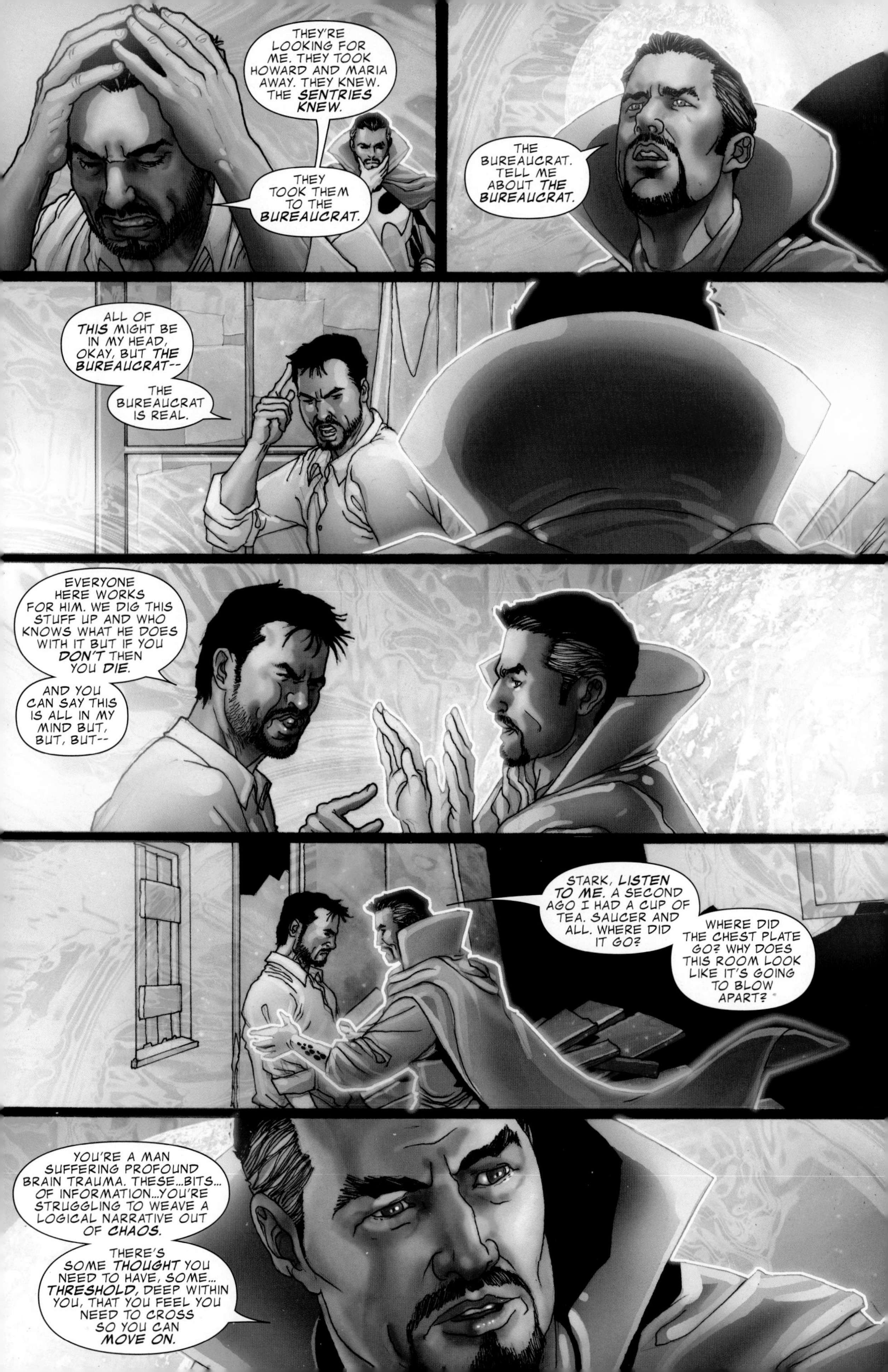
THEY'RE LOOKING FOR ME. THEY TOOK HOWARD AND MARIA AWAY. THEY KNEW. THE SENTRIES KNEW.
THEY TOOK THEM TO THE BUREAUCRAT.
THE BUREAUCRAT. TELL ME ABOUT THE BUREAUCRAT.
ALL OF THIS MIGHT BE IN MY HEAD, OKAY, BUT THE BUREAUCRAT--
THE BUREAUCRAT IS REAL.
EVERYONE HERE WORKS FOR HIM. WE DIG THIS STUFF UP AND WHO KNOWS WHAT HE DOES WITH IT BUT IF YOU DON'T THEN YOU DIE.
AND YOU CAN SAY THIS IS ALL IN MY MIND BUT, BUT, BUT--
STARK, LISTEN TO ME. A SECOND AGO I HAD A CUP OF TEA. SAUCER AND ALL. WHERE DID IT GO?
WHERE DID THE CHEST PLATE GO? WHY DOES THIS ROOM LOOK LIKE IT'S GOING TO BLOW APART?
YOU'RE A MAN SUFFERING PROFOUND BRAIN TRAUMA. THESE...BITS... OF INFORMATION...YOU'RE STRUGGLING TO WEAVE A LOGICAL NARRATIVE OUT OF CHAOS.
THERE'S SOME THOUGHT YOU NEED TO HAVE, SOME... THRESHOLD, DEEP WITHIN YOU, THAT YOU FEEL YOU NEED TO CROSS SO YOU CAN MOVE ON.

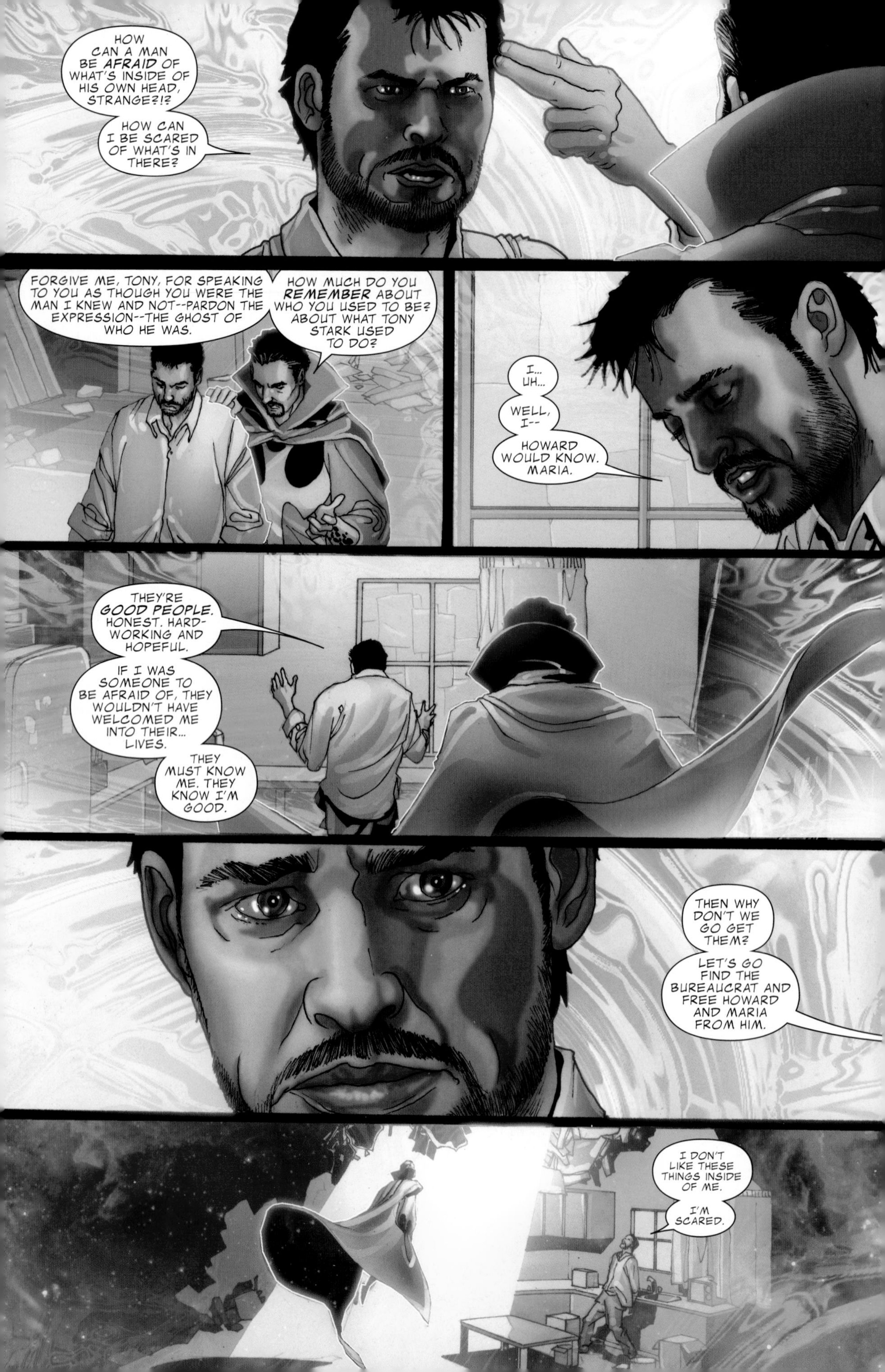
HOW CAN A MAN BE AFRAID OF WHAT'S INSIDE OF HIS OWN HEAD, STRANGE?!?
HOW CAN I BE SCARED OF WHAT'S IN THERE?
FORGIVE ME, TONY, FOR SPEAKING TO YOU AS THOUGH YOU WERE THE MAN I KNEW AND NOT--PARDON THE EXPRESSION--THE GHOST OF WHO HE WAS.
HOW MUCH DO YOU REMEMBER ABOUT WHO YOU USED TO BE? ABOUT WHAT TONY STARK USED TO DO?
I... UH...
WELL, I--
HOWARD WOULD KNOW. MARIA.
THEY'RE GOOD PEOPLE. HONEST. HARD-WORKING AND HOPEFUL.
IF I WAS SOMEONE TO BE AFRAID OF, THEY WOULDN'T HAVE WELCOMED ME INTO THEIR... LIVES.
THEY MUST KNOW ME. THEY KNOW I'M GOOD.
THEN WHY DON'T WE GO GET THEM?
LET'S GO FIND THE BUREAUCRAT AND FREE HOWARD AND MARIA FROM HIM.
I DON'T LIKE THESE THINGS INSIDE OF ME.
I'M SCARED.

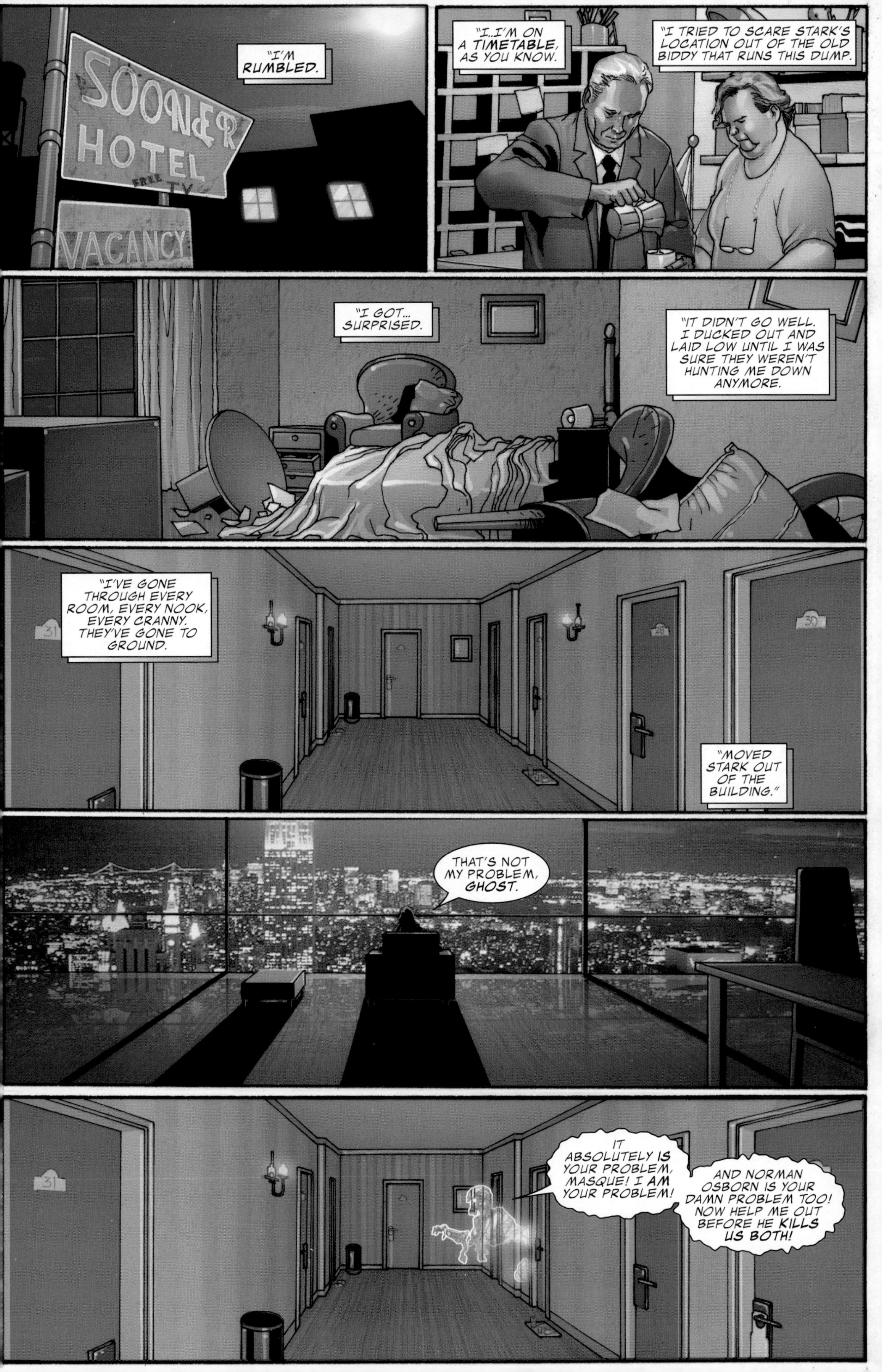
SOONER HOTEL
FREE TV
VACANCY
"I'M RUMBLED.
"I..I'M ON A TIMETABLE, AS YOU KNOW.
"I TRIED TO SCARE STARK'S LOCATION OUT OF THE OLD BIDDY THAT RUNS THIS DUMP.
"I GOT... SURPRISED.
"IT DIDN'T GO WELL. I DUCKED OUT AND LAID LOW UNTIL I WAS SURE THEY WEREN'T HUNTING ME DOWN ANYMORE.
"I'VE GONE THROUGH EVERY ROOM, EVERY NOOK, EVERY CRANNY. THEY'VE GONE TO GROUND.
31
28
30
"MOVED STARK OUT OF THE BUILDING."
THAT'S NOT MY PROBLEM, GHOST.
31
IT ABSOLUTELY IS YOUR PROBLEM, MASQUE! I AM YOUR PROBLEM!
AND NORMAN OSBORN IS YOUR DAMN PROBLEM TOO! NOW HELP ME OUT BEFORE HE KILLS US BOTH!

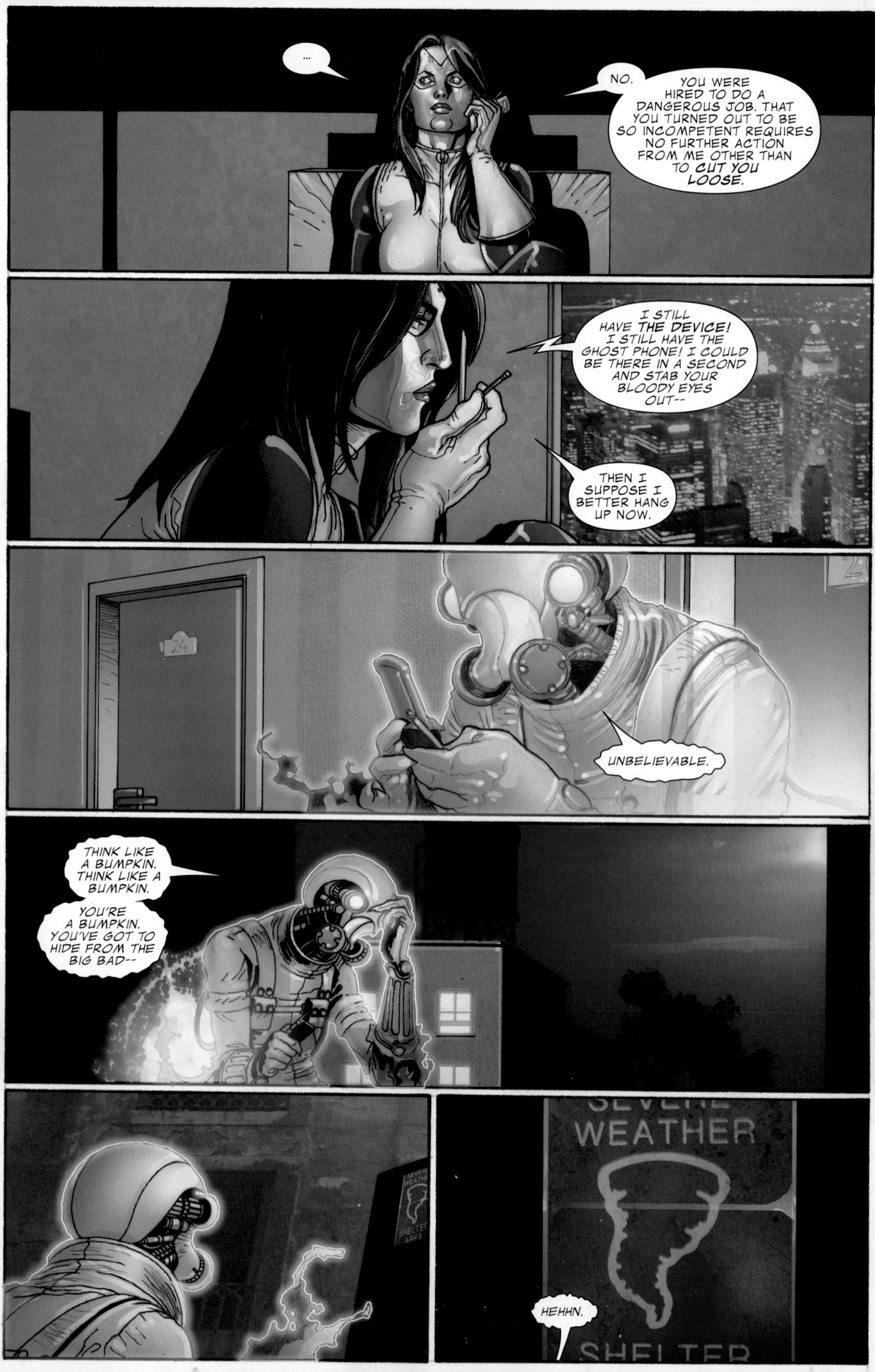
...
NO.
YOU WERE HIRED TO DO A DANGEROUS JOB. THAT YOU TURNED OUT TO BE SO INCOMPETENT REQUIRES NO FURTHER ACTION FROM ME OTHER THAN TO CUT YOU LOOSE.
I STILL HAVE THE DEVICE! I STILL HAVE THE GHOST PHONE! I COULD BE THERE IN A SECOND AND STAB YOUR BLOODY EYES OUT--
THEN I SUPPOSE I BETTER HANG UP NOW.
24
UNBELIEVABLE.
THINK LIKE A BUMPKIN. THINK LIKE A BUMPKIN.
YOU'RE A BUMPKIN. YOU'VE GOT TO HIDE FROM THE BIG BAD--
WEATHER
HEHHN.

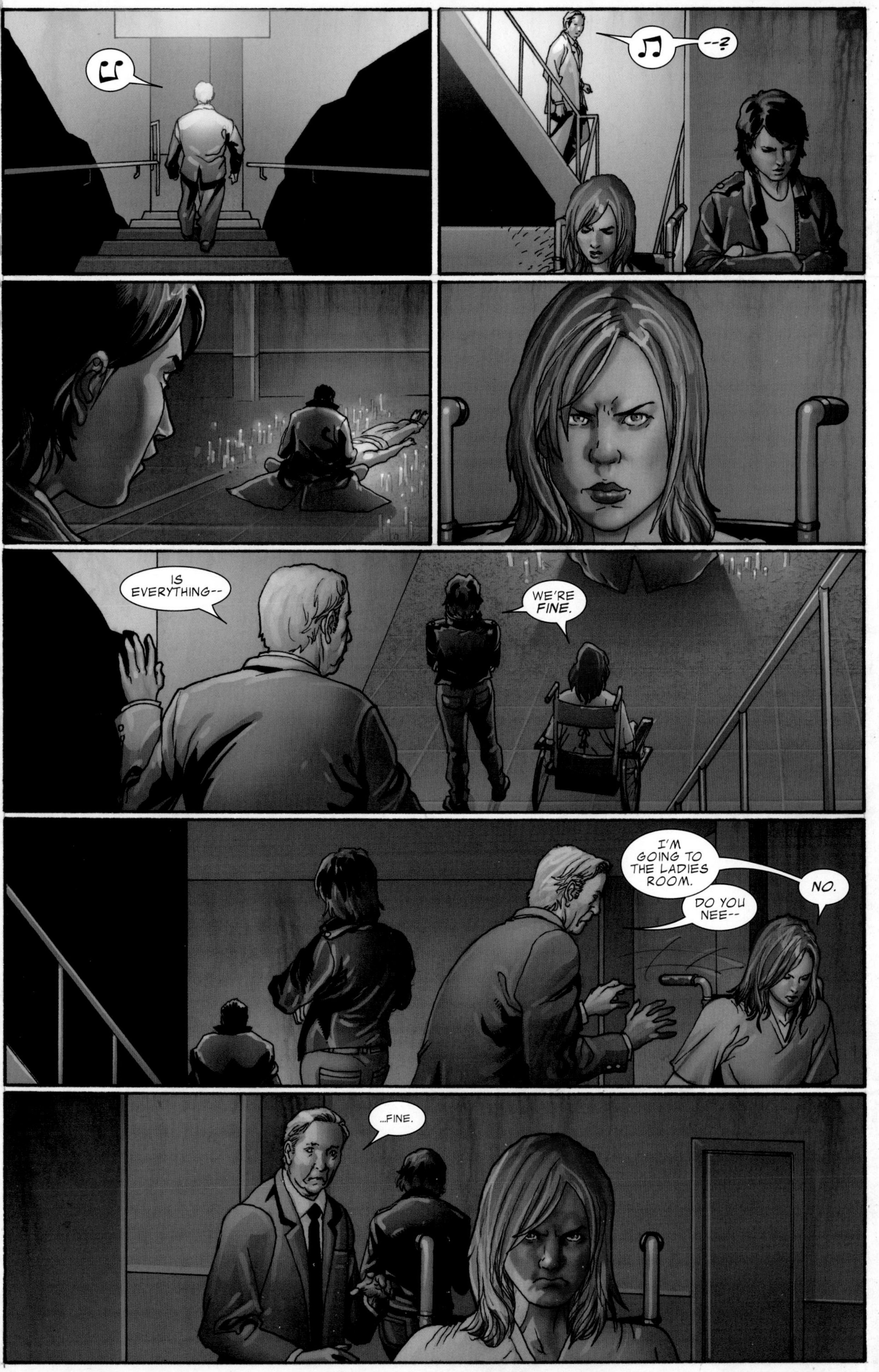
♫
--?
IS EVERYTHING--
WE'RE FINE.
I'M GOING TO THE LADIES ROOM.
DO YOU NEE--
NO.
...FINE.

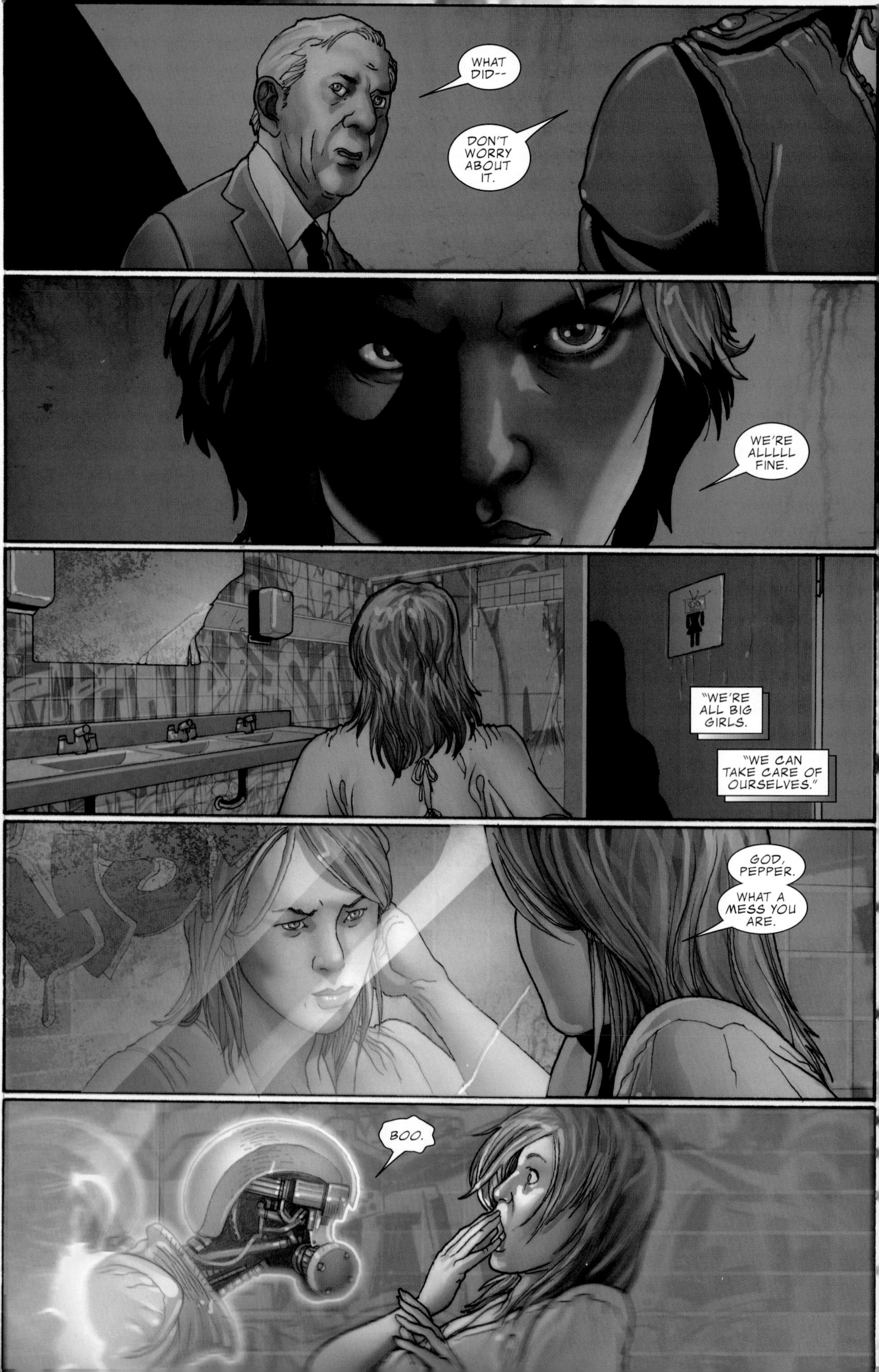
WHAT DID--
DON'T WORRY ABOUT IT.
WE'RE ALLLLL FINE.
"WE'RE ALL BIG GIRLS.
"WE CAN TAKE CARE OF OURSELVES."
GOD, PEPPER.
WHAT A MESS YOU ARE.
BOO.

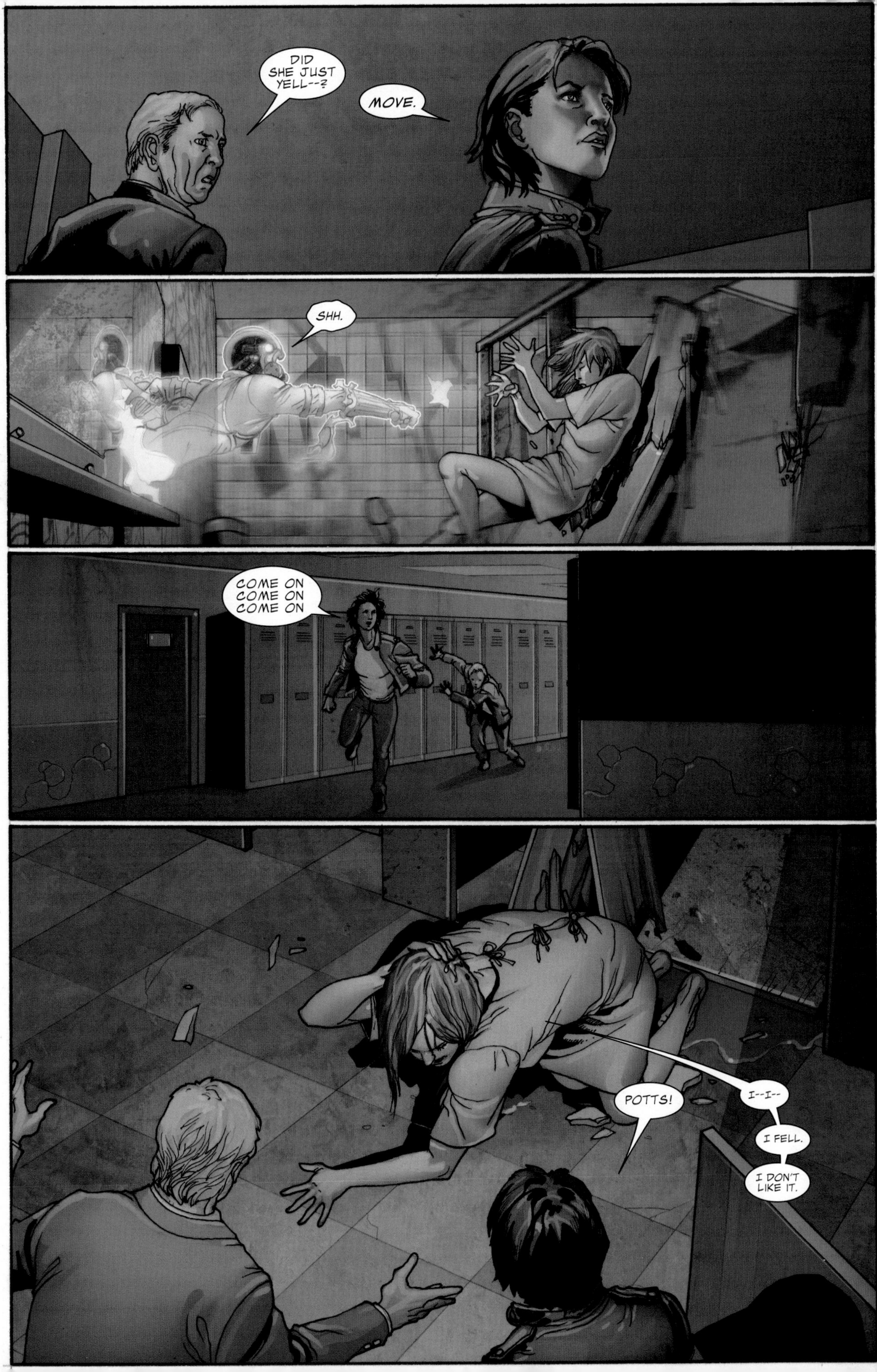
DID SHE JUST YELL--?
MOVE.
SHH.
COME ON COME ON COME ON
POTTS!
I--I--
I FELL.
I DON'T LIKE IT.

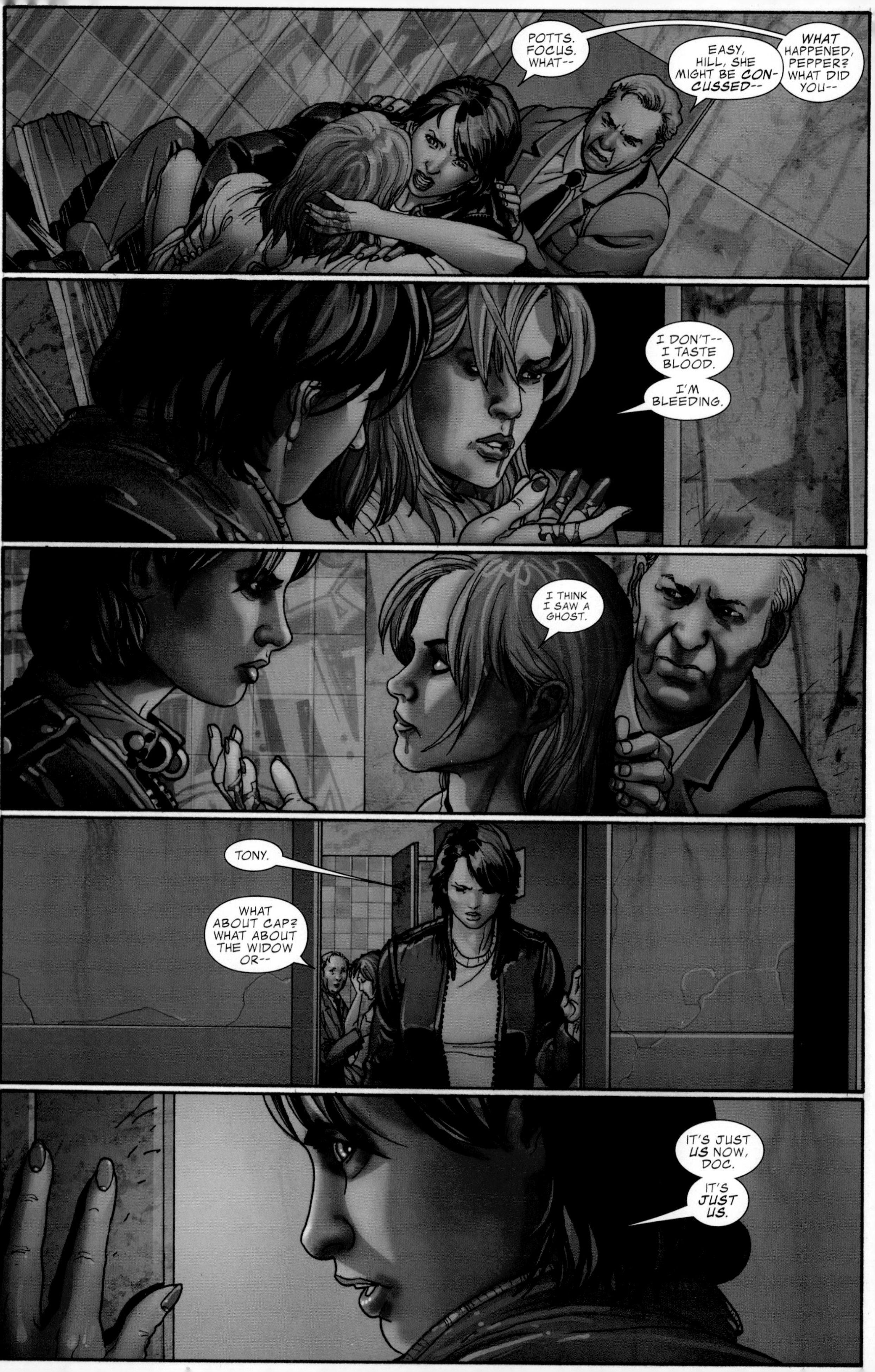
POTTS. FOCUS. WHAT--
WHAT HAPPENED, PEPPER? WHAT DID YOU--
EASY, HILL, SHE MIGHT BE CONCUSSED--
I DON'T-- I TASTE BLOOD.
I'M BLEEDING.
I THINK I SAW A GHOST.
TONY.
WHAT ABOUT CAP? WHAT ABOUT THE WIDOW OR--
IT'S JUST US NOW, DOC.
IT'S JUST US.

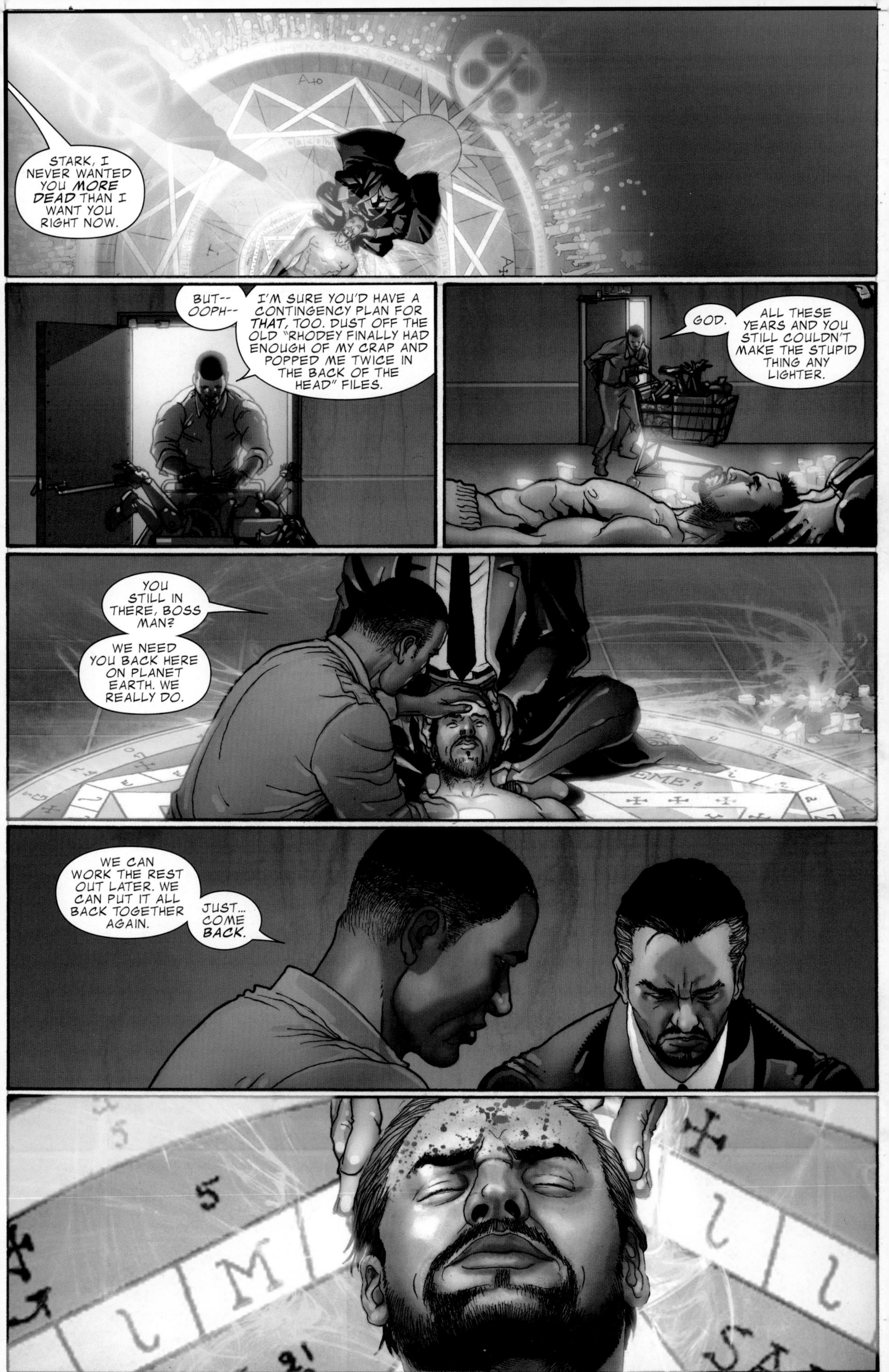
STARK, I NEVER WANTED YOU MORE DEAD THAN I WANT YOU RIGHT NOW.
BUT-- OOPH--
I'M SURE YOU'D HAVE A CONTINGENCY PLAN FOR THAT, TOO. DUST OFF THE OLD "RHODEY FINALLY HAD ENOUGH OF MY CRAP AND POPPED ME TWICE IN THE BACK OF THE HEAD" FILES.
GOD.
ALL THESE YEARS AND YOU STILL COULDN'T MAKE THE STUPID THING ANY LIGHTER.
YOU STILL IN THERE, BOSS MAN?
WE NEED YOU BACK HERE ON PLANET EARTH. WE REALLY DO.
WE CAN WORK THE REST OUT LATER. WE CAN PUT IT ALL BACK TOGETHER AGAIN.
JUST... COME BACK.

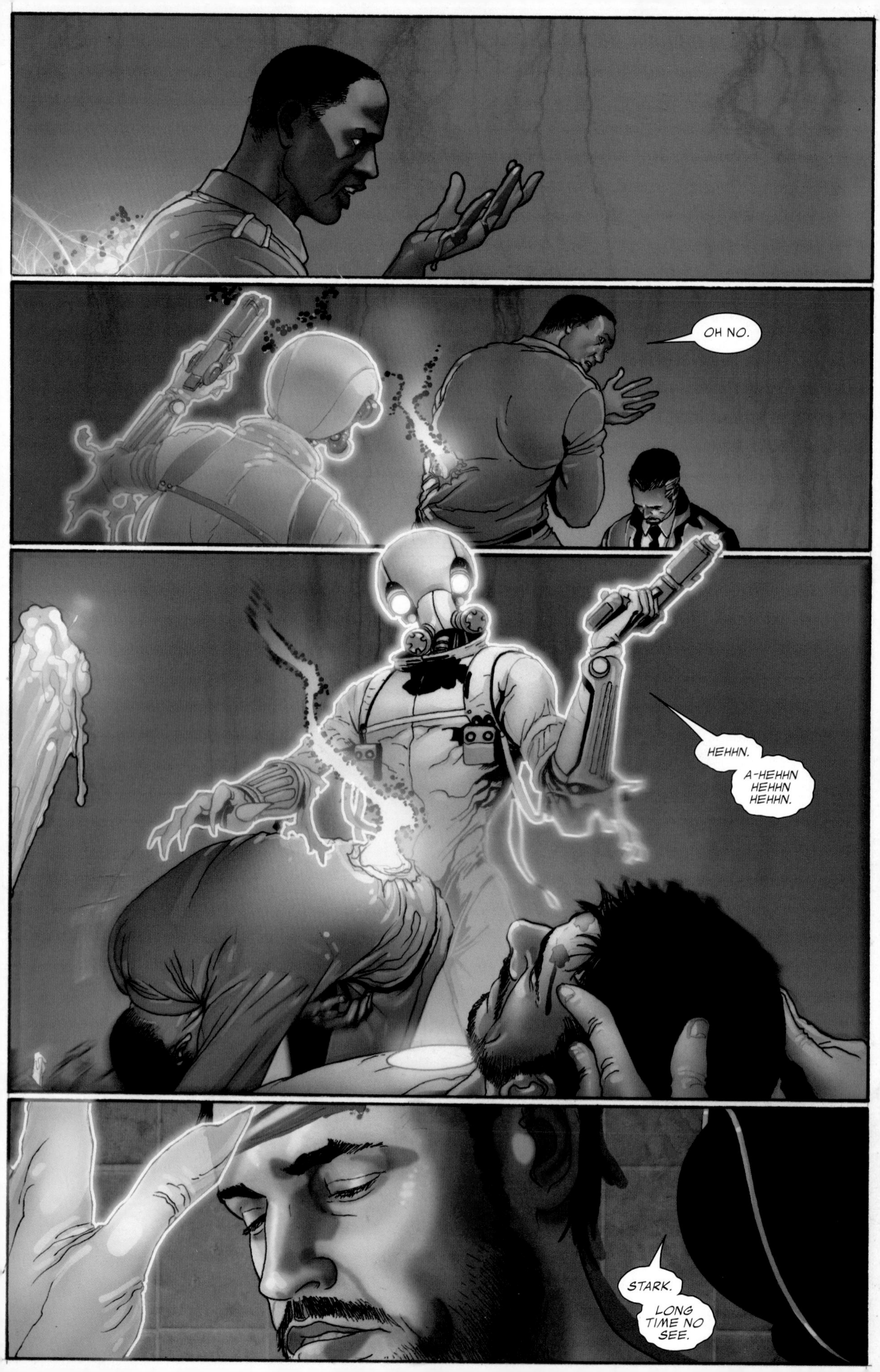
OH NO.
HEHHN.
A-HEHHN HEHHN HEHHN.
STARK.
LONG TIME NO SEE.

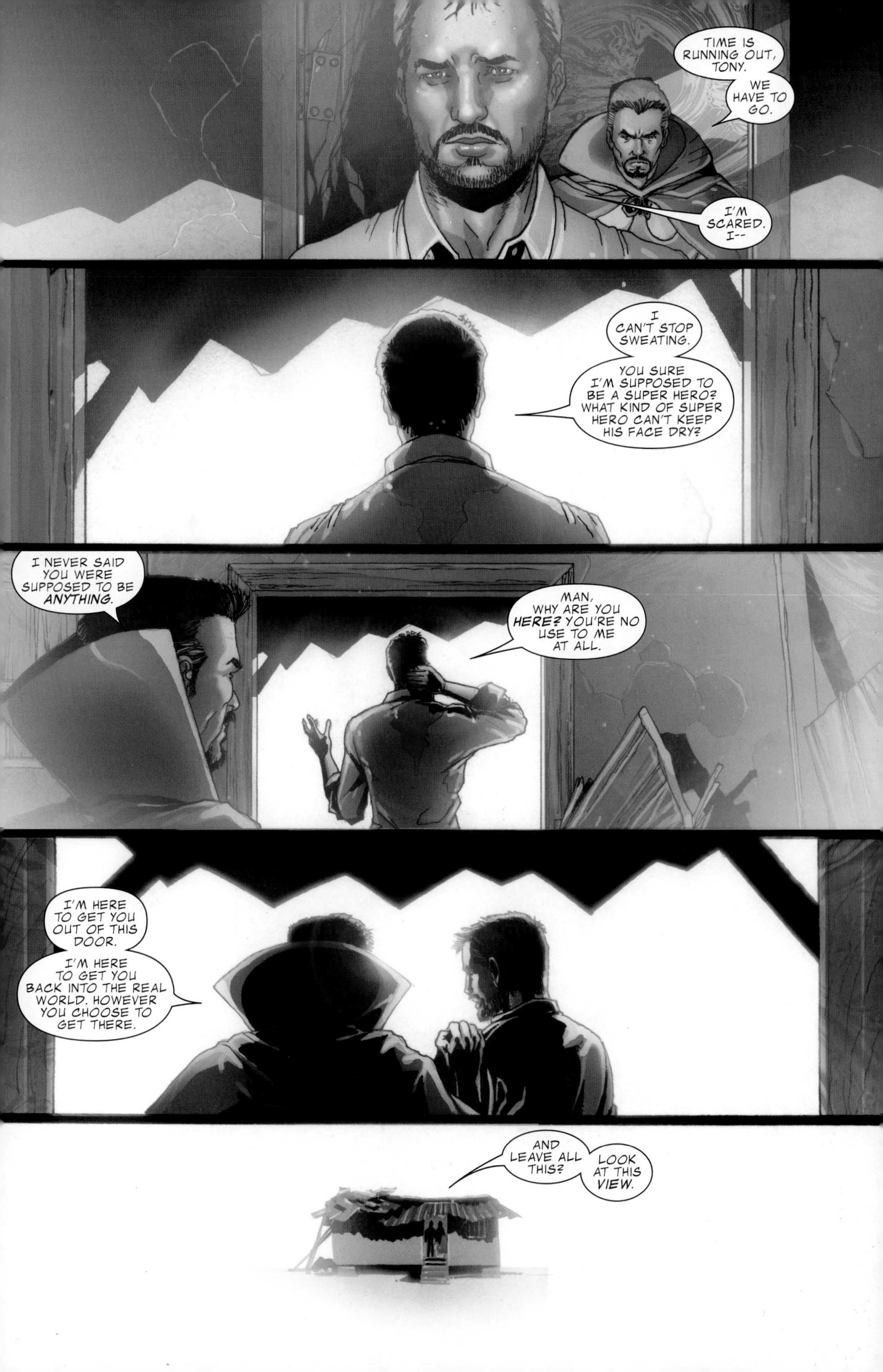
TIME IS RUNNING OUT, TONY.
WE HAVE TO GO.
I'M SCARED. I--
I CAN'T STOP SWEATING.
YOU SURE I'M SUPPOSED TO BE A SUPER HERO? WHAT KIND OF SUPER HERO CAN'T KEEP HIS FACE DRY?
I NEVER SAID YOU WERE SUPPOSED TO BE *ANYTHING*.
MAN, WHY ARE YOU *HERE?* YOU'RE NO USE TO ME AT ALL.
I'M HERE TO GET YOU OUT OF THIS DOOR.
I'M HERE TO GET YOU BACK INTO THE REAL WORLD. HOWEVER YOU CHOOSE TO GET THERE.
AND LEAVE ALL THIS?
LOOK AT THIS *VIEW*.

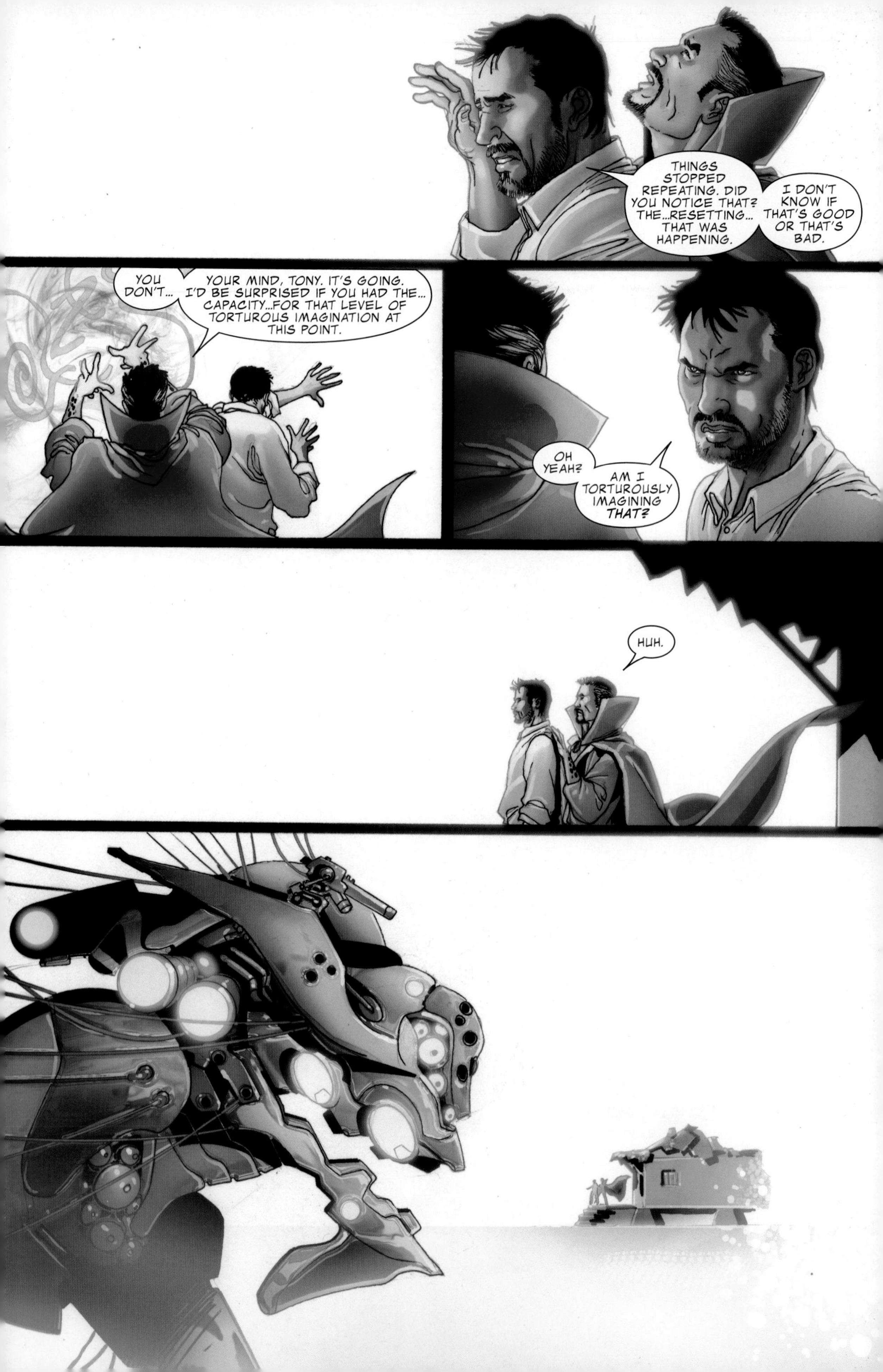
THINGS STOPPED REPEATING. DID YOU NOTICE THAT? THE...RESETTING... THAT WAS HAPPENING.
I DON'T KNOW IF THAT'S GOOD OR THAT'S BAD.
YOU DON'T...
YOUR MIND, TONY. IT'S GOING. I'D BE SURPRISED IF YOU HAD THE... CAPACITY...FOR THAT LEVEL OF TORTUROUS IMAGINATION AT THIS POINT.
OH YEAH?
AM I TORTUROUSLY IMAGINING THAT?
HUH.

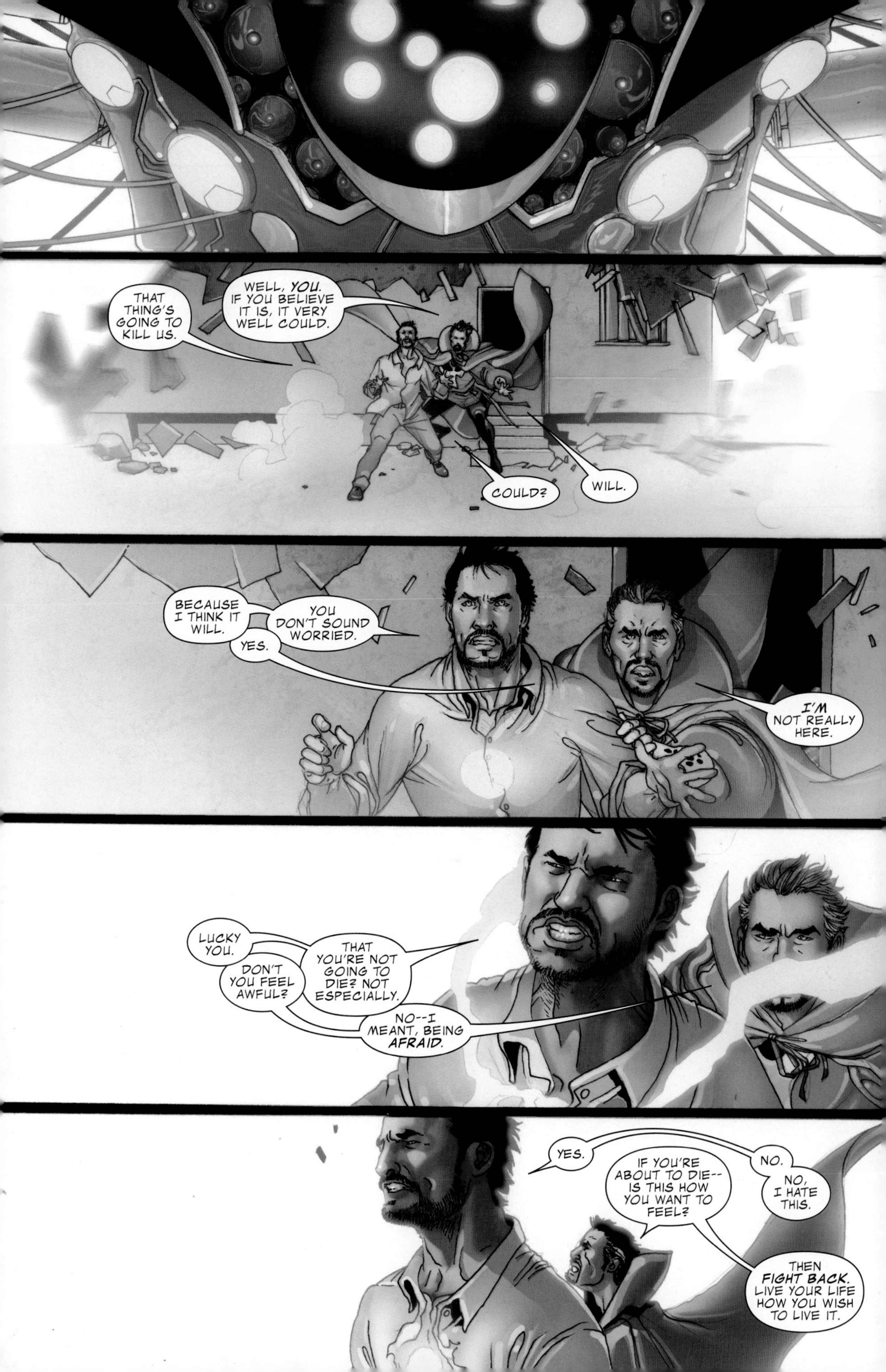
THAT THING'S GOING TO KILL US.
WELL, YOU. IF YOU BELIEVE IT IS, IT VERY WELL COULD.
COULD?
WILL.
YOU DON'T SOUND WORRIED.
BECAUSE I THINK IT WILL.
YES.
I'M NOT REALLY HERE.
LUCKY YOU.
THAT YOU'RE NOT GOING TO DIE? NOT ESPECIALLY.
DON'T YOU FEEL AWFUL?
NO--I MEANT, BEING AFRAID.
YES.
IF YOU'RE ABOUT TO DIE-- IS THIS HOW YOU WANT TO FEEL?
NO.
NO, I HATE THIS.
THEN FIGHT BACK. LIVE YOUR LIFE HOW YOU WISH TO LIVE IT.

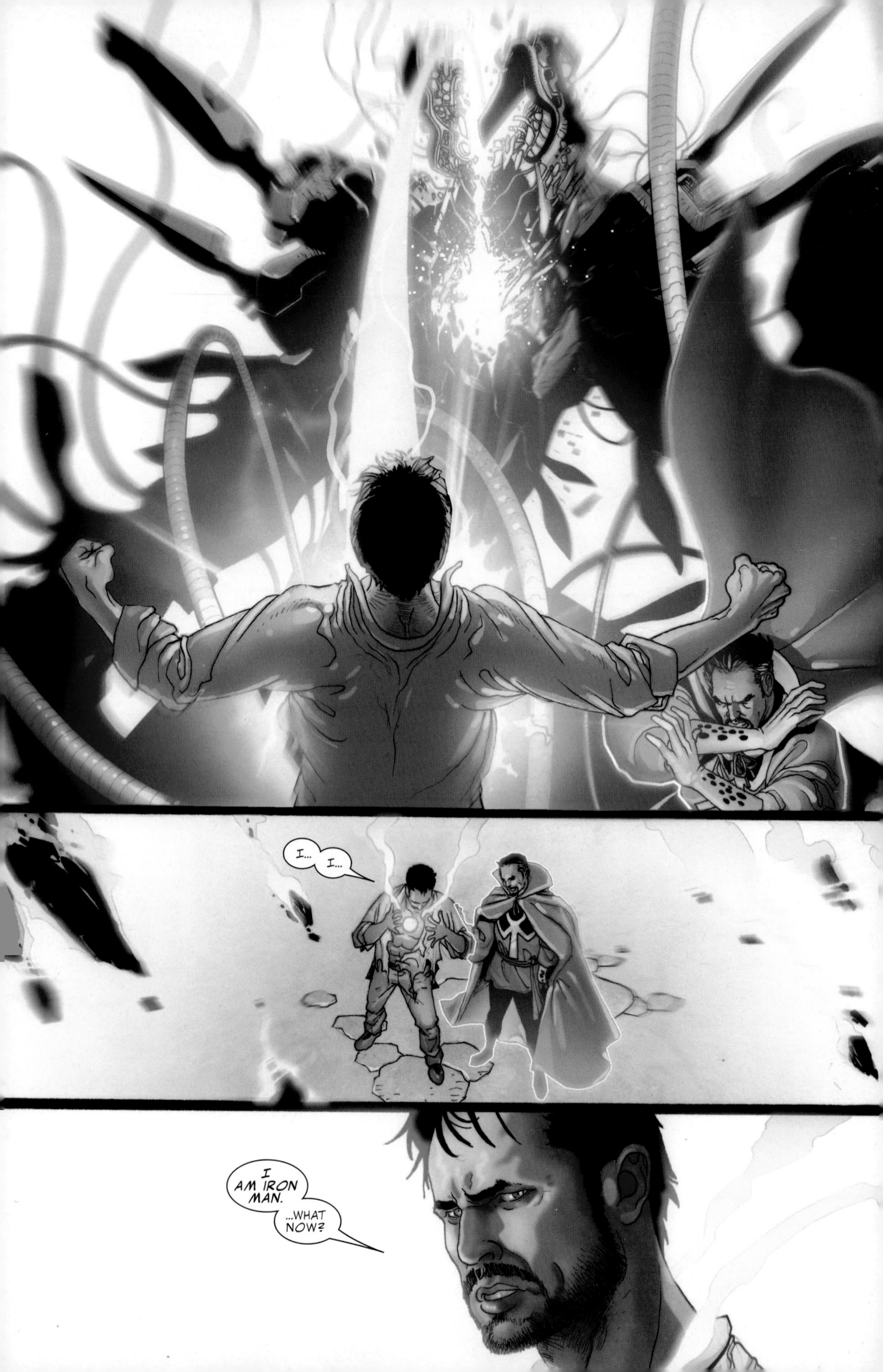
I...
I...
I AM IRON MAN.
...WHAT NOW?

The Invincible

IRON MAN

Stark: Disassembled 5 of 5

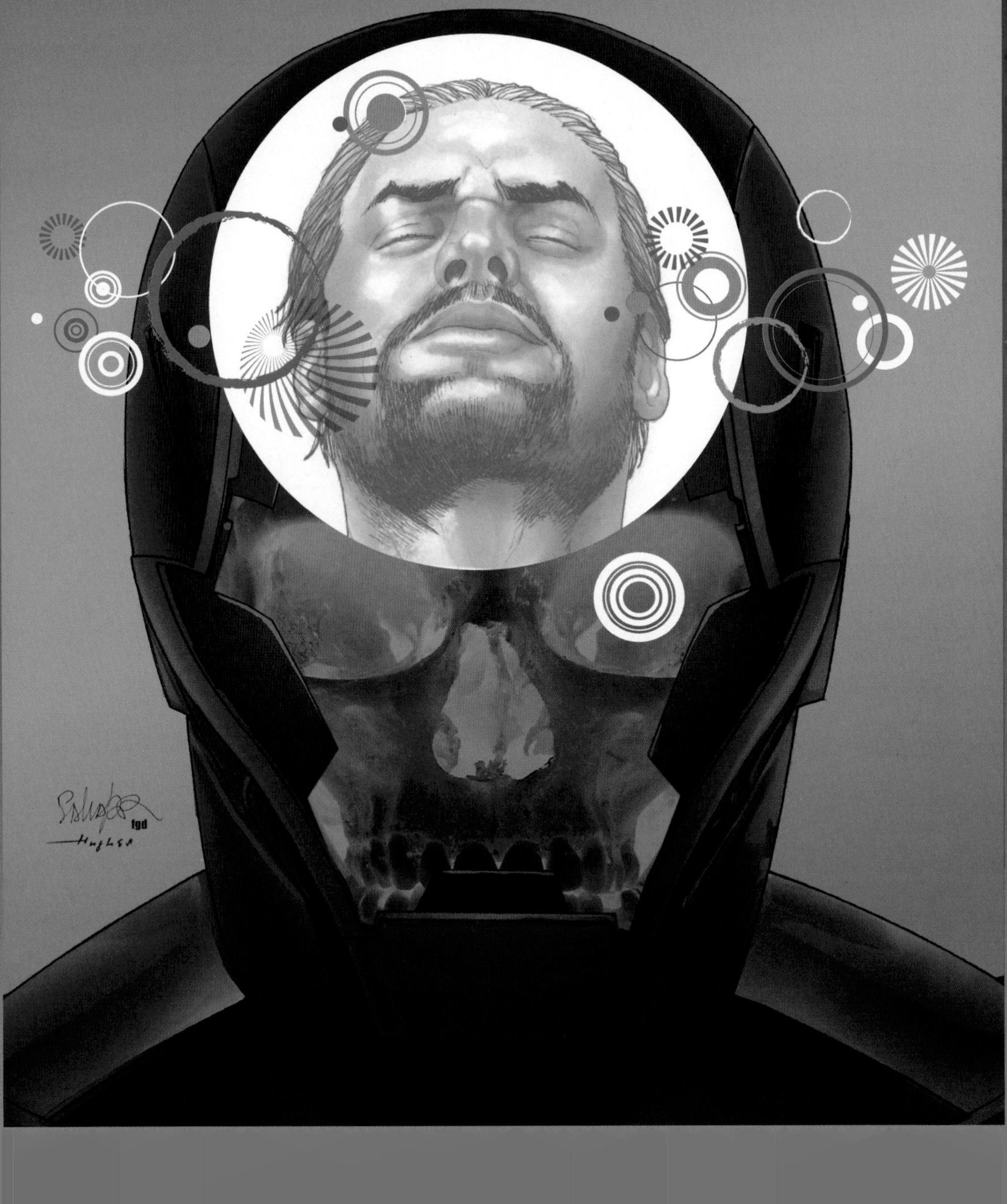

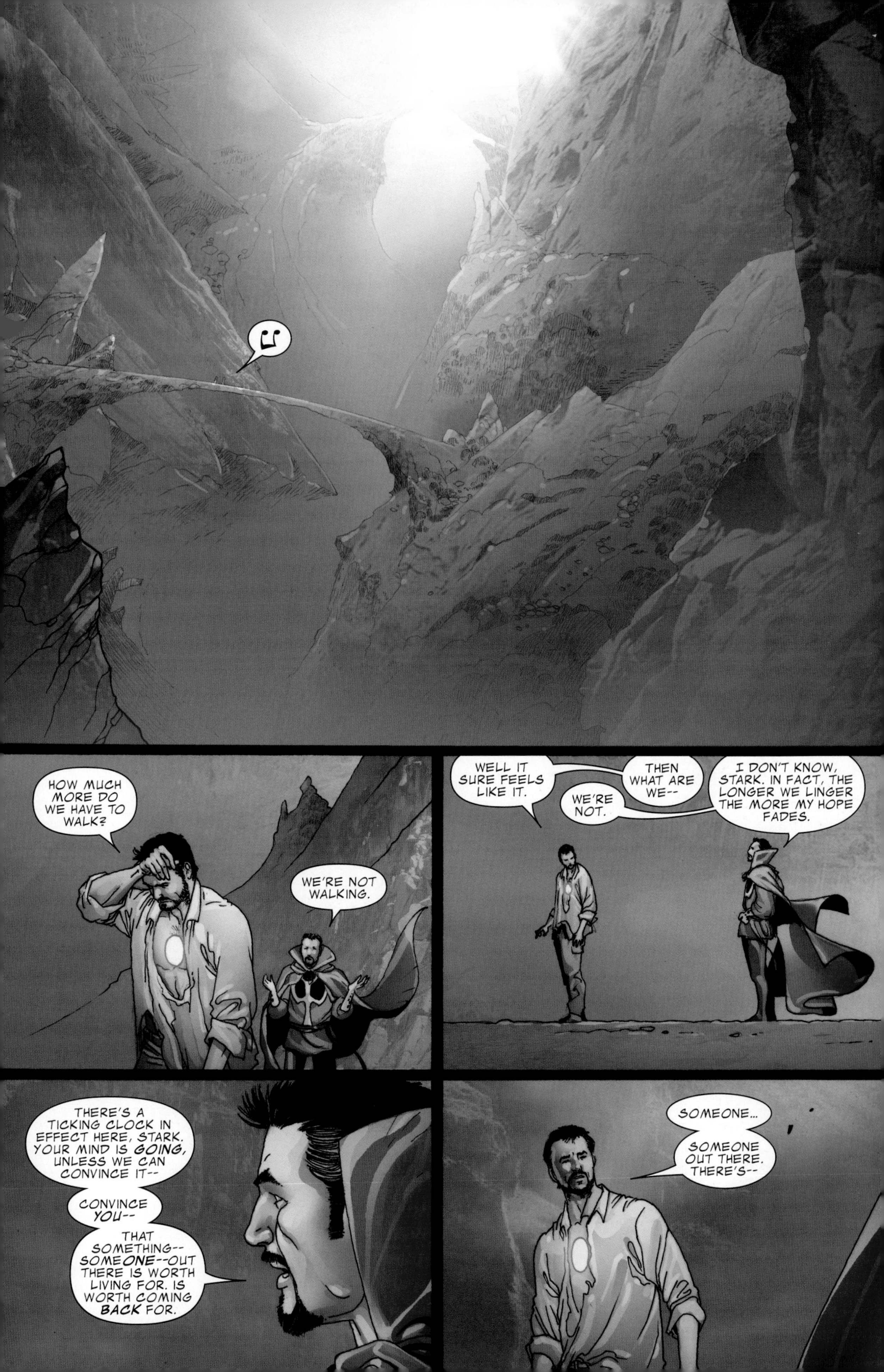
HOW MUCH MORE DO WE HAVE TO WALK?
WE'RE NOT WALKING.
WELL IT SURE FEELS LIKE IT.
WE'RE NOT.
THEN WHAT ARE WE--
I DON'T KNOW, STARK. IN FACT, THE LONGER WE LINGER THE MORE MY HOPE FADES.
THERE'S A TICKING CLOCK IN EFFECT HERE, STARK. YOUR MIND IS GOING, UNLESS WE CAN CONVINCE IT--
CONVINCE YOU--
THAT SOMETHING-- SOMEONE--OUT THERE IS WORTH LIVING FOR. IS WORTH COMING BACK FOR.
SOMEONE...
SOMEONE OUT THERE. THERE'S--

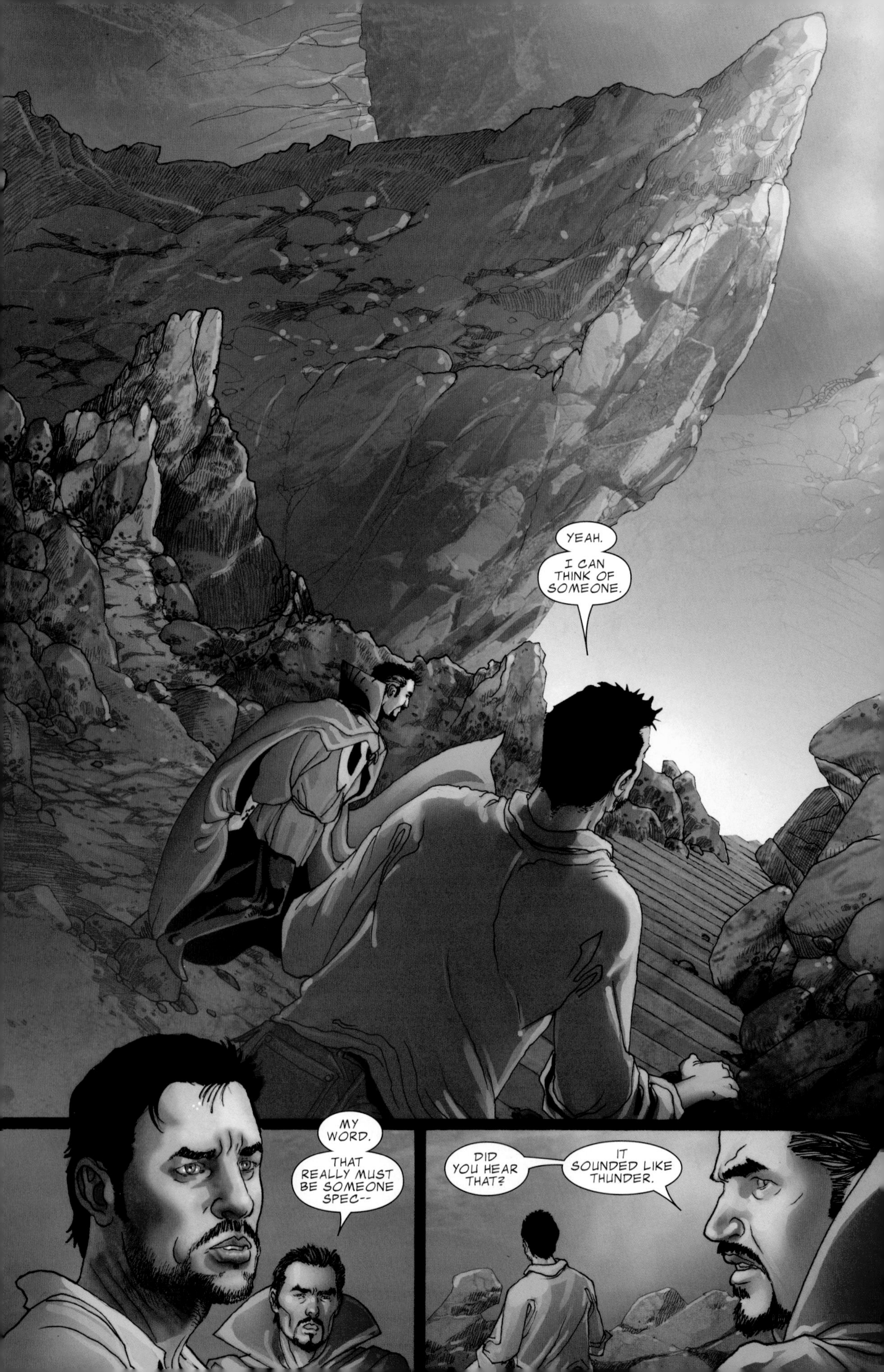
YEAH.
I CAN THINK OF SOMEONE.
MY WORD.
THAT REALLY MUST BE SOMEONE SPEC--
DID YOU HEAR THAT?
IT SOUNDED LIKE THUNDER.

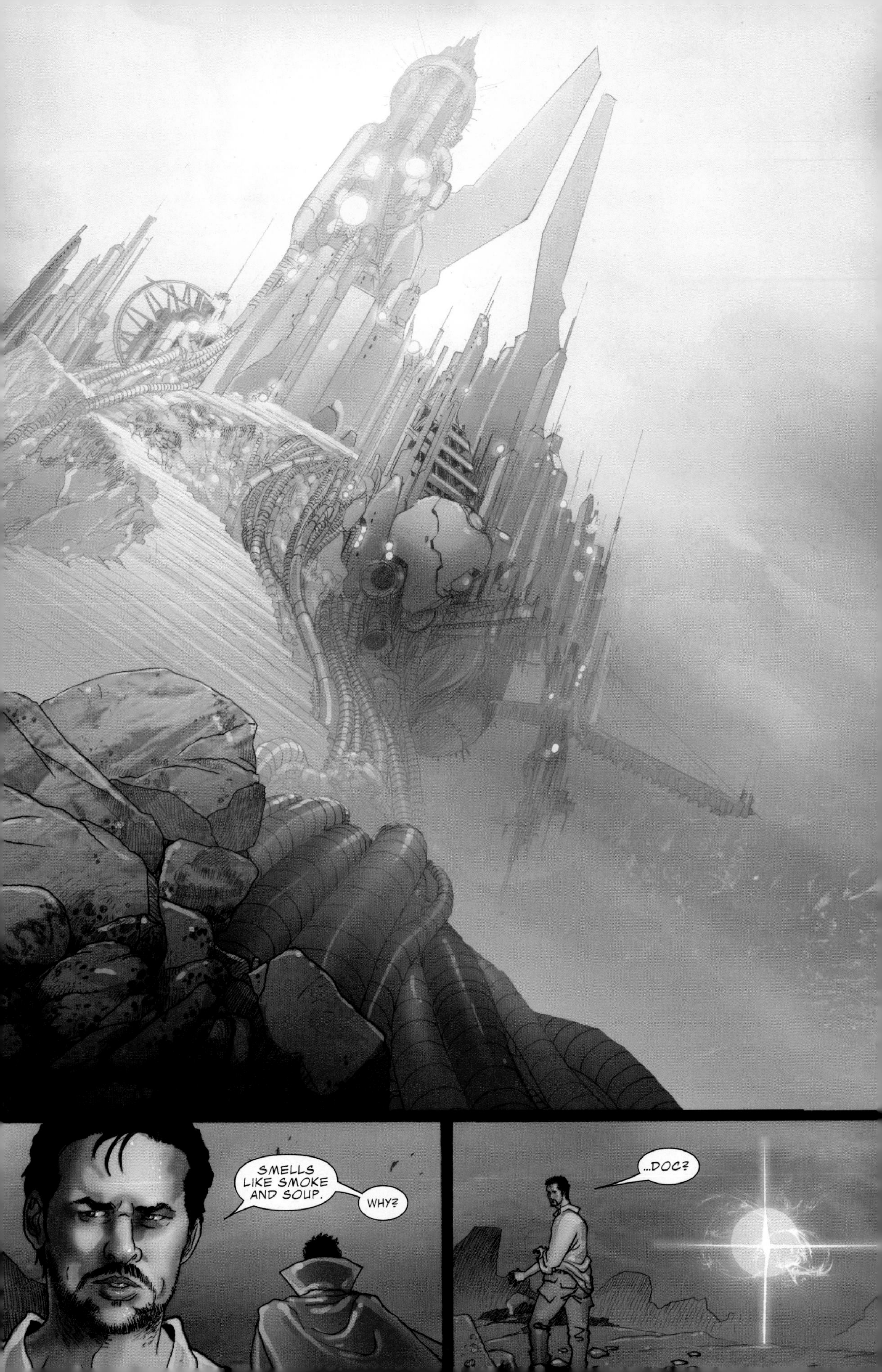
SMELLS LIKE SMOKE AND SOUP.
WHY?
...DOC?

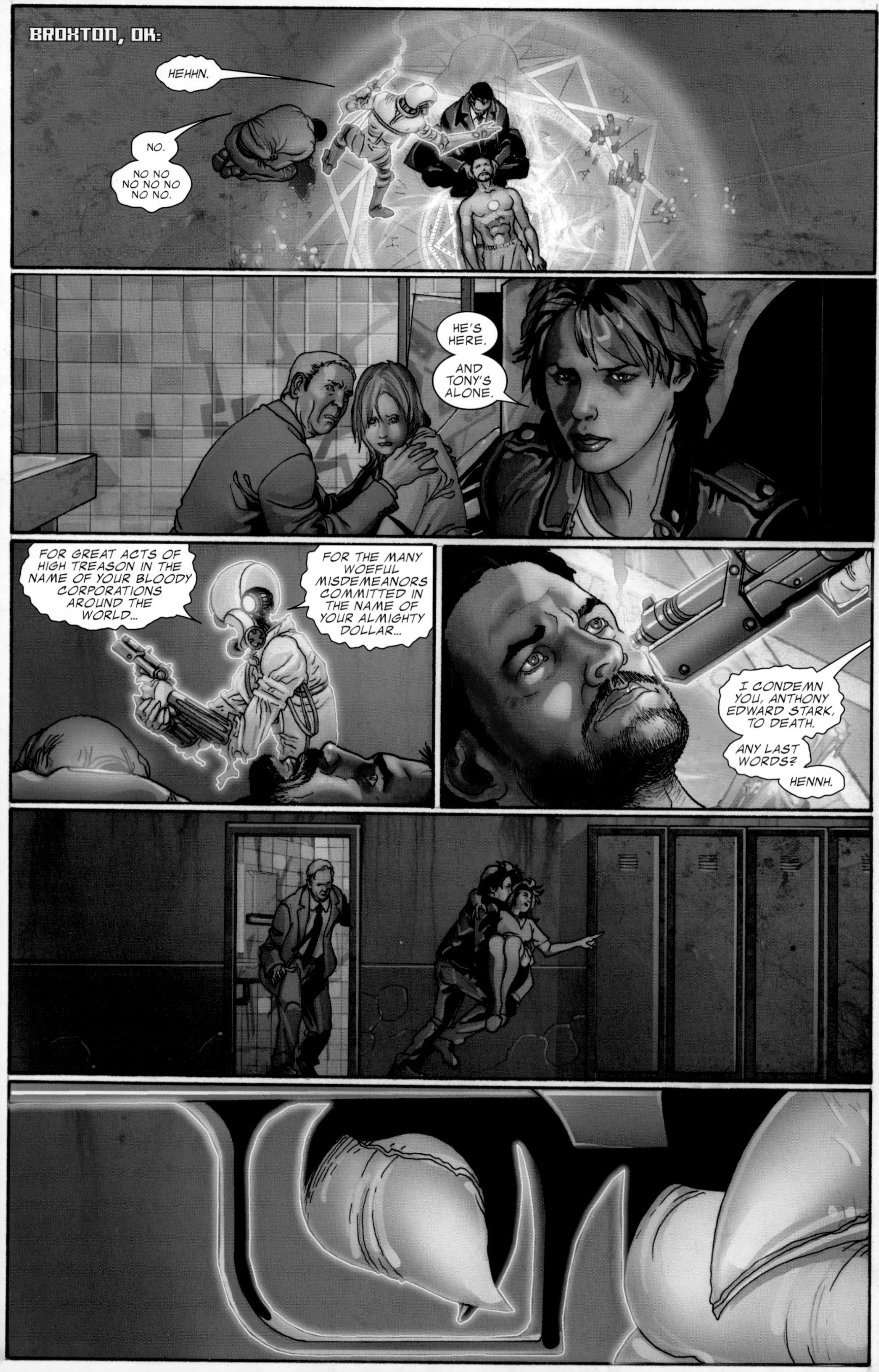
BROXTON, OK:
HEHHN.
NO.
NO NO NO NO NO NO NO.
HE'S HERE.
AND TONY'S ALONE.
FOR GREAT ACTS OF HIGH TREASON IN THE NAME OF YOUR BLOODY CORPORATIONS AROUND THE WORLD...
FOR THE MANY WOEFUL MISDEMEANORS COMMITTED IN THE NAME OF YOUR ALMIGHTY DOLLAR...
I CONDEMN YOU, ANTHONY EDWARD STARK, TO DEATH.
ANY LAST WORDS?
HENNH.

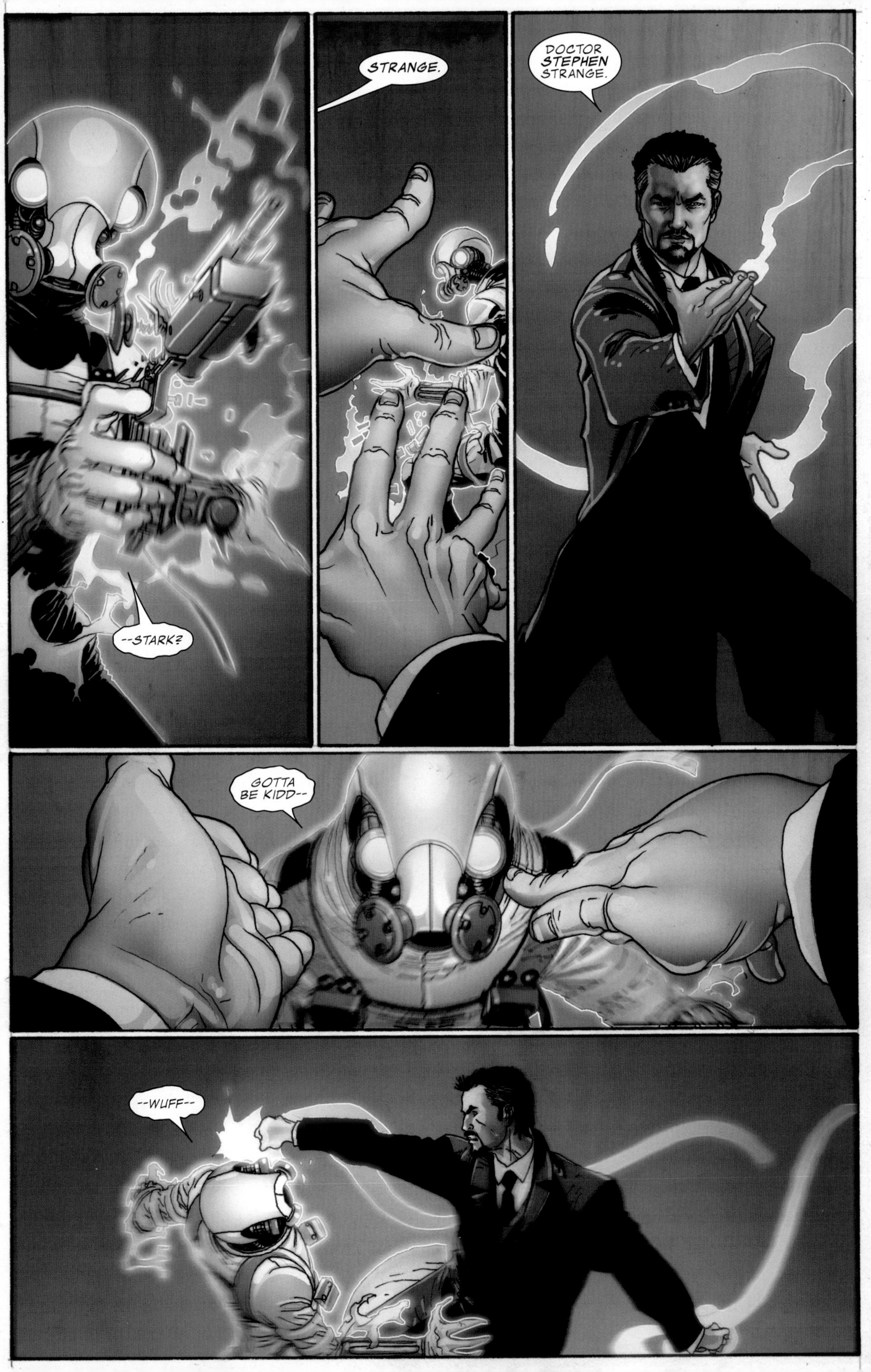
--STARK?
STRANGE.
DOCTOR STEPHEN STRANGE.
GOTTA BE KIDD--
--WUFF--

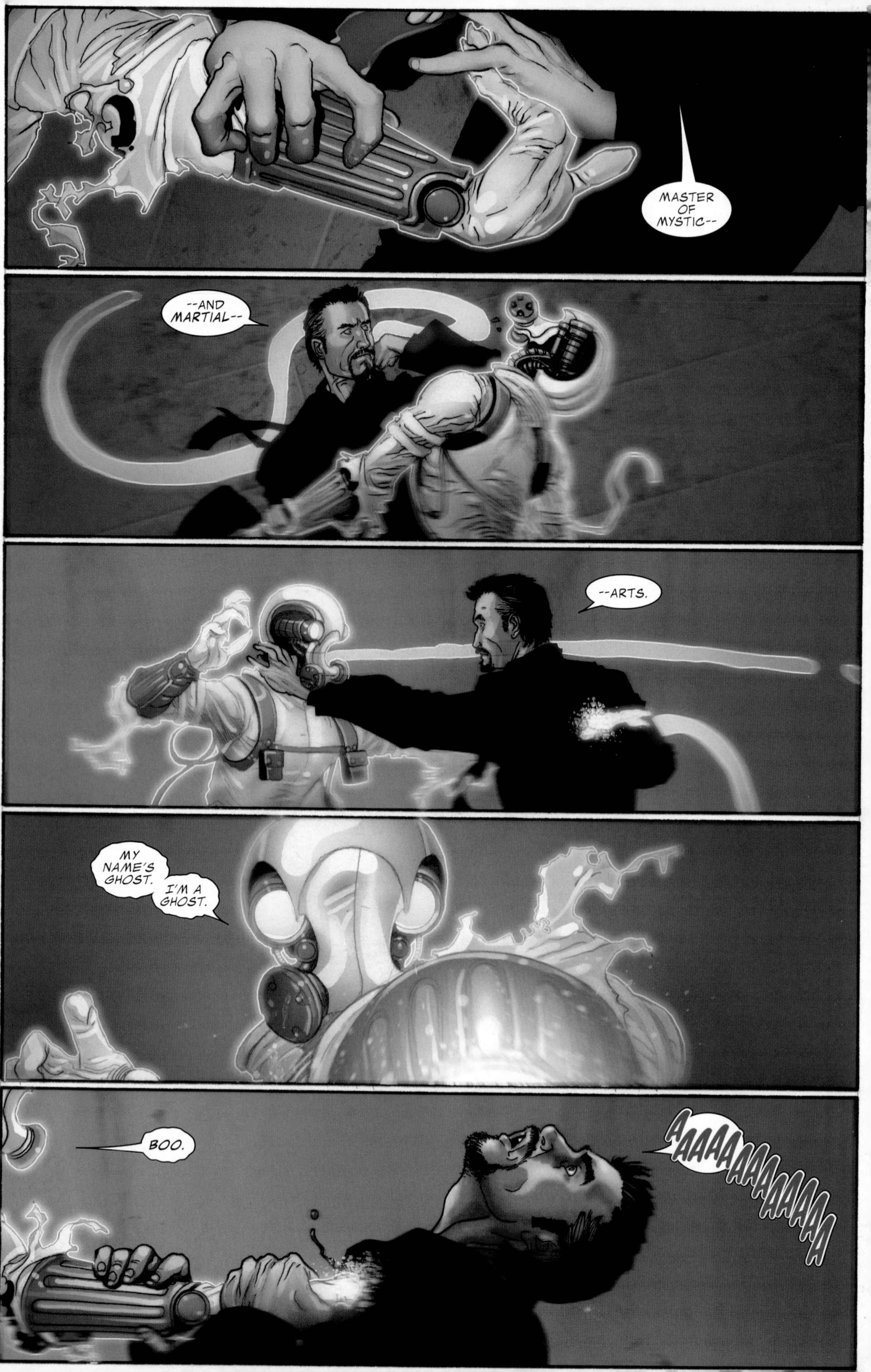
MASTER OF MYSTIC--
--AND MARTIAL--
--ARTS.
MY NAME'S GHOST.
I'M A GHOST.
BOO.
AAAAAAAAAAAAAA

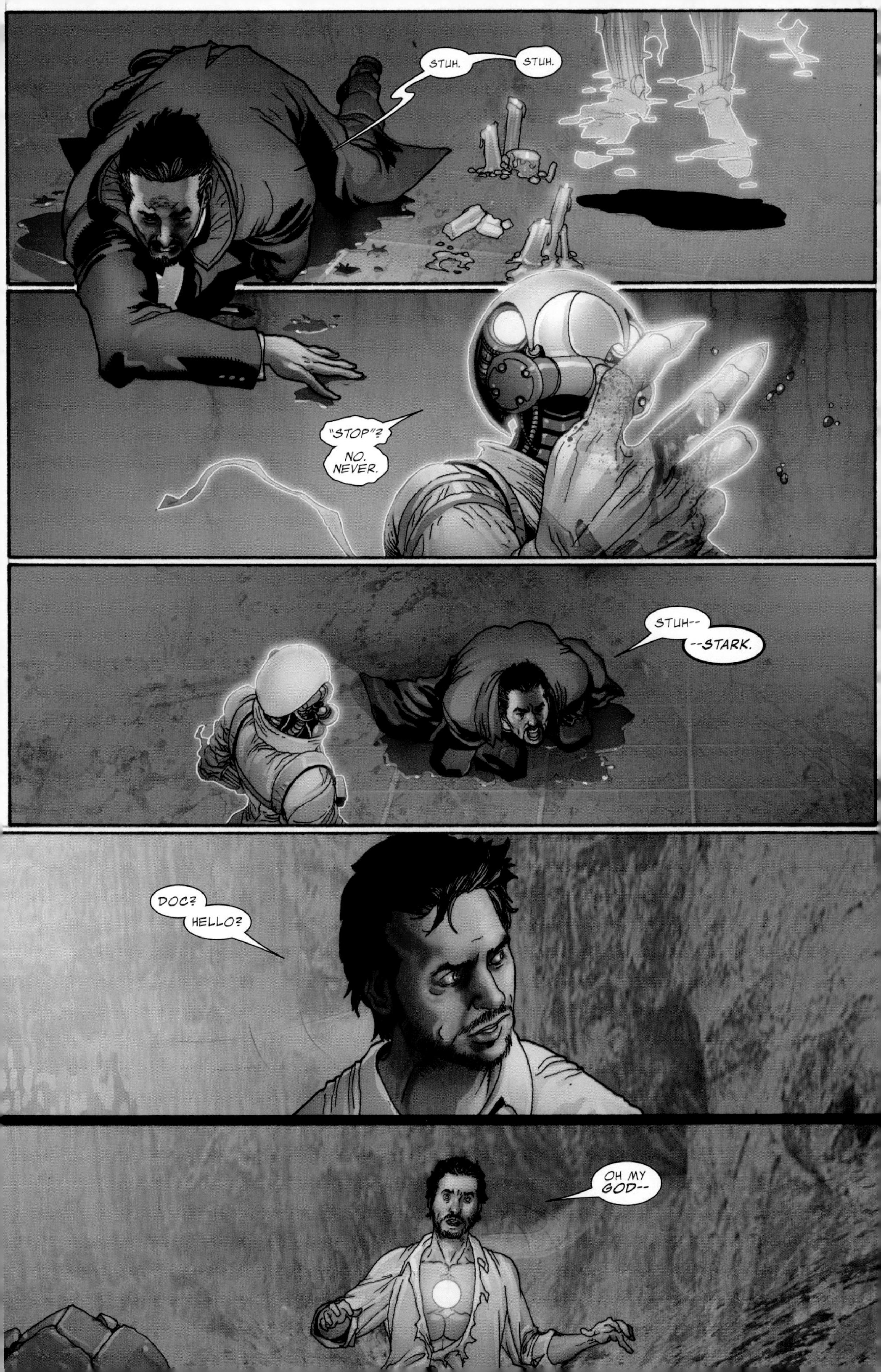
STUH.
STUH.
"STOP"? NO. NEVER.
STUH--
--STARK.
DOC? HELLO?
OH MY GOD--

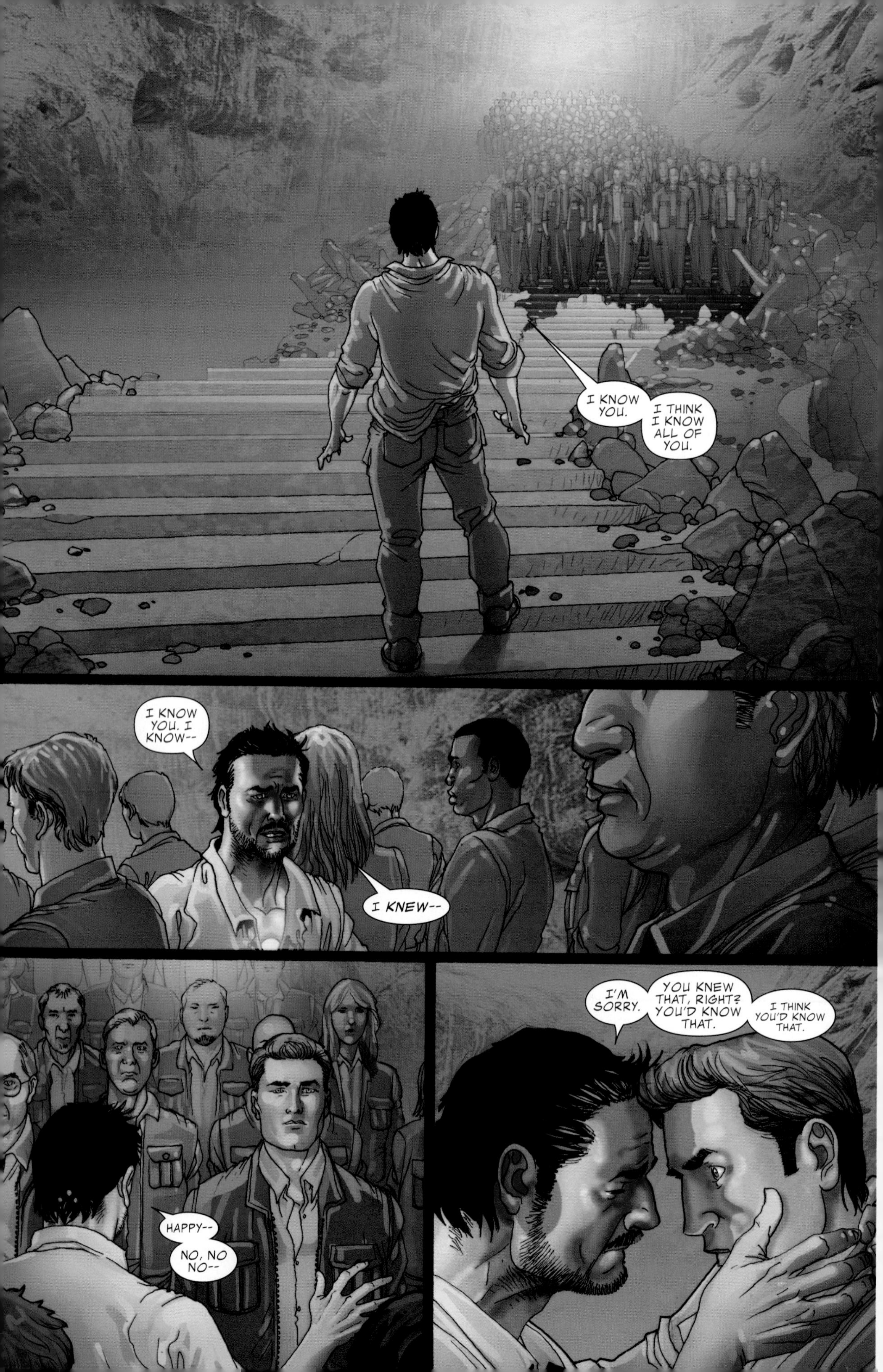
I KNOW YOU.
I THINK I KNOW ALL OF YOU.
I KNOW YOU. I KNOW--
I KNEW--
HAPPY--
NO, NO NO--
I'M SORRY.
YOU KNEW THAT, RIGHT? YOU'D KNOW THAT.
I THINK YOU'D KNOW THAT.

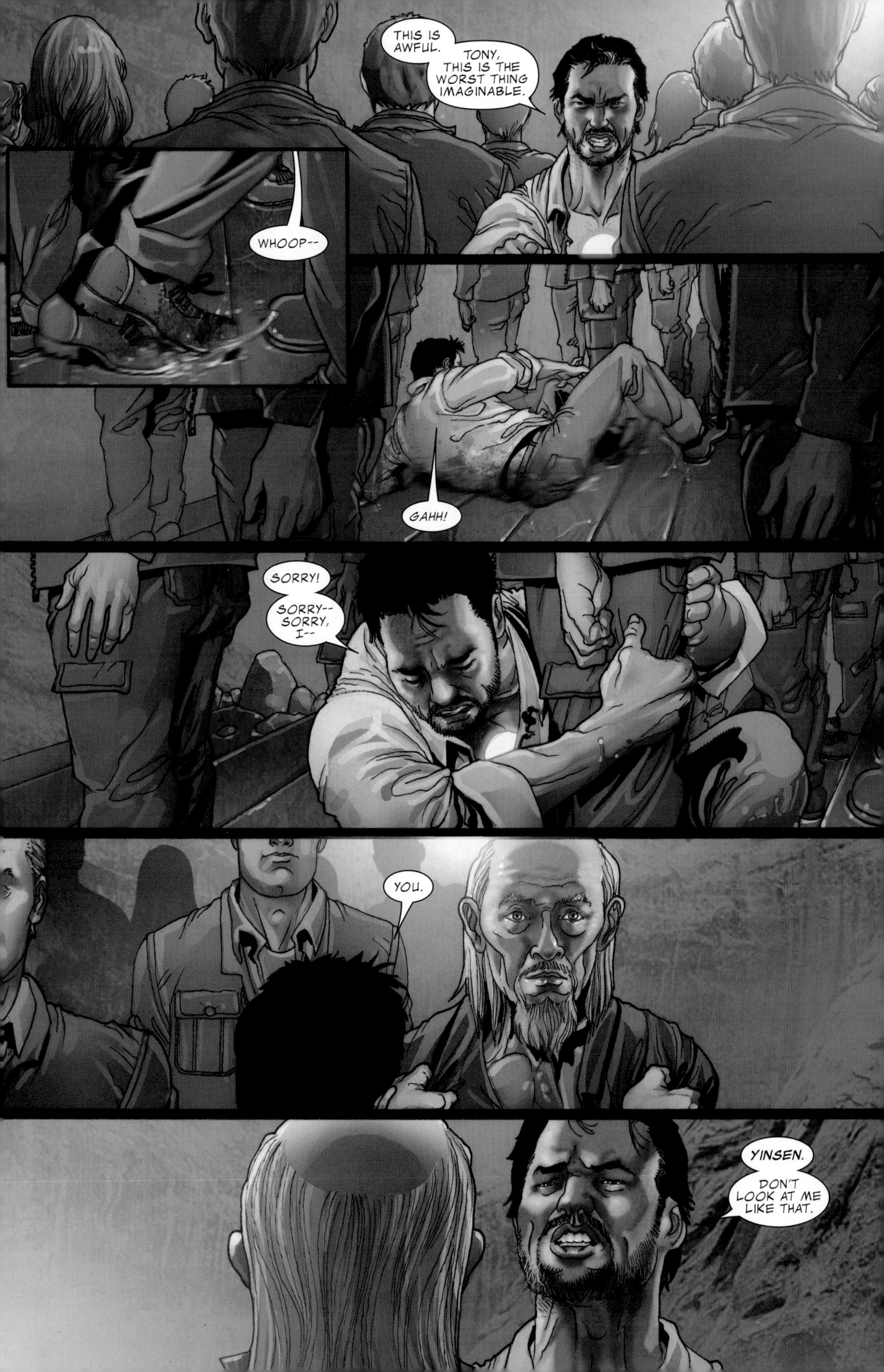
THIS IS AWFUL.
TONY, THIS IS THE WORST THING IMAGINABLE.
WHOOP--
GAHH!
SORRY!
SORRY-- SORRY, I--
YOU.
YINSEN.
DON'T LOOK AT ME LIKE THAT.

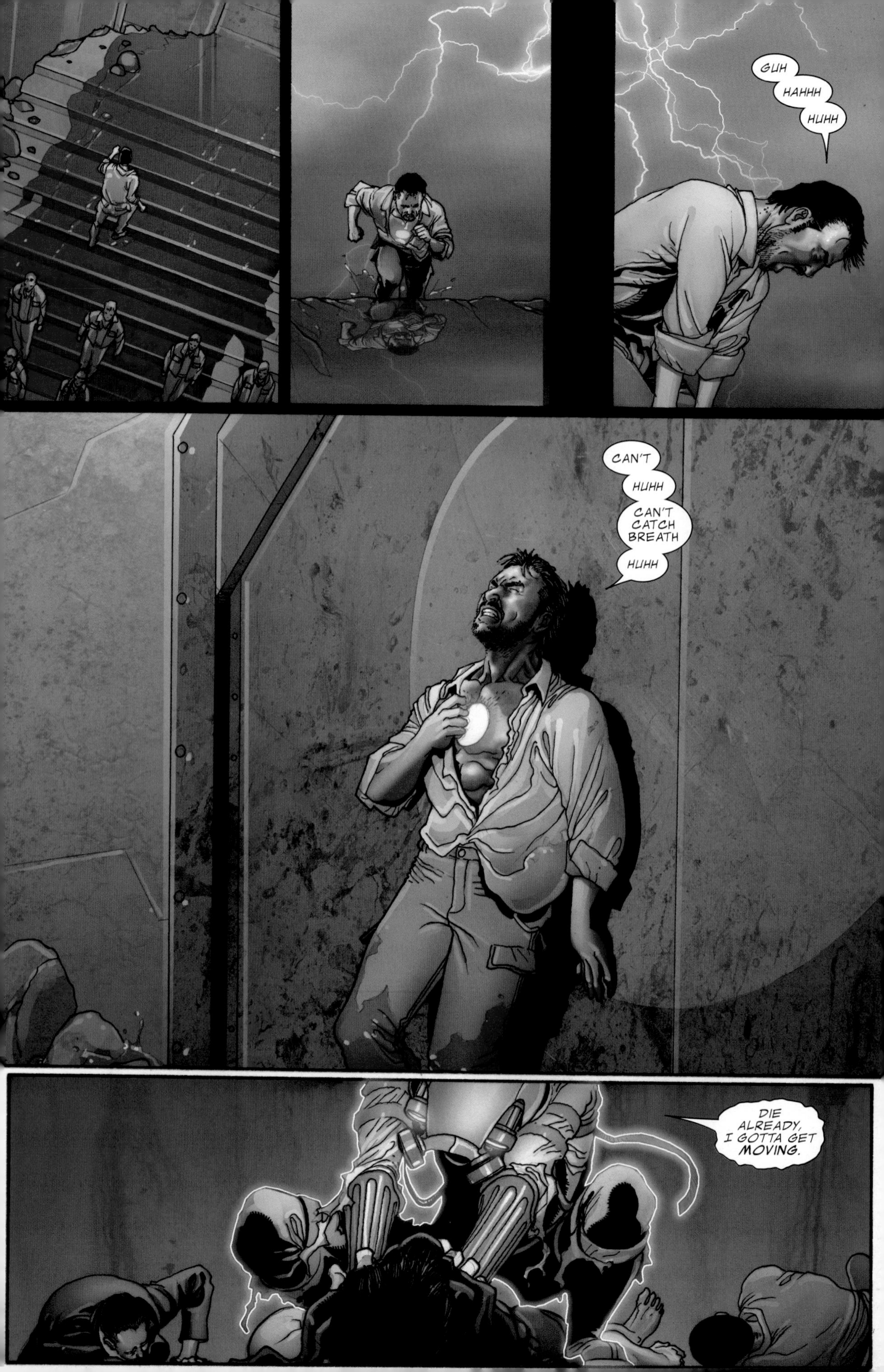
GUH
HAHHH
HUHH
CAN'T
HUHH
CAN'T CATCH BREATH
HUHH
DIE ALREADY, I GOTTA GET MOVING.

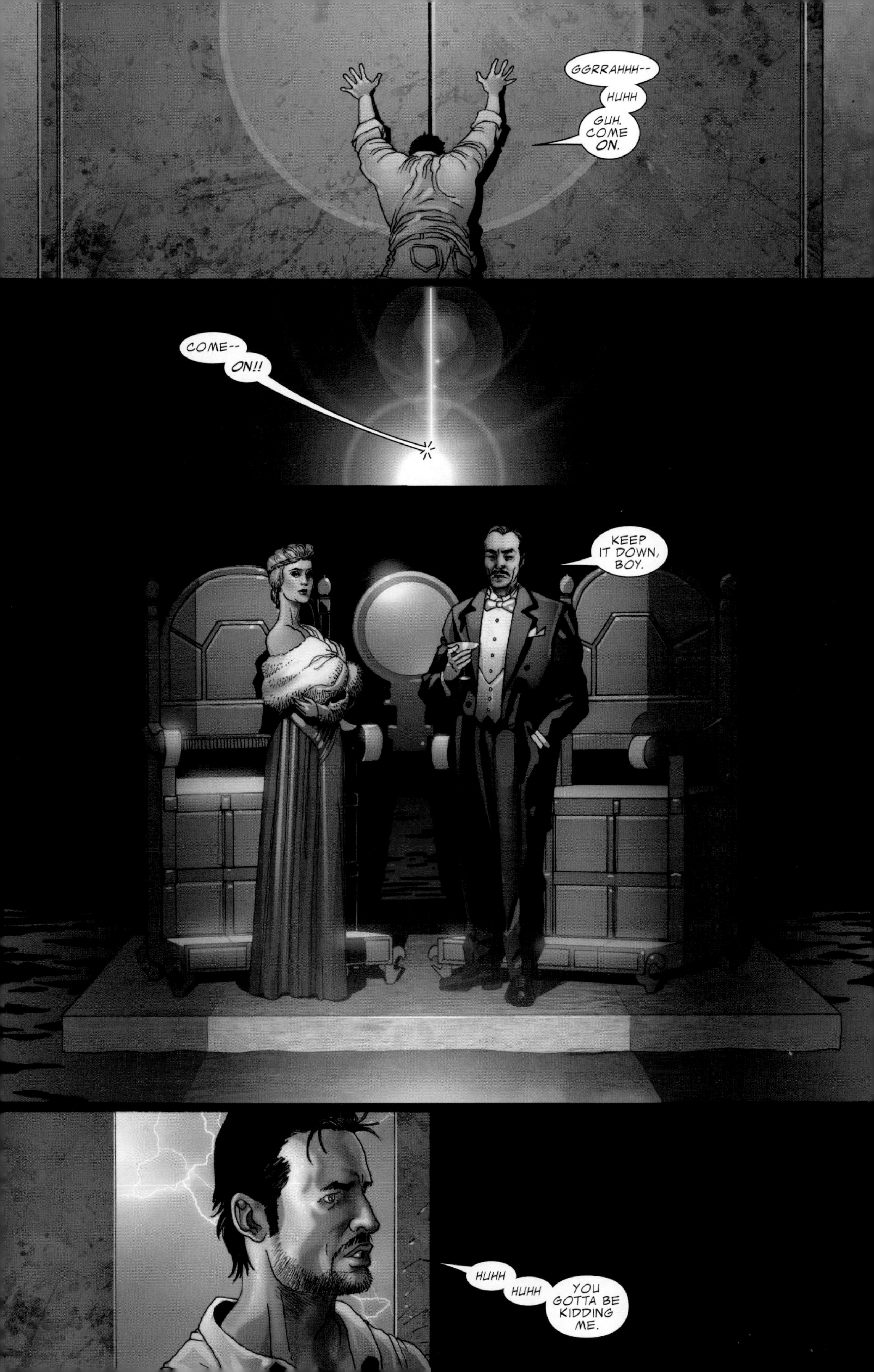
GGRRAHHH--
HUHH
GUH. COME ON.
COME--
ON!!
KEEP IT DOWN, BOY.
HUHH
HUHH
YOU GOTTA BE KIDDING ME.

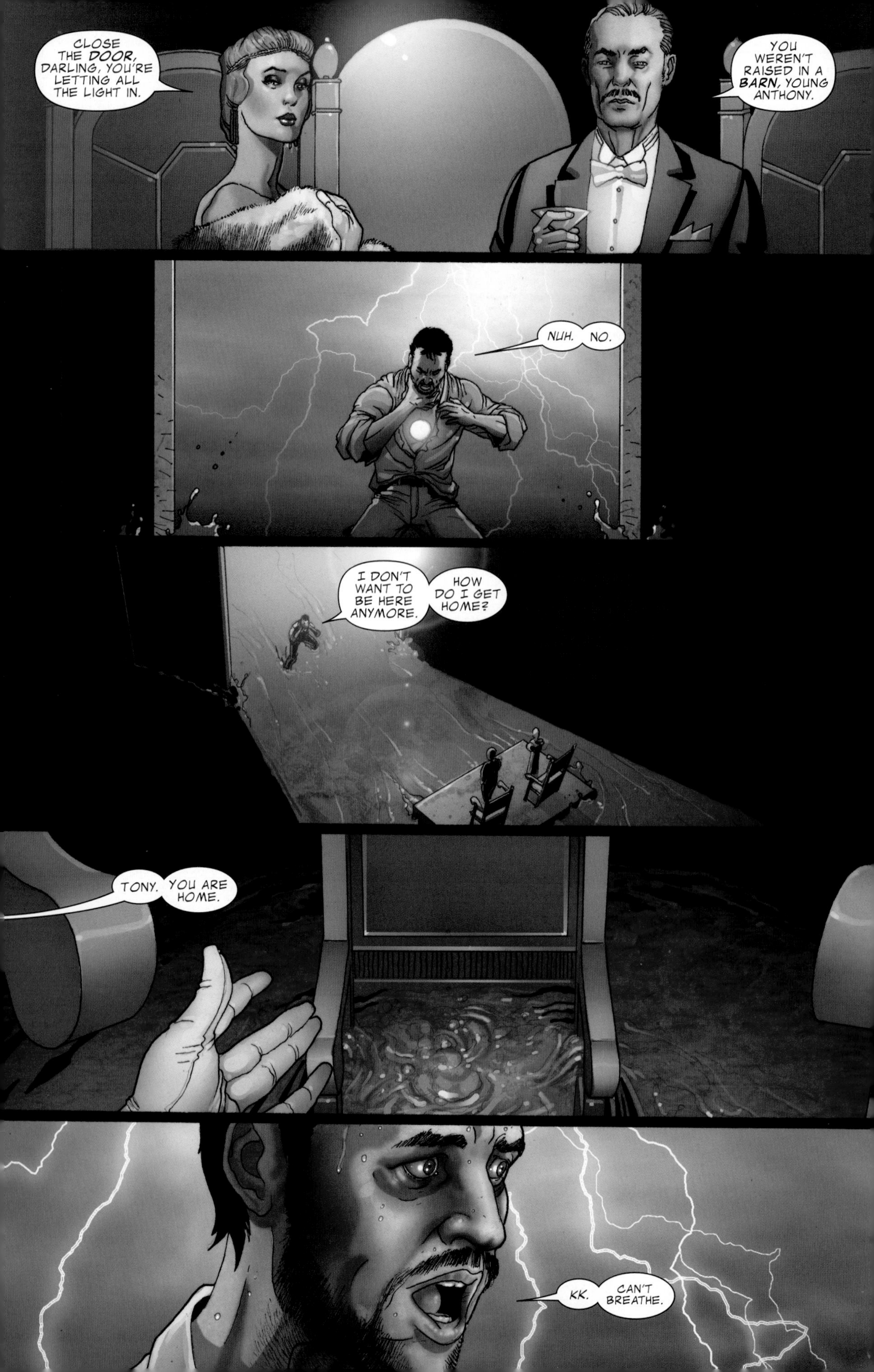
CLOSE THE DOOR, DARLING, YOU'RE LETTING ALL THE LIGHT IN.
YOU WEREN'T RAISED IN A BARN, YOUNG ANTHONY.
NUH.
NO.
I DON'T WANT TO BE HERE ANYMORE.
HOW DO I GET HOME?
TONY.
YOU ARE HOME.
KK.
CAN'T BREATHE.

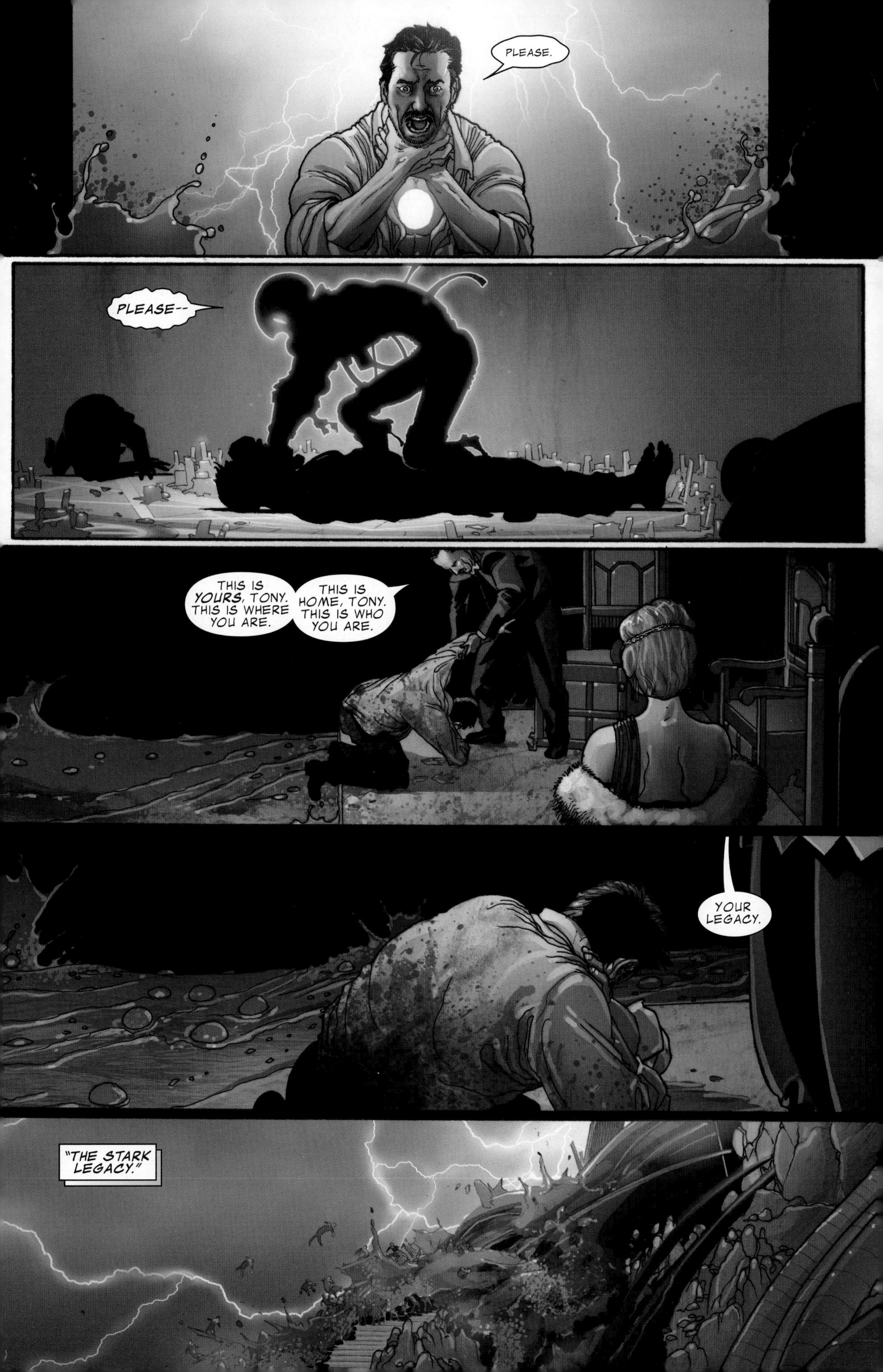
PLEASE.
PLEASE--
THIS IS YOURS, TONY. THIS IS WHERE YOU ARE.
THIS IS HOME, TONY. THIS IS WHO YOU ARE.
YOUR LEGACY.
"THE STARK LEGACY."

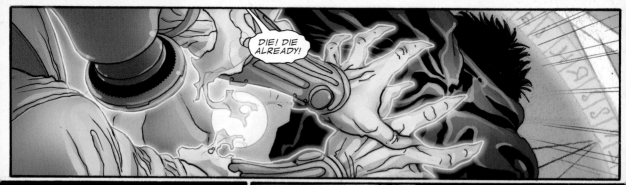

DIE! DIE ALREADY!

MOTHER-- HELP ME.

NO. GOD, NO.

YOU HAVE BLOOD ON YOUR HANDS.

NOW TAKE YOUR SEAT.

GET OFF OF HIM--

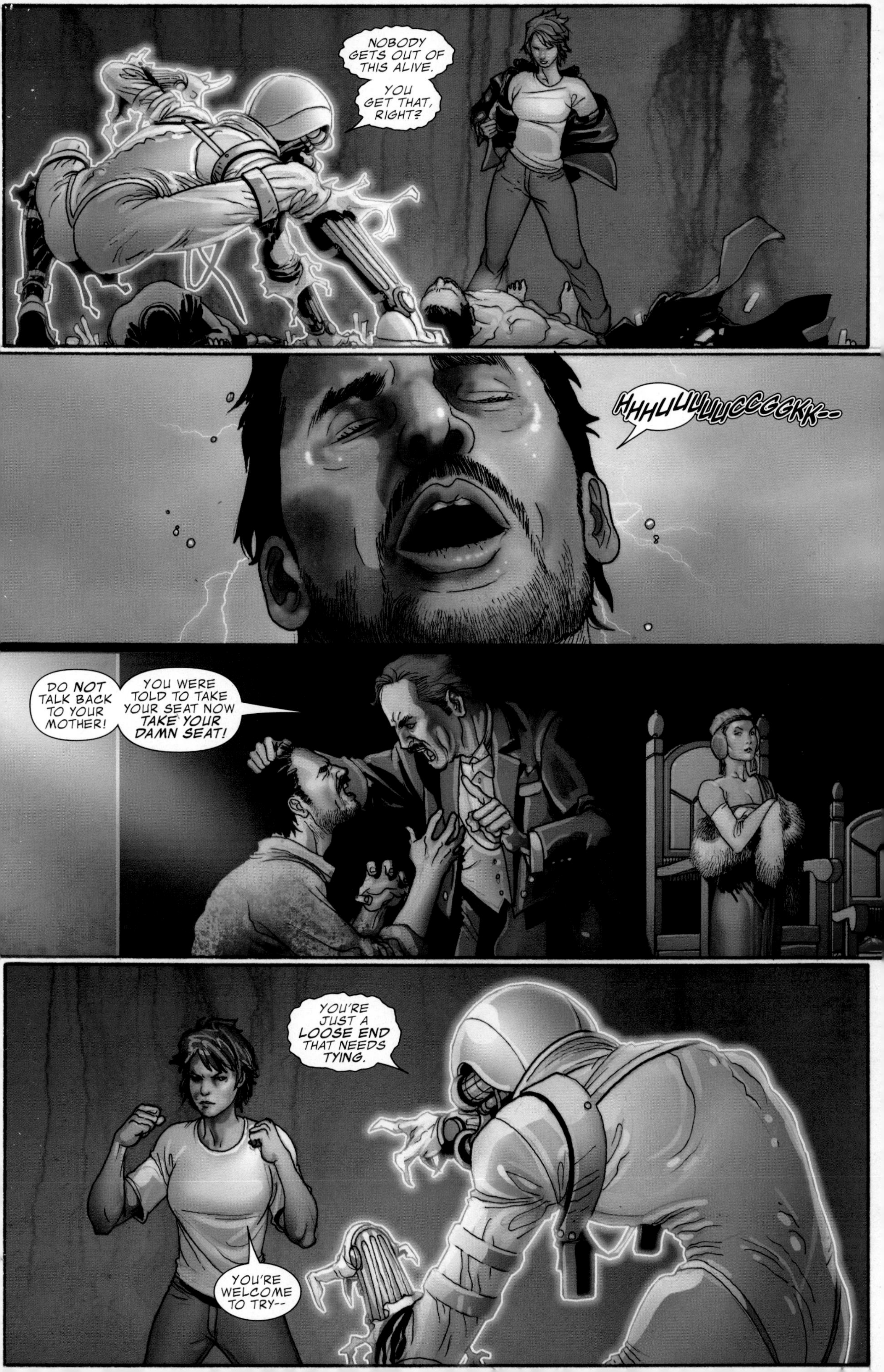
NOBODY GETS OUT OF THIS ALIVE.
YOU GET THAT, RIGHT?
HHHUUUUUCCCCKK--
DO NOT TALK BACK TO YOUR MOTHER!
YOU WERE TOLD TO TAKE YOUR SEAT NOW TAKE YOUR DAMN SEAT!
YOU'RE JUST A LOOSE END THAT NEEDS TYING.
YOU'RE WELCOME TO TRY--

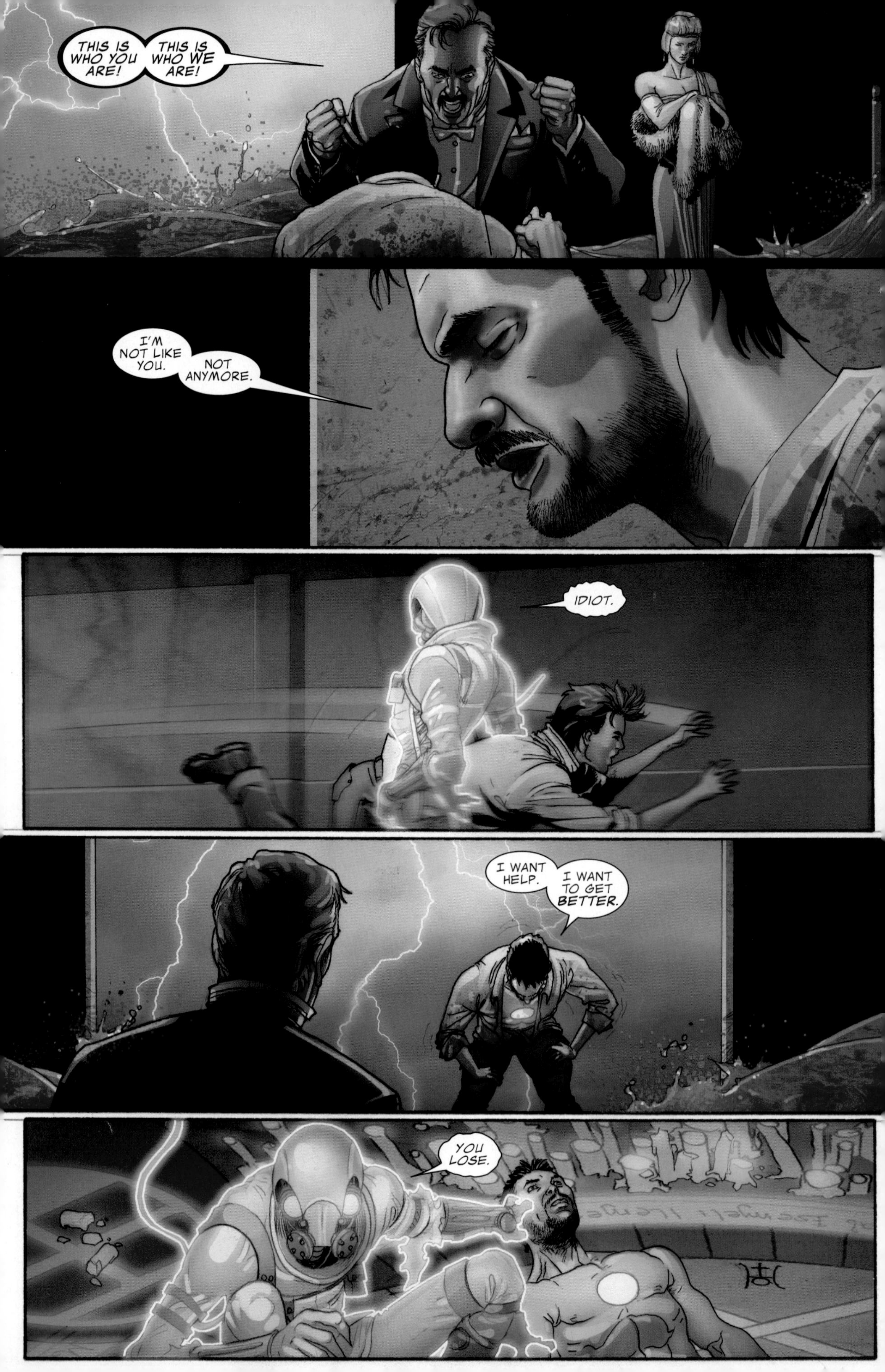
THIS IS WHO YOU ARE!
THIS IS WHO WE ARE!
I'M NOT LIKE YOU.
NOT ANYMORE.
IDIOT.
I WANT HELP.
I WANT TO GET BETTER.
YOU LOSE.

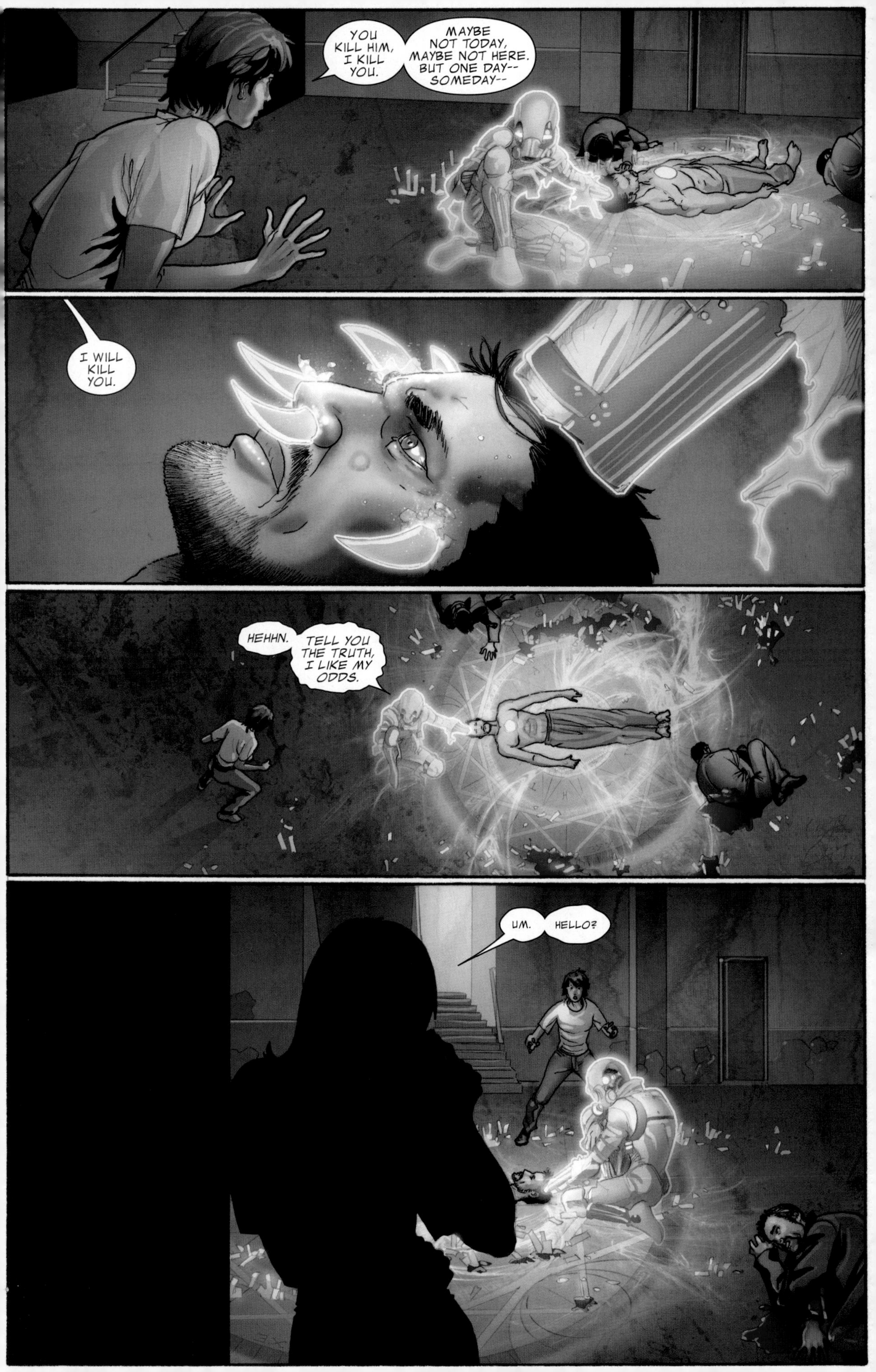
YOU KILL HIM, I KILL YOU.
MAYBE NOT TODAY, MAYBE NOT HERE. BUT ONE DAY-- SOMEDAY--
I WILL KILL YOU.
HEHHN.
TELL YOU THE TRUTH, I LIKE MY ODDS.
UM.
HELLO?

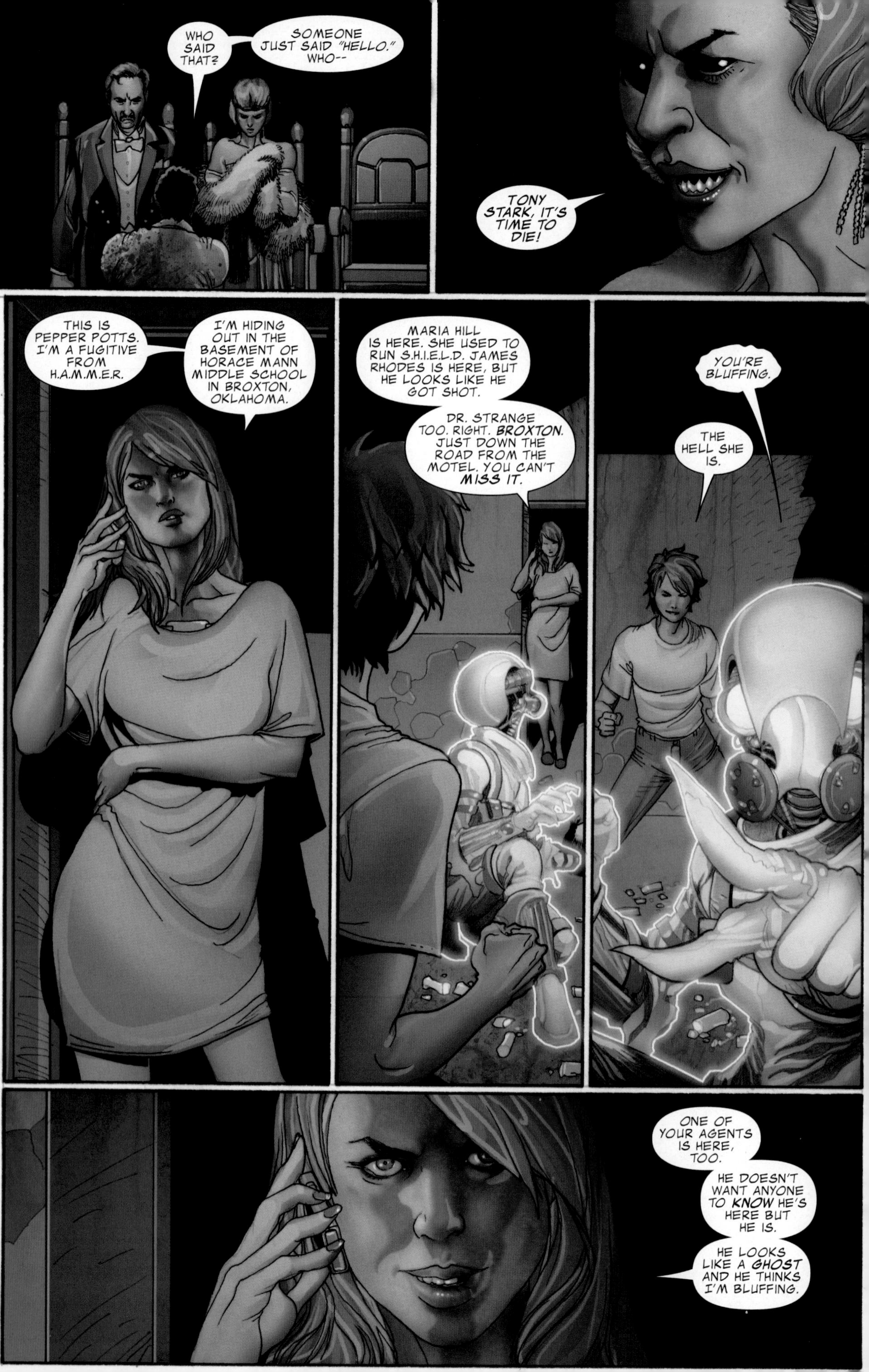

WHO SAID THAT?
SOMEONE JUST SAID "HELLO." WHO--
TONY STARK, IT'S TIME TO DIE!
THIS IS PEPPER POTTS. I'M A FUGITIVE FROM H.A.M.M.E.R.
I'M HIDING OUT IN THE BASEMENT OF HORACE MANN MIDDLE SCHOOL IN BROXTON, OKLAHOMA.
MARIA HILL IS HERE. SHE USED TO RUN S.H.I.E.L.D. JAMES RHODES IS HERE, BUT HE LOOKS LIKE HE GOT SHOT.
DR. STRANGE TOO. RIGHT. BROXTON. JUST DOWN THE ROAD FROM THE MOTEL. YOU CAN'T MISS IT.
YOU'RE BLUFFING.
THE HELL SHE IS.
ONE OF YOUR AGENTS IS HERE, TOO.
HE DOESN'T WANT ANYONE TO KNOW HE'S HERE BUT HE IS.
HE LOOKS LIKE A GHOST AND HE THINKS I'M BLUFFING.

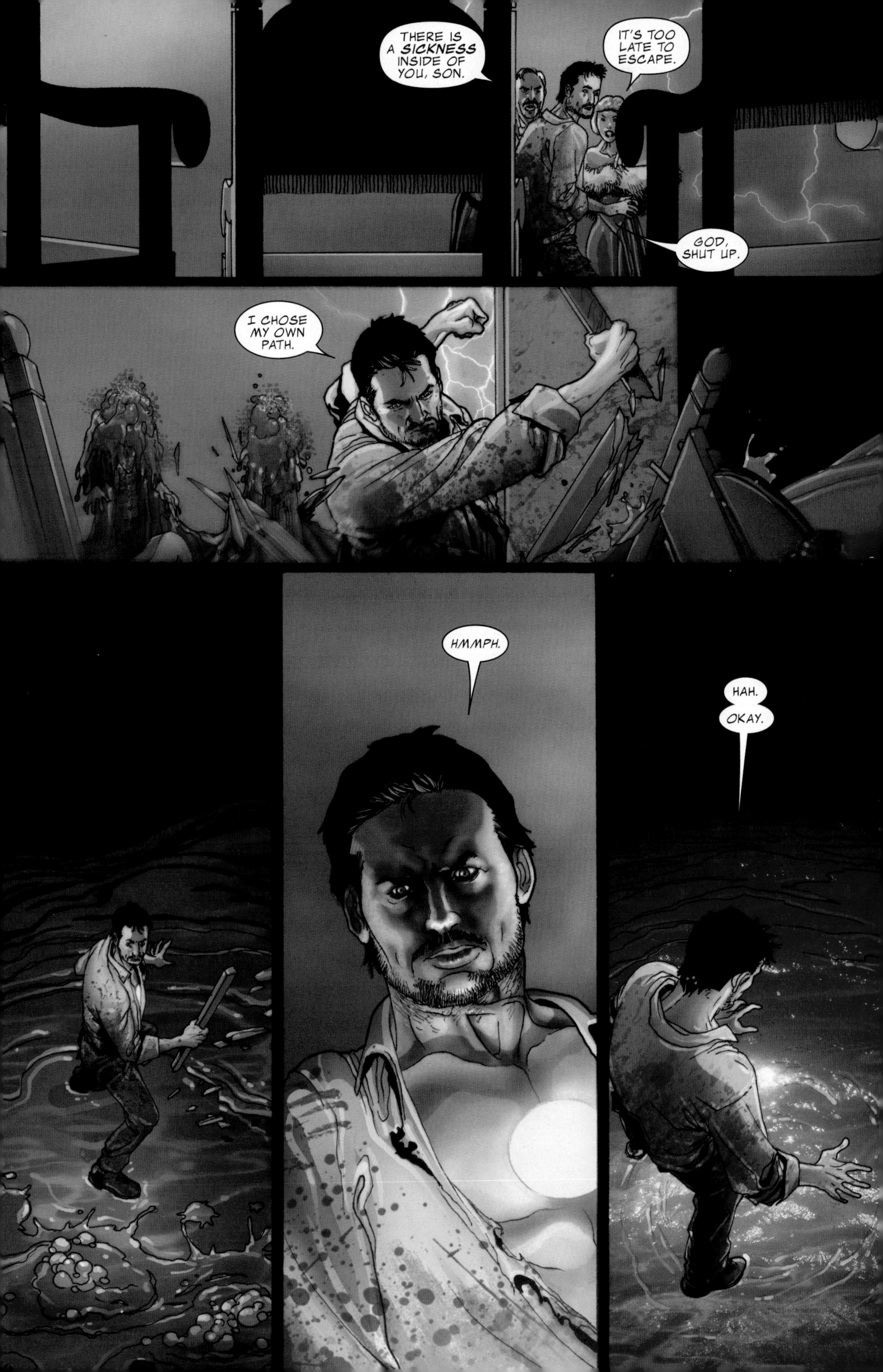
THERE IS A SICKNESS INSIDE OF YOU, SON.
IT'S TOO LATE TO ESCAPE.
GOD, SHUT UP.
I CHOSE MY OWN PATH.
HMMPH.
HAH.
OKAY.

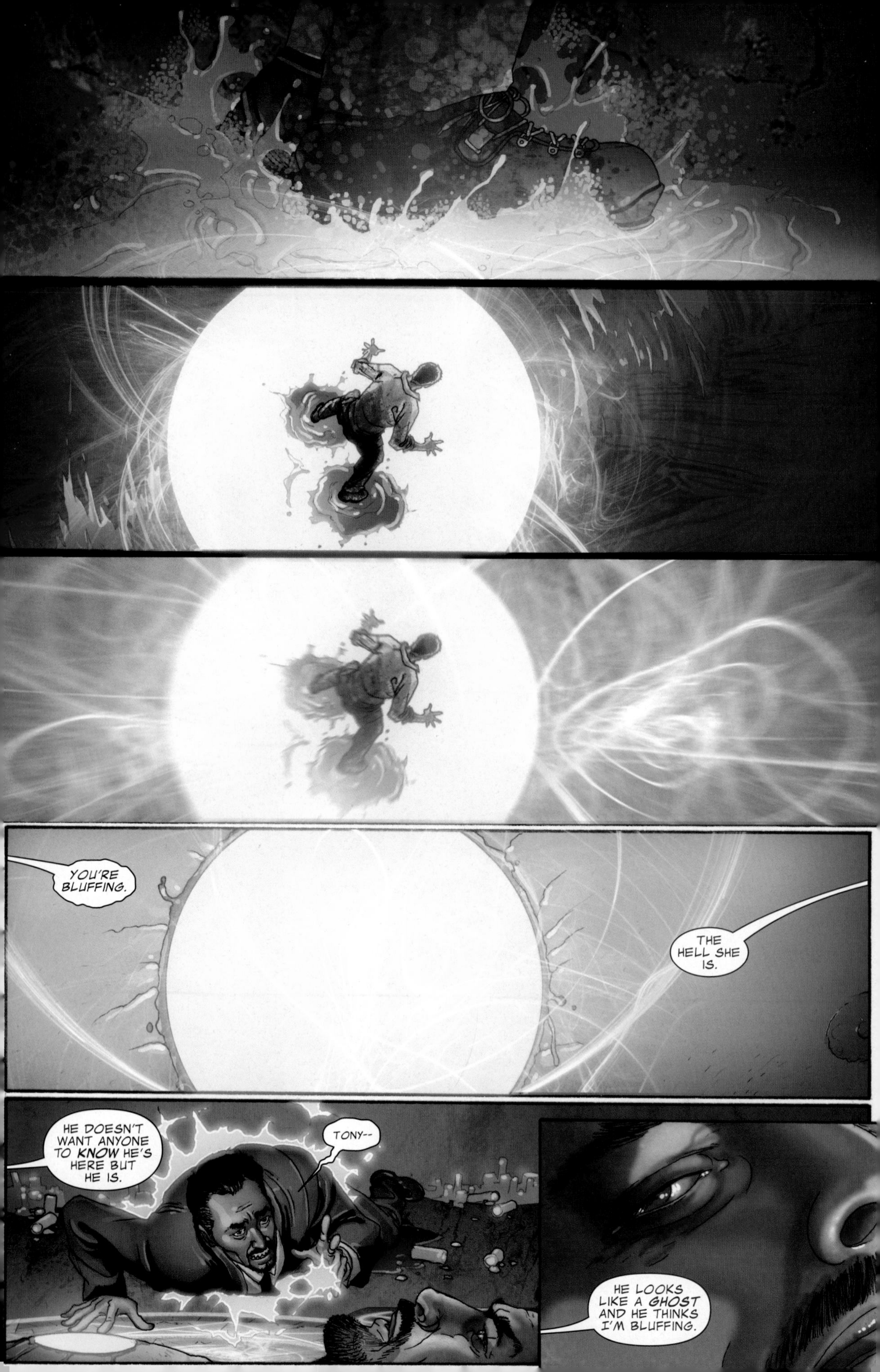

YOU'RE BLUFFING.
THE HELL SHE IS.
HE DOESN'T WANT ANYONE TO KNOW HE'S HERE BUT HE IS.
TONY--
HE LOOKS LIKE A GHOST AND HE THINKS I'M BLUFFING.

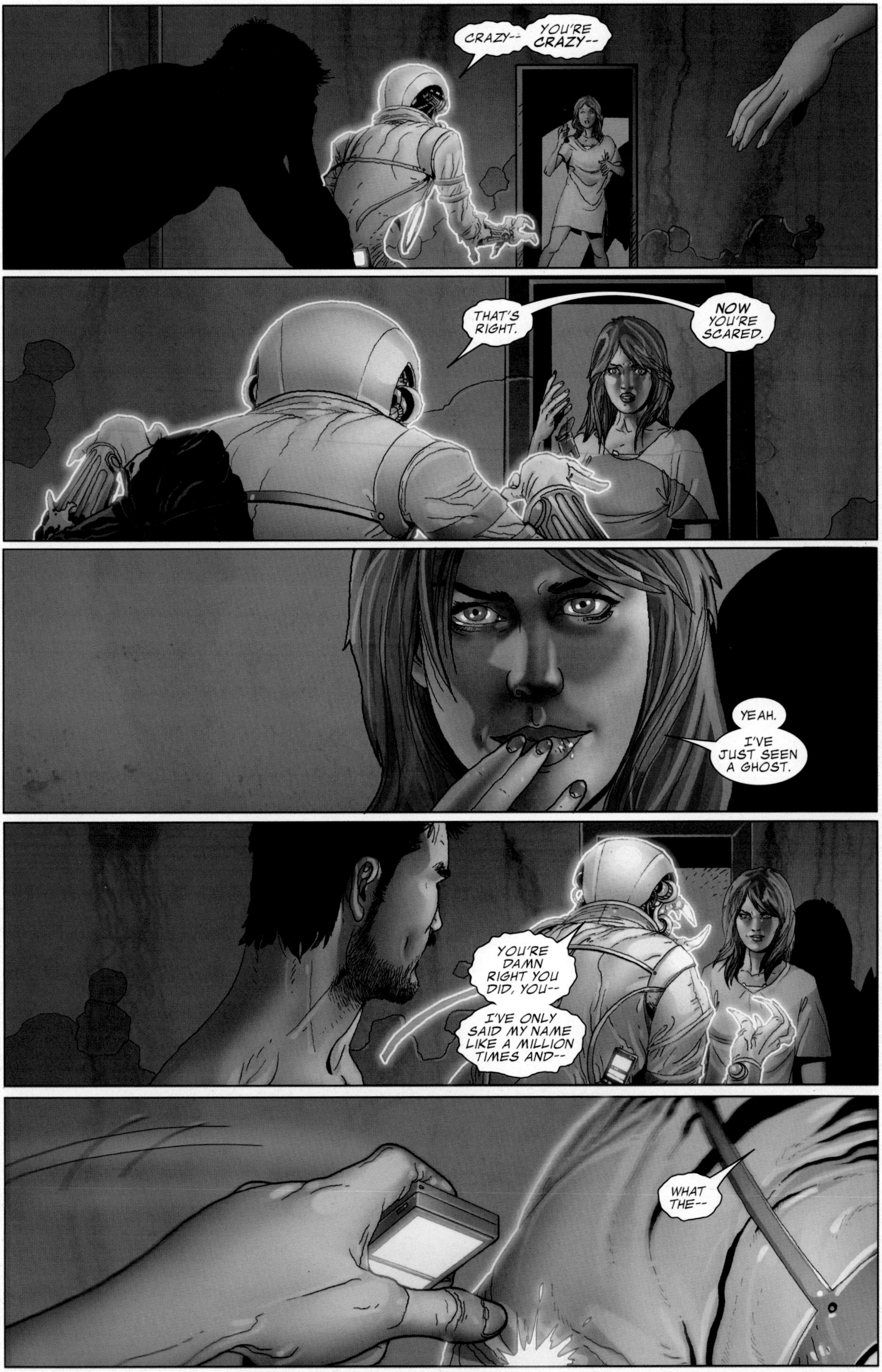
CRAZY--
YOU'RE CRAZY--
THAT'S RIGHT.
NOW YOU'RE SCARED.
YEAH.
I'VE JUST SEEN A GHOST.
YOU'RE DAMN RIGHT YOU DID, YOU--
I'VE ONLY SAID MY NAME LIKE A MILLION TIMES AND--
WHAT THE--

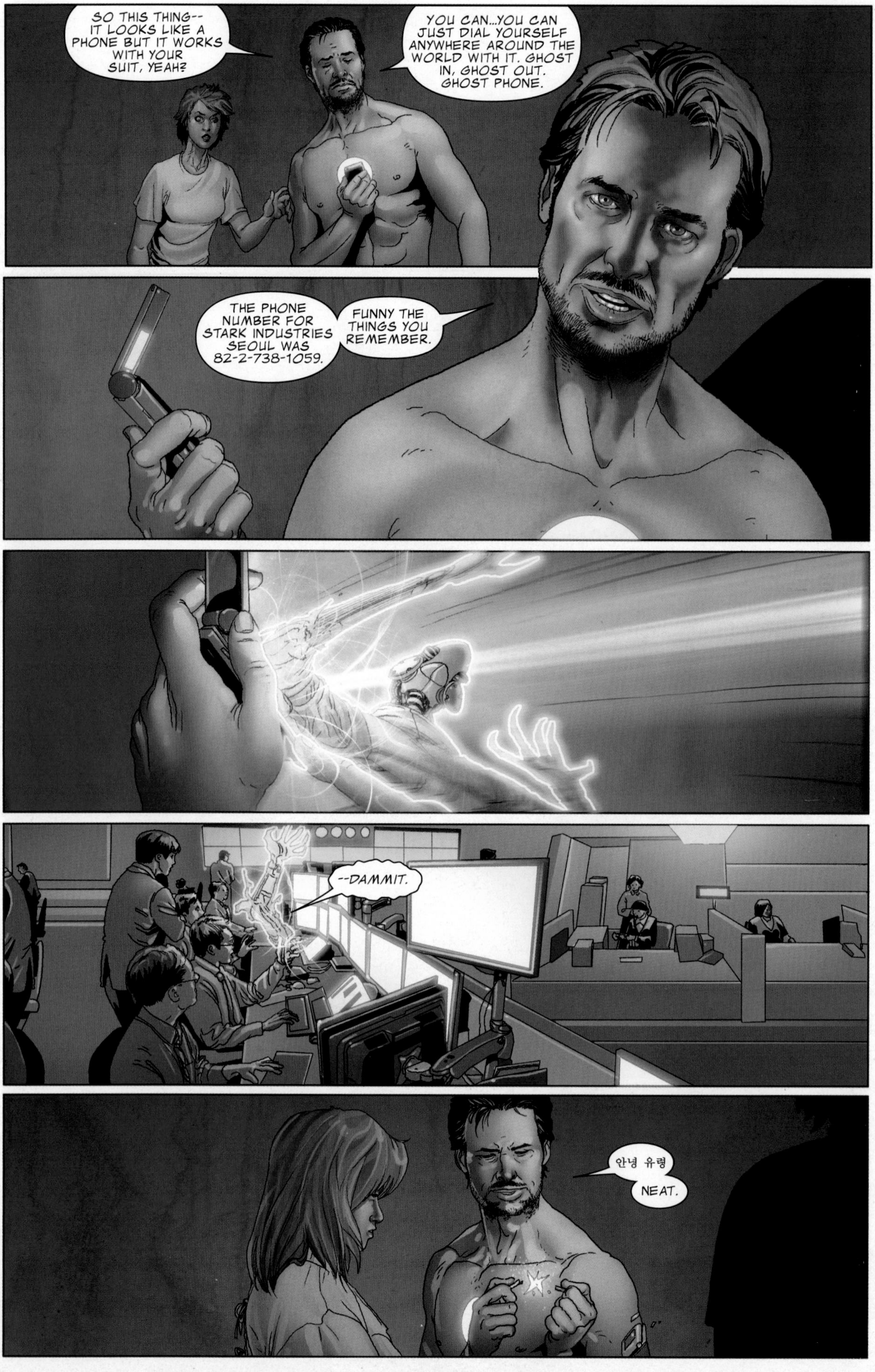
SO THIS THING-- IT LOOKS LIKE A PHONE BUT IT WORKS WITH YOUR SUIT, YEAH?
YOU CAN...YOU CAN JUST DIAL YOURSELF ANYWHERE AROUND THE WORLD WITH IT. GHOST IN, GHOST OUT. GHOST PHONE.
THE PHONE NUMBER FOR STARK INDUSTRIES SEOUL WAS 82-2-738-1059.
FUNNY THE THINGS YOU REMEMBER.
--DAMMIT.
안녕 유령
NEAT.

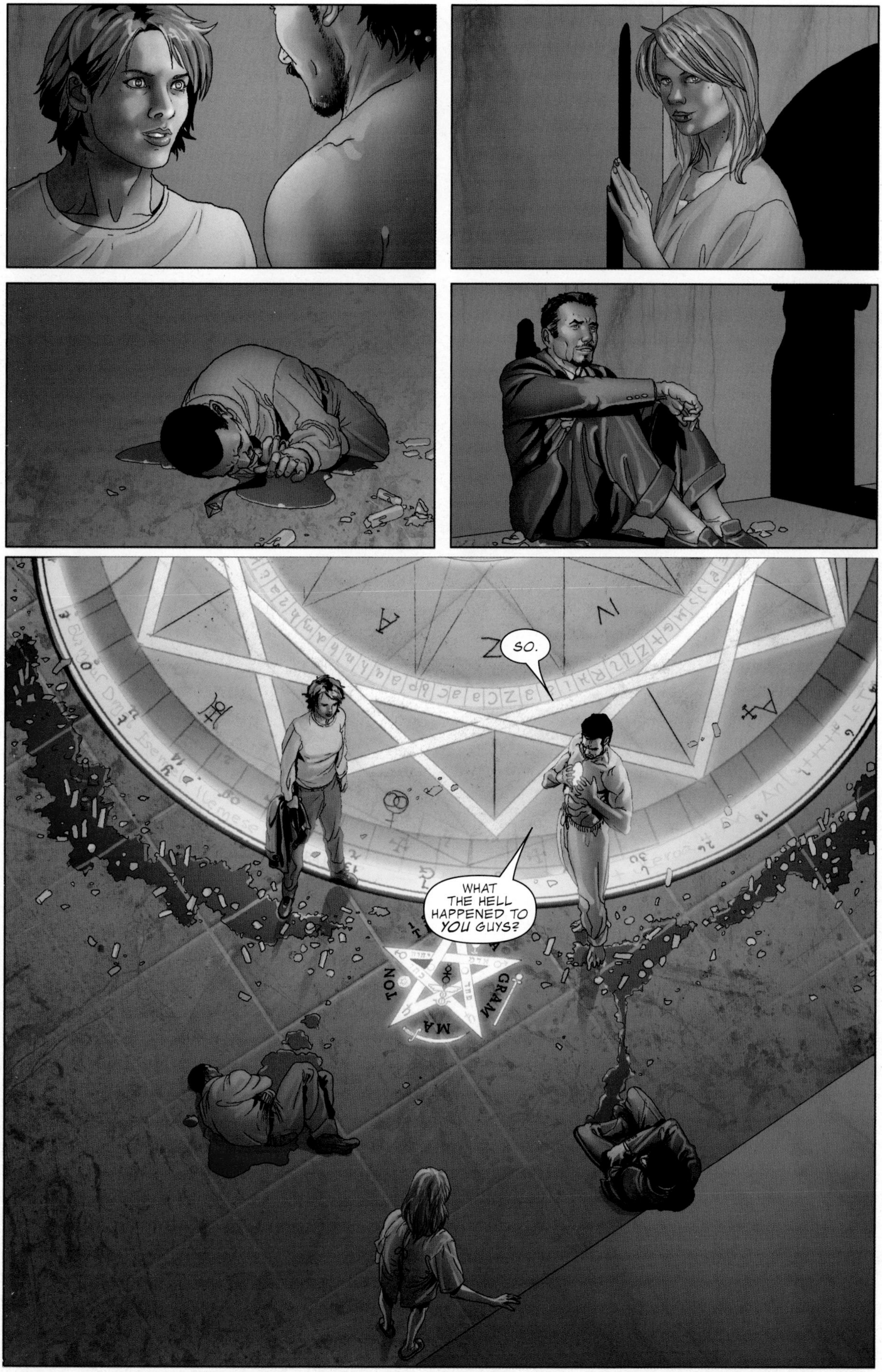
SO.
WHAT THE HELL HAPPENED TO YOU GUYS?

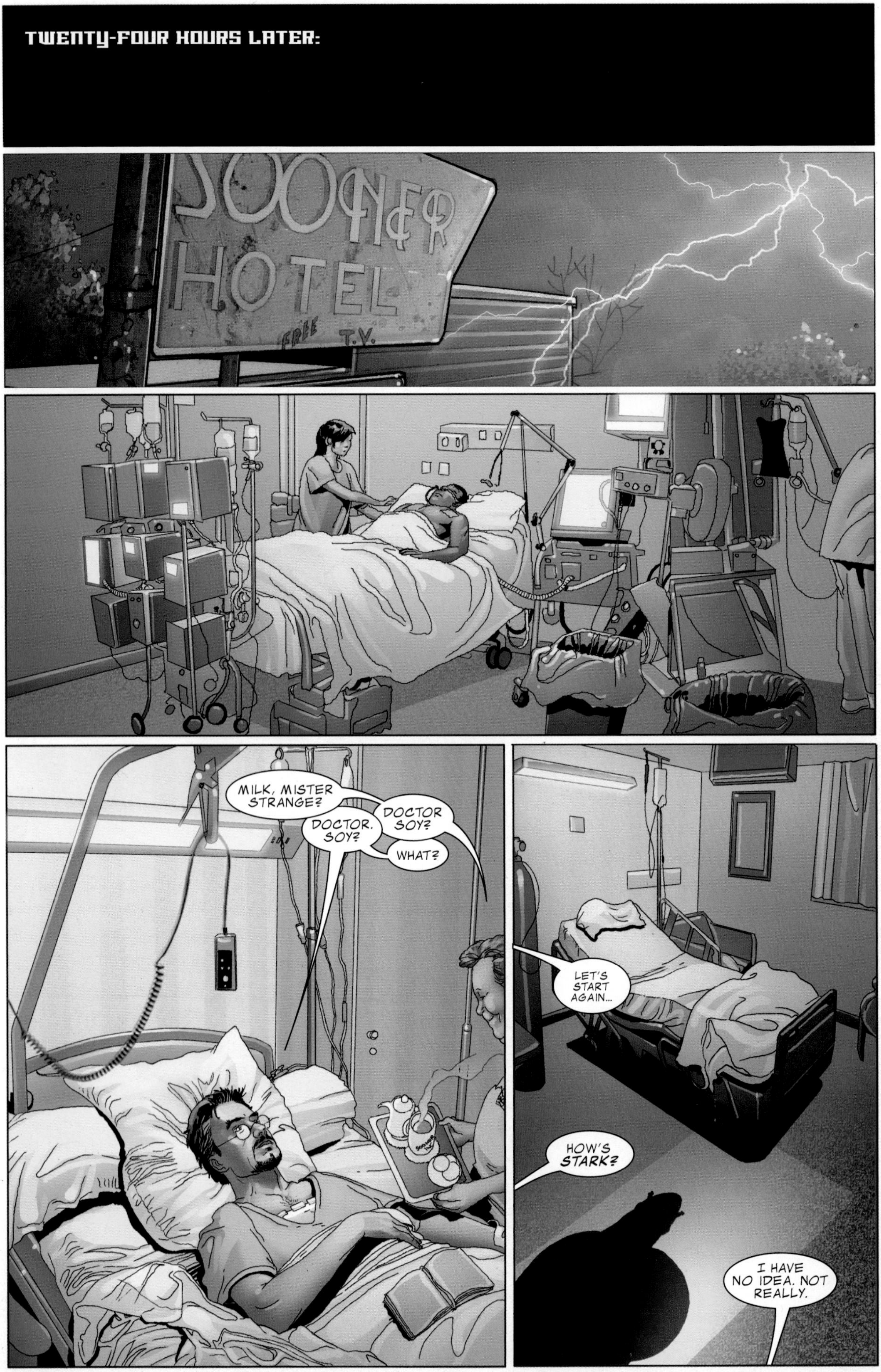
TWENTY-FOUR HOURS LATER:
SOONER
HOTEL
FREE T.V.
MILK, MISTER STRANGE?
DOCTOR SOY?
DOCTOR. SOY?
WHAT?
LET'S START AGAIN...
HOW'S STARK?
I HAVE NO IDEA. NOT REALLY.

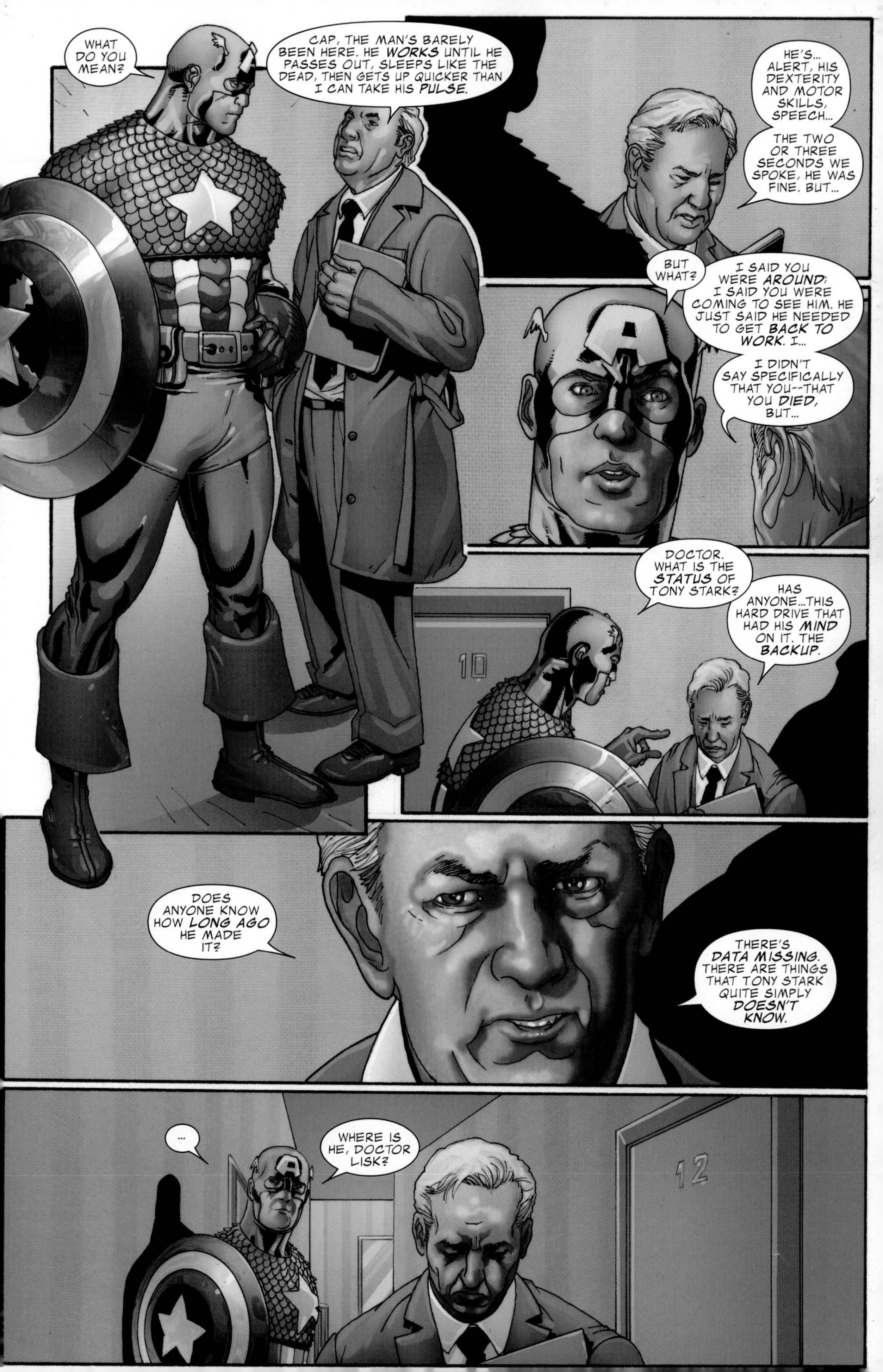
WHAT DO YOU MEAN?
CAP, THE MAN'S BARELY BEEN HERE. HE WORKS UNTIL HE PASSES OUT, SLEEPS LIKE THE DEAD, THEN GETS UP QUICKER THAN I CAN TAKE HIS PULSE.
HE'S... ALERT, HIS DEXTERITY AND MOTOR SKILLS, SPEECH...
THE TWO OR THREE SECONDS WE SPOKE, HE WAS FINE. BUT...
BUT WHAT?
I SAID YOU WERE AROUND; I SAID YOU WERE COMING TO SEE HIM. HE JUST SAID HE NEEDED TO GET BACK TO WORK. I...
I DIDN'T SAY SPECIFICALLY THAT YOU--THAT YOU DIED, BUT...
DOCTOR. WHAT IS THE STATUS OF TONY STARK?
HAS ANYONE...THIS HARD DRIVE THAT HAD HIS MIND ON IT. THE BACKUP.
10
DOES ANYONE KNOW HOW LONG AGO HE MADE IT?
THERE'S DATA MISSING. THERE ARE THINGS THAT TONY STARK QUITE SIMPLY DOESN'T KNOW.
...
WHERE IS HE, DOCTOR LISK?
12

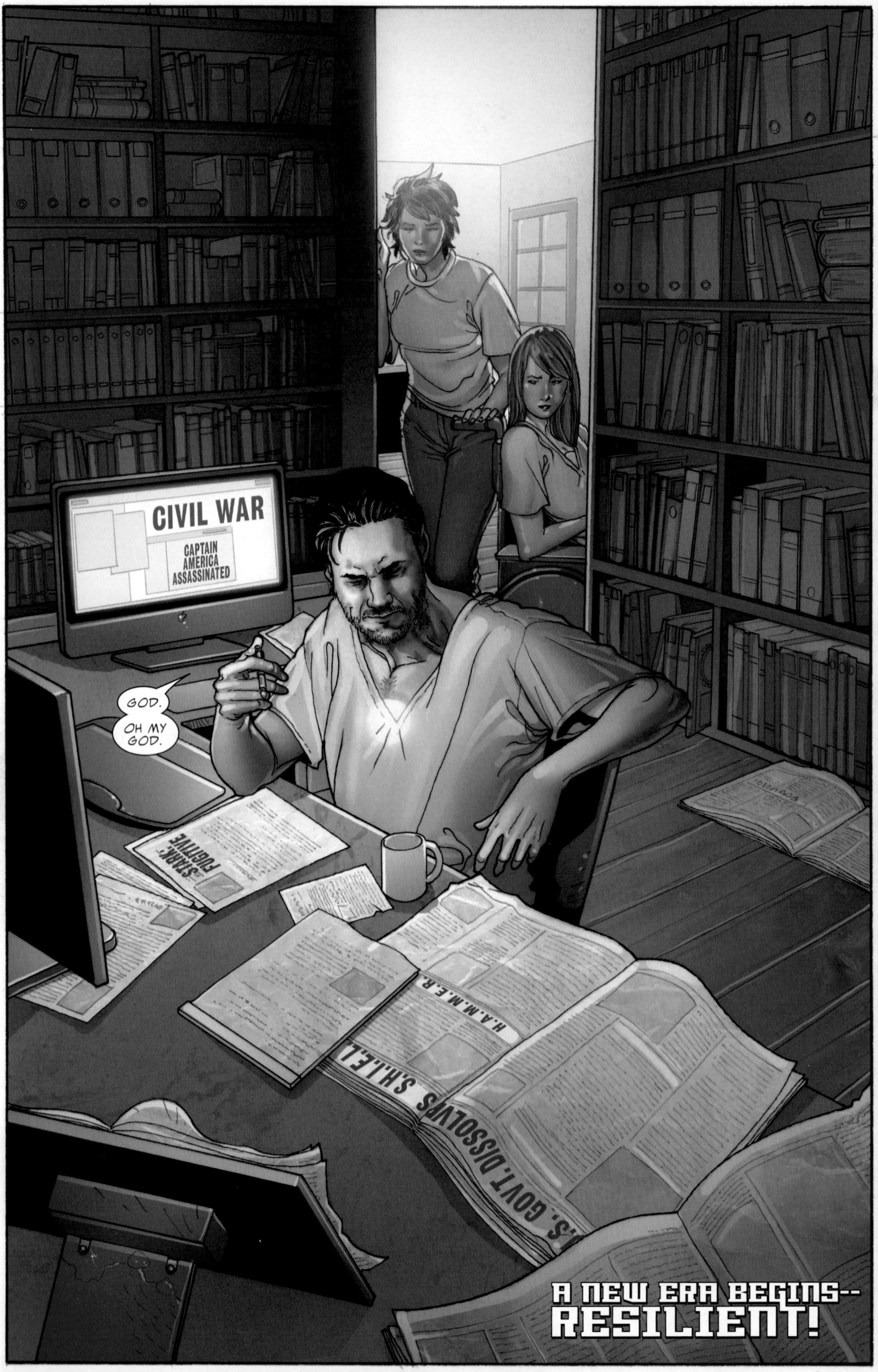
CIVIL WAR
CAPTAIN AMERICA ASSASSINATED
GOD. OH MY GOD.
STARK: FUGITIVE
H.A.M.M.E.R.
U.S. GOVT. DISSOLVES S.H.I.E.L.D.
A NEW ERA BEGINS--
RESILIENT!

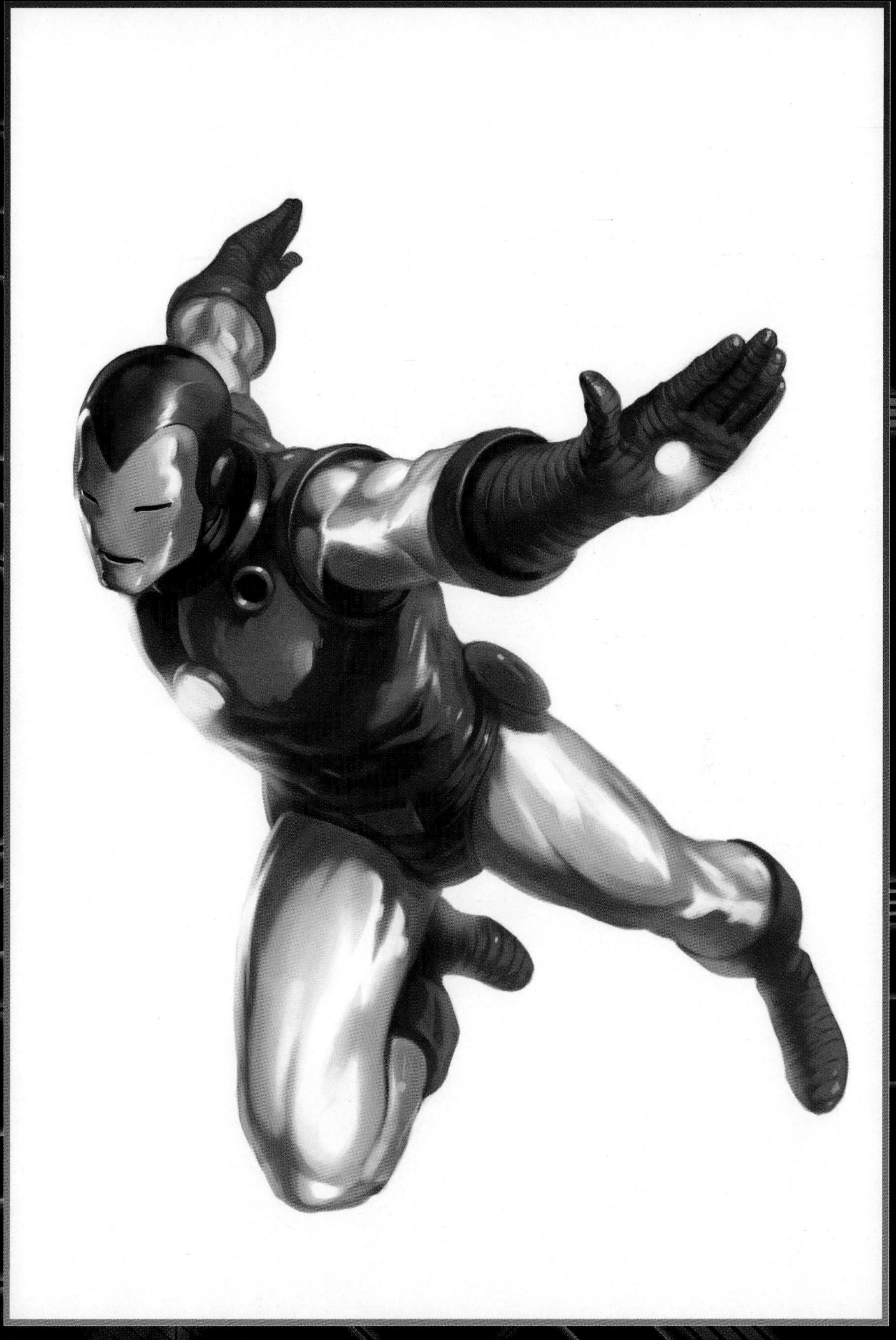

#20 70TH ANNIVERSARY VARIANT
BY MARKO DJURDJEVIC

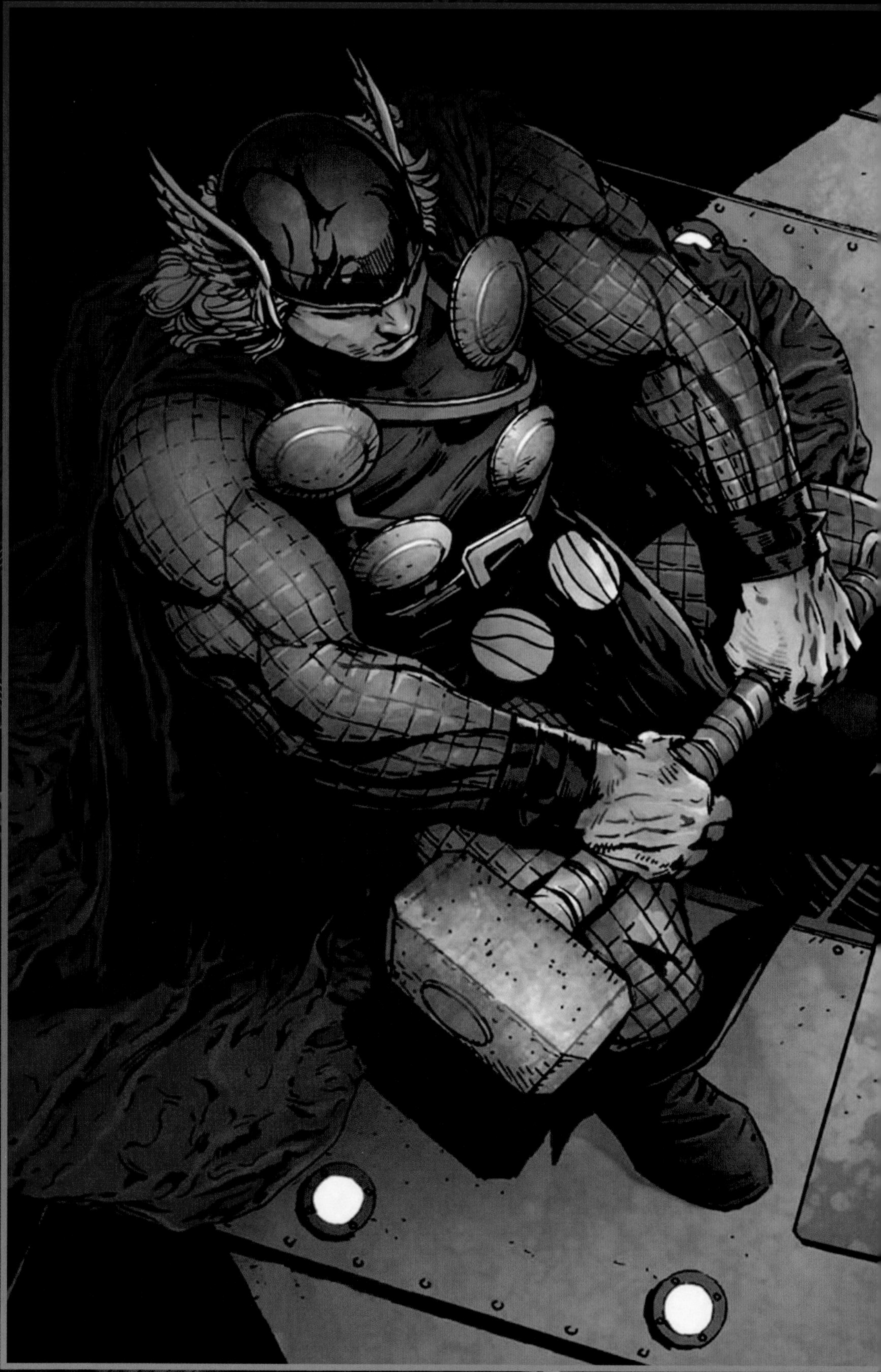

#20 VARIANT BY PATRICK ZIRCHER & JUNE CHUNG

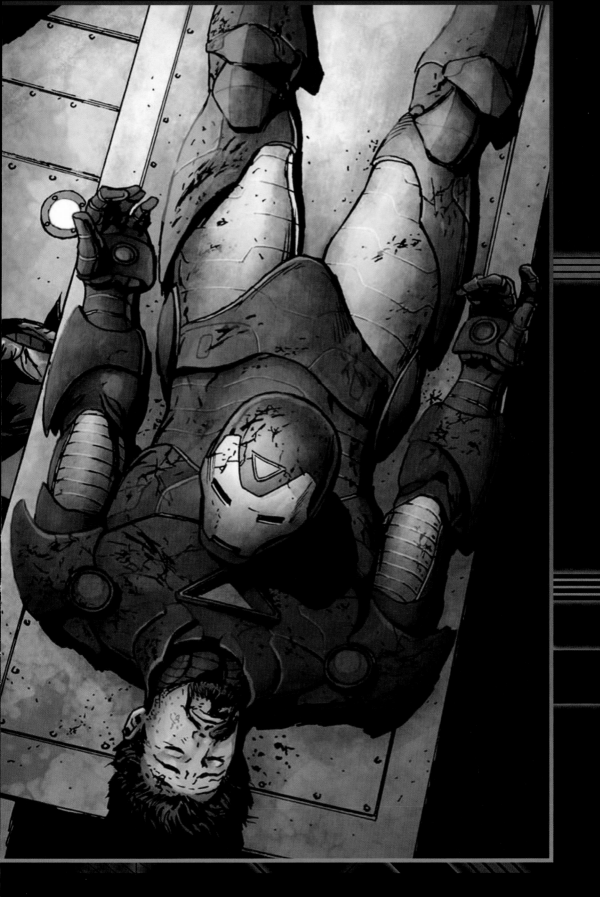

#20 SKETCH VARIANT by Patrick Zircher

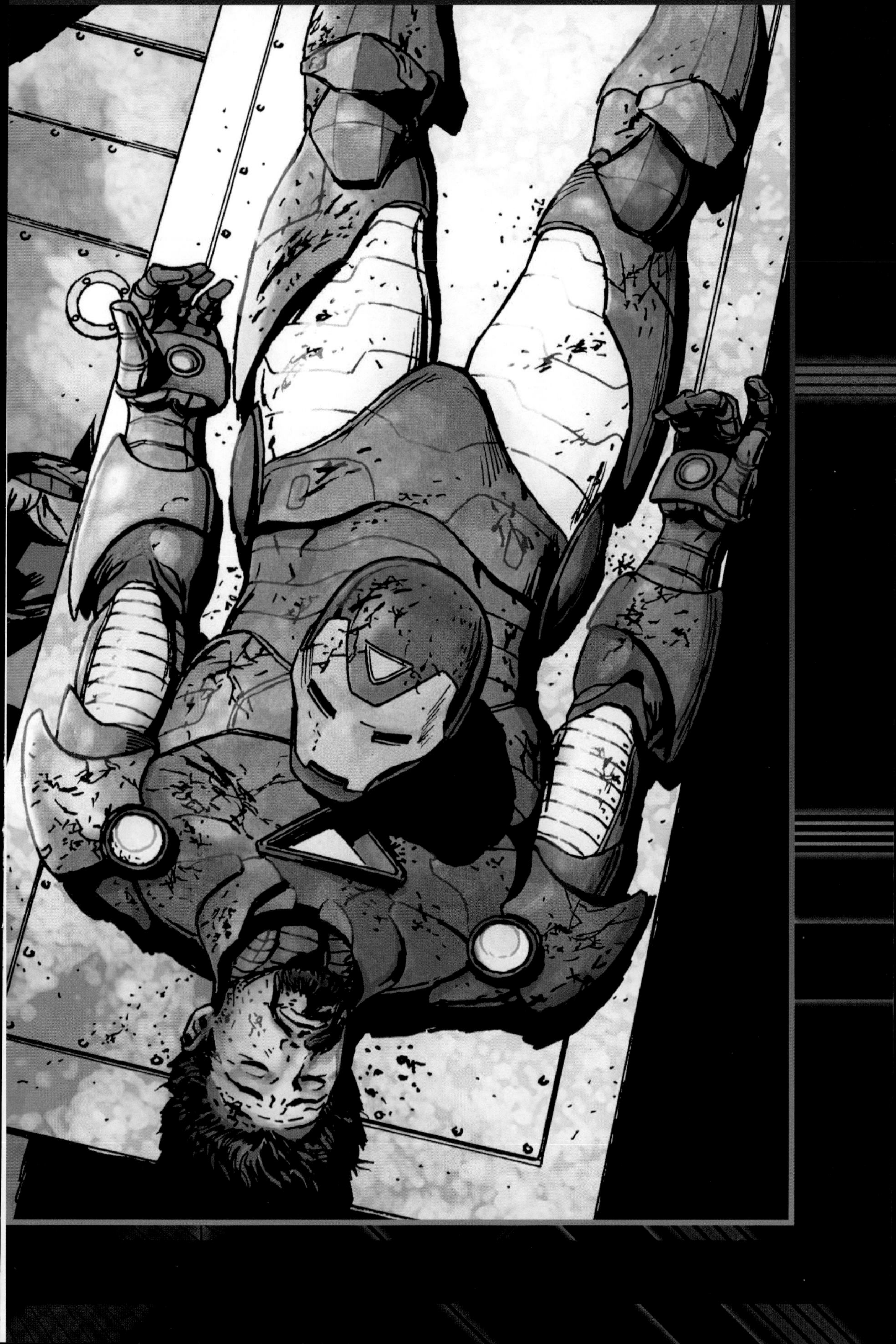

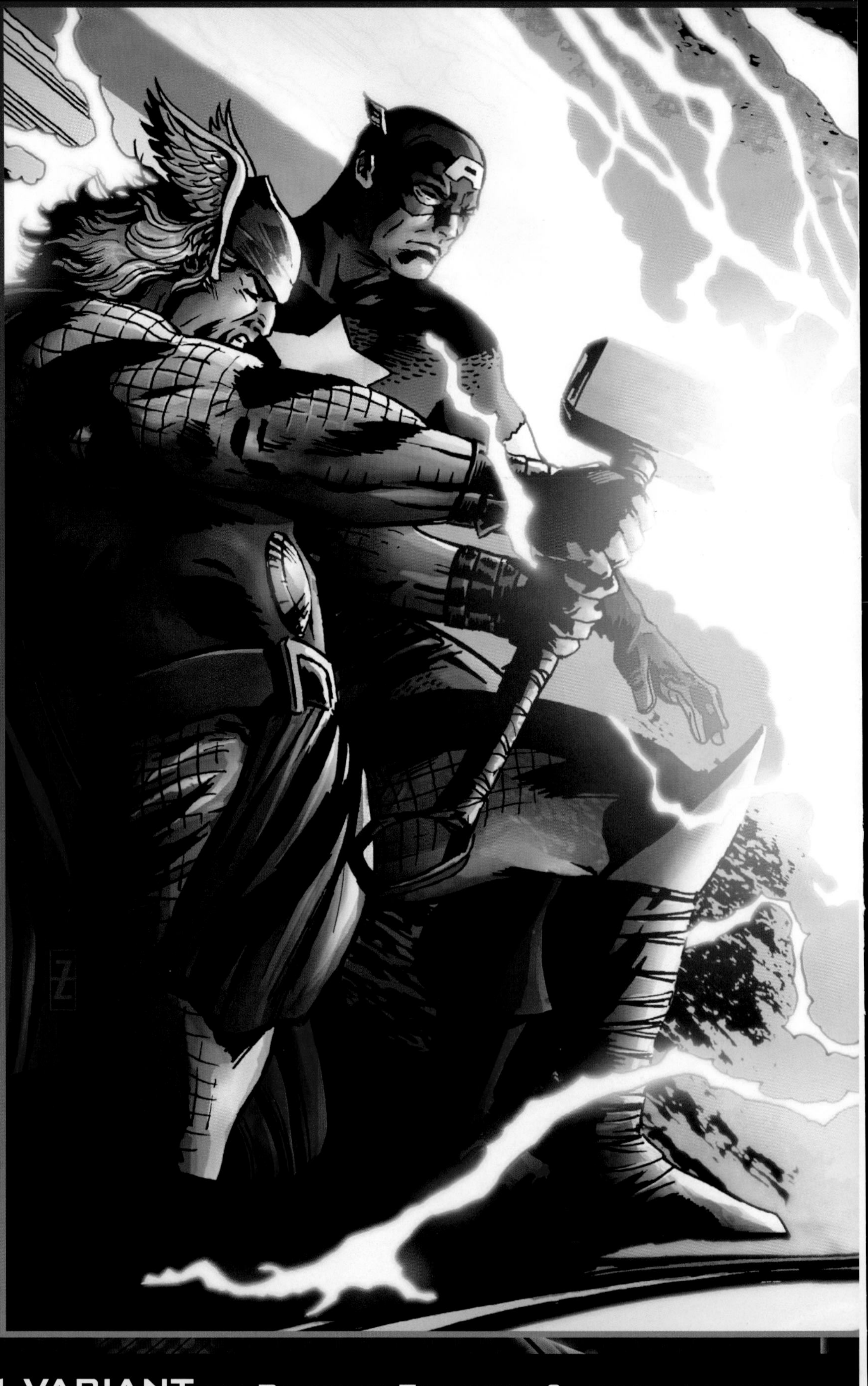

#21 VARIANT BY PATRICK ZIRCHER & JUNE CHUNG

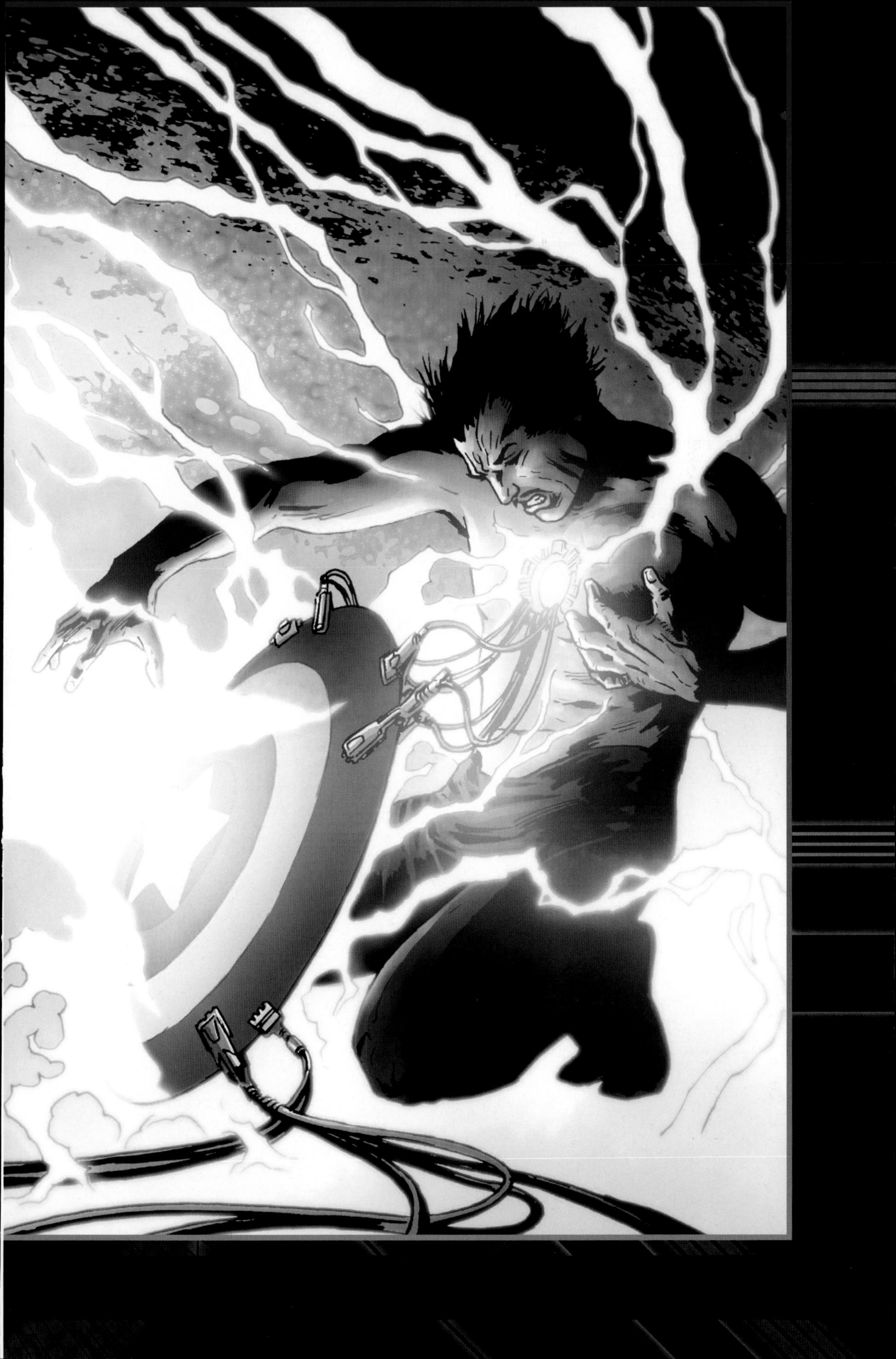

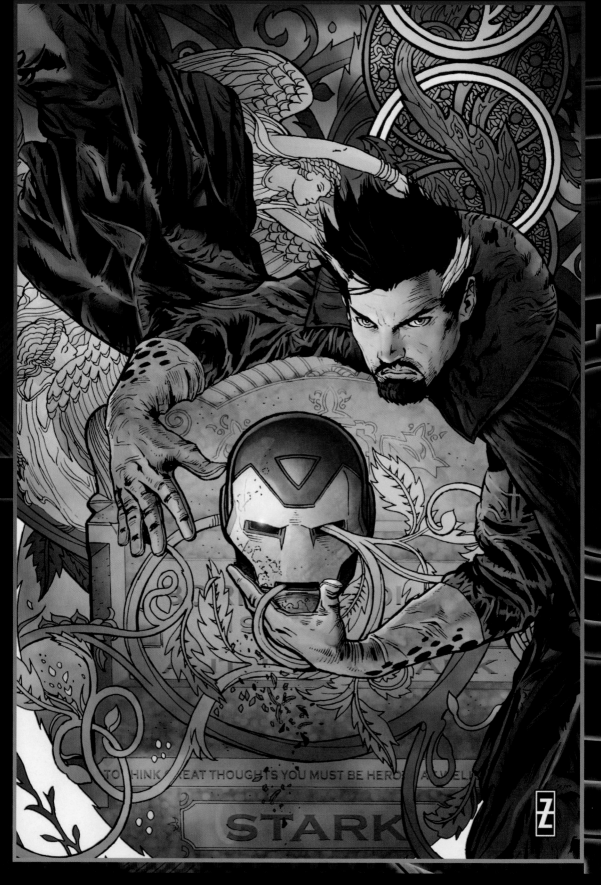

#22 VARIANT by Patrick Zircher & June Chung

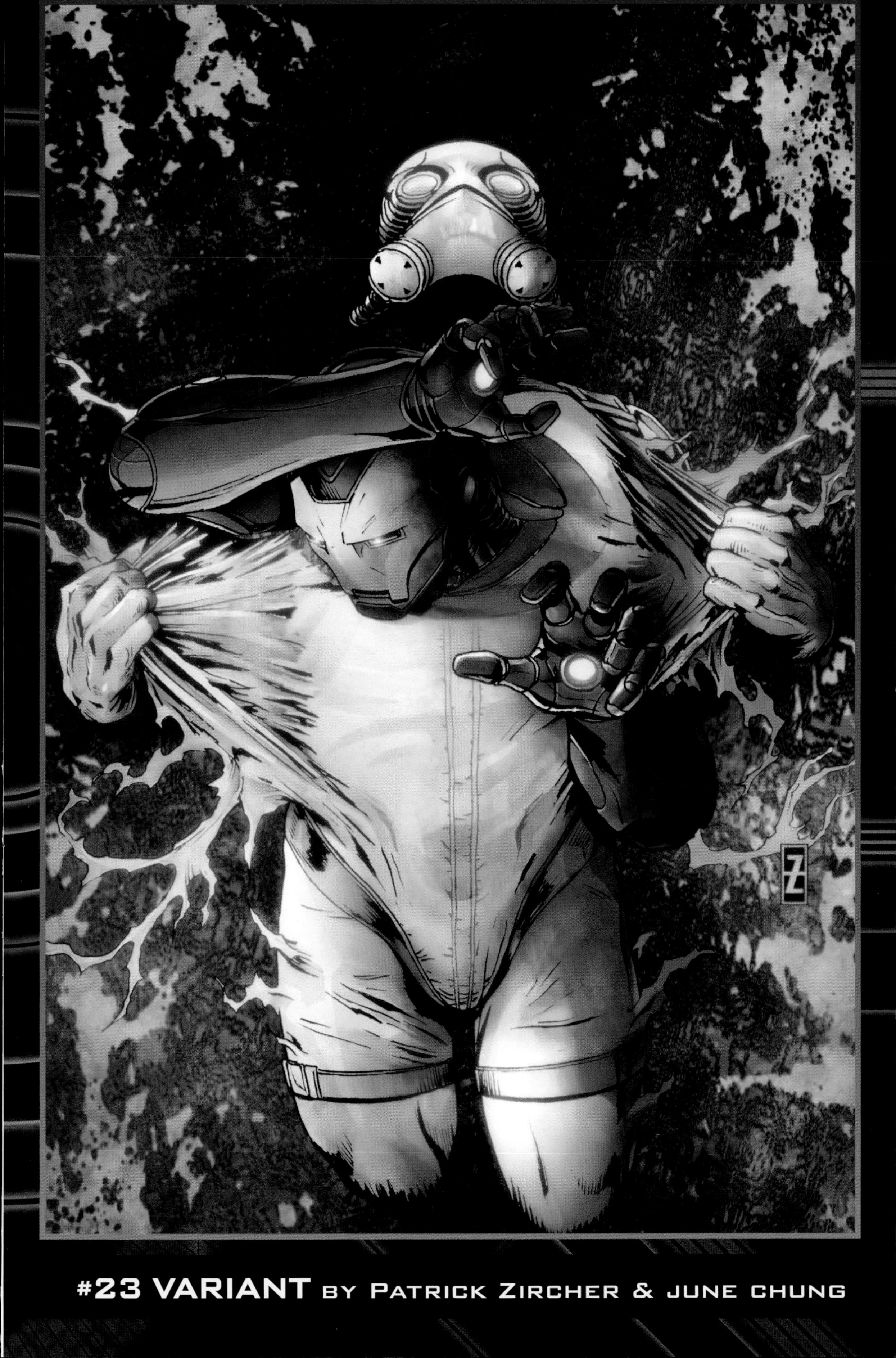
ZZ

#23 VARIANT BY PATRICK ZIRCHER & JUNE CHUNG

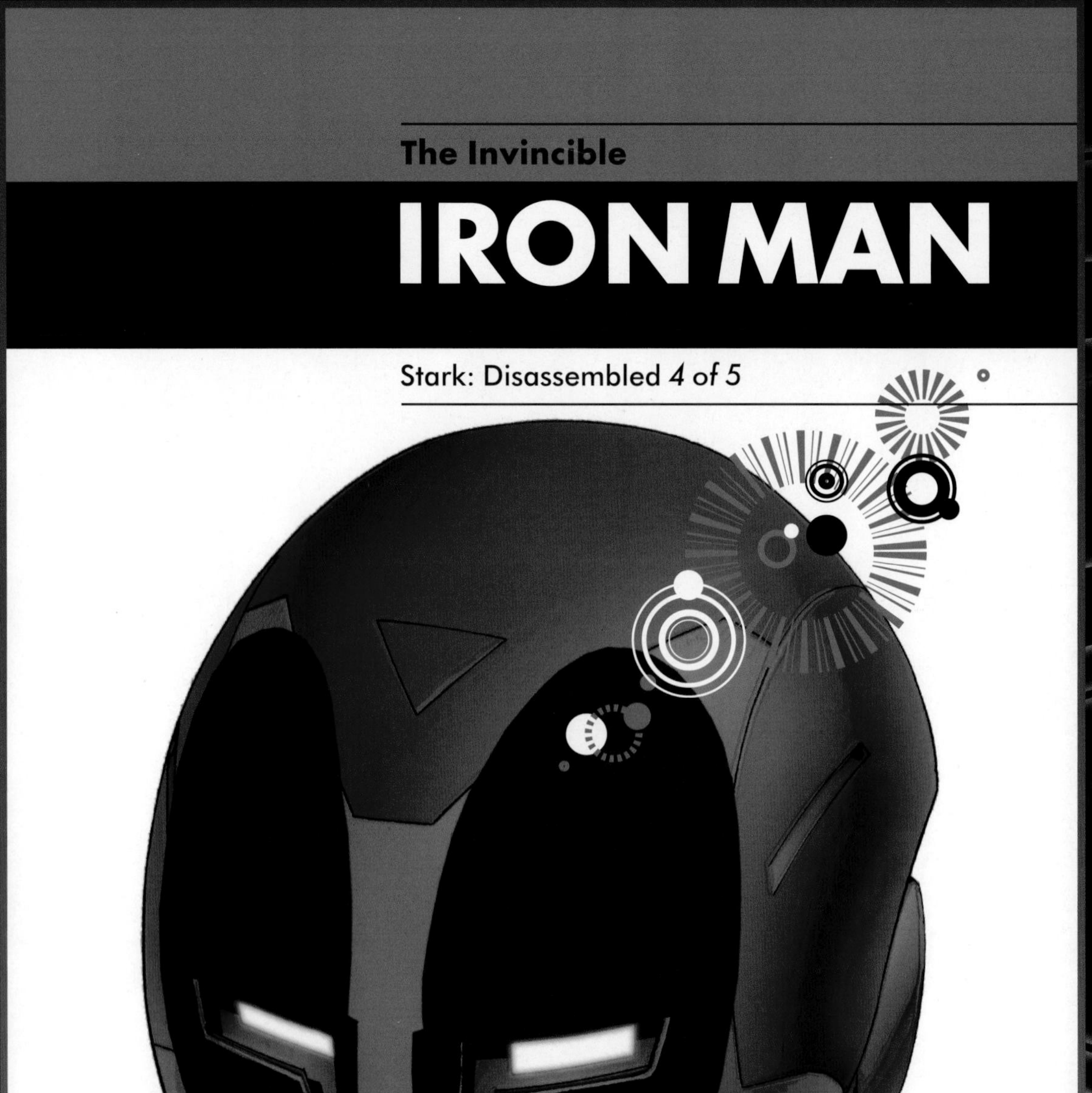
The Invincible
IRON MAN
Stark: Disassembled 4 of 5

#23 DEADPOOL VARIANT
BY SALVADOR LARROCA & RIAN HUGHES

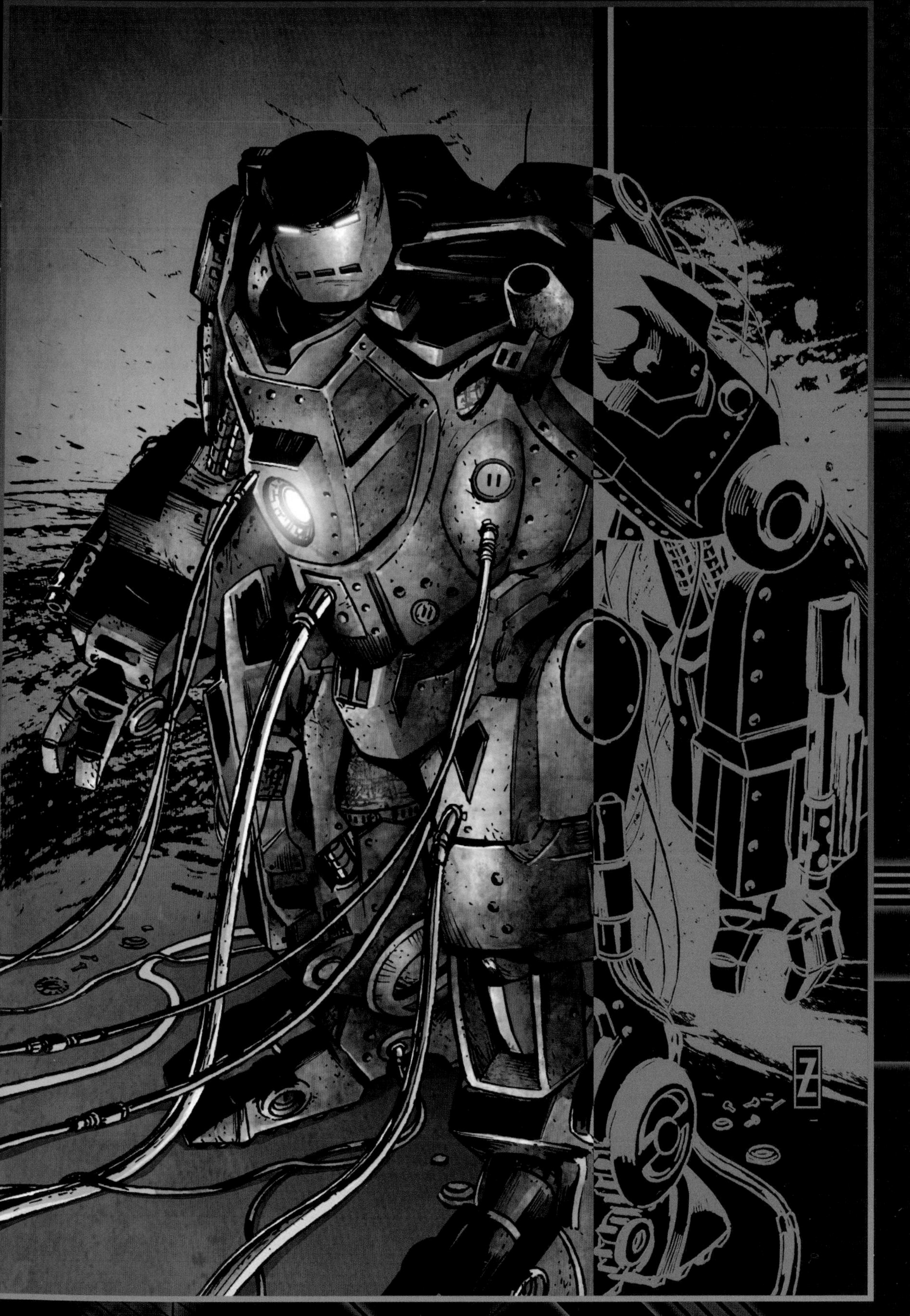
Z

#24 VARIANT BY PATRICK ZIRCHER & JUNE CHUNG

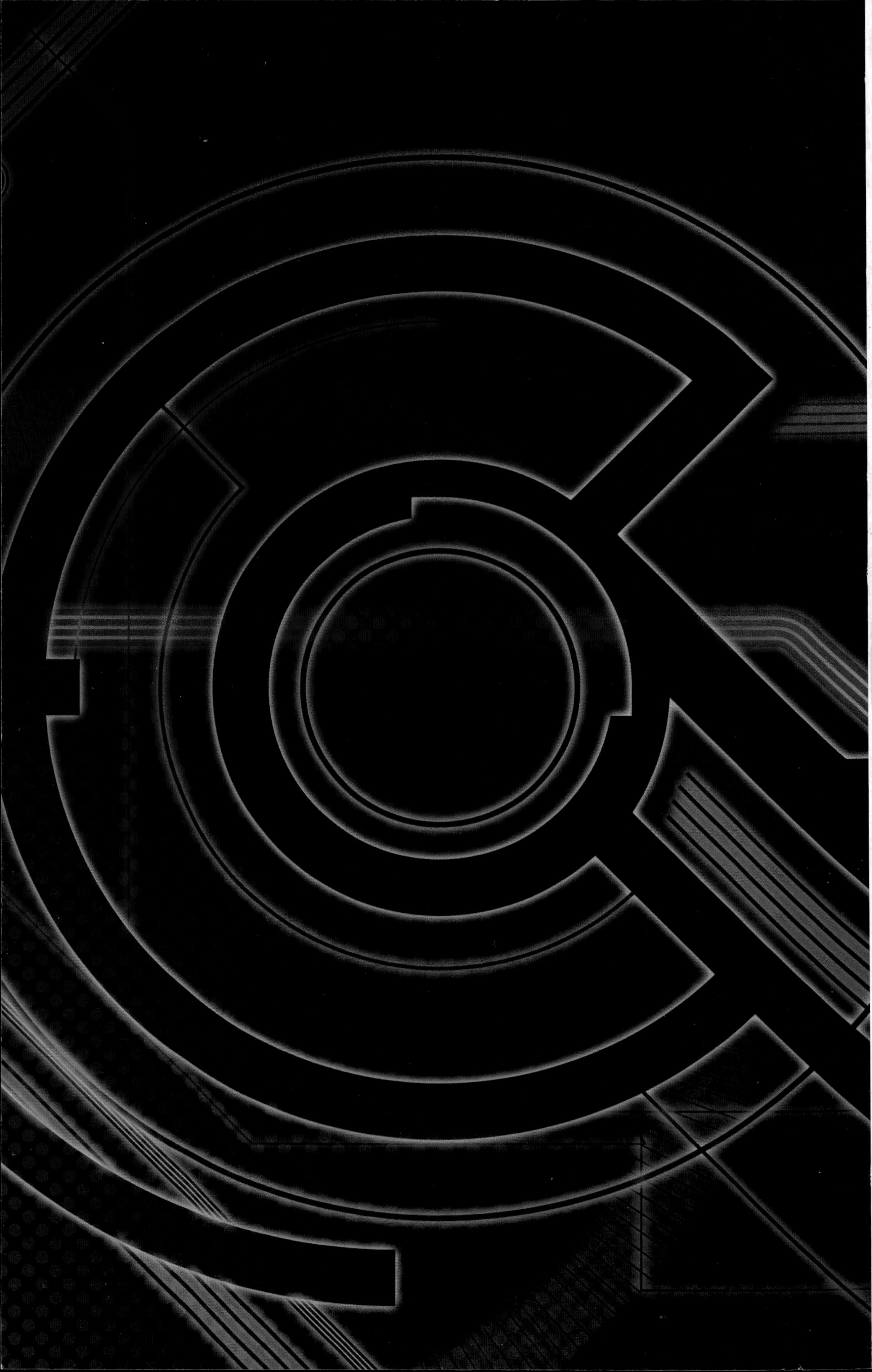